ESCAPING DYSTOPIA

ESCAPING DYSTOPIA

Rebuilding a Public Domain

Stephen McBride

BRISTOL
UNIVERSITY
PRESS

First published in Great Britain in 2022 by

Bristol University Press
University of Bristol
1-9 Old Park Hill
Bristol
BS2 8BB
UK
t: +44 (0)117 374 6645
e: bup-info@bristol.ac.uk

Details of international sales and distribution partners are available at
bristoluniversitypress.co.uk

British Library Cataloguing in Publication Data
A catalogue record for this book is available from the British Library

ISBN 978-1-5292-2061-2 paperback
ISBN 978-1-5292-2062-9 ePub
ISBN 978-1-5292-2063-6 ePdf

Cover design: blu inc
Front cover image: Unsplash/Jason Wong

Bristol University Press uses environmentally responsible
print partners.

Printed and bound in Great Britain by TJ Books, Padstow

Contents

List of Figures and Tables

Figures

Tables

List of Abbreviations

AfD	Alternative for Germany
AI	artificial intelligence
ASEAN	Association of Southeast Asian Nations
B3W	Build Back Better World
BRI	One Belt, One Road initiative
BUI	basic universal income
CARES Act	Coronavirus Aid, Relief, and Economic Security Act
CBI	central bank independence
CDO	collateralized debt obligation
CDS	credit default swap
CEO	chief executive officer
CES	clean electricity standard
CETA	EU–Canada Comprehensive Economic and Trade Agreement
CIA	Central Intelligence Agency
CPTPP	Comprehensive and Progressive Agreement for Trans-Pacific Partnership
CSRs	Country-Specific Recommendations
ECB	European Central Bank
ECJ	European Court of Justice
EES	European Employment Strategy
EMU	European Monetary Union
ESG	Environmental, Social, Governance
EU	European Union
Eurodad	European Network on Debt and Development
FN	National Front (Front National)
GCHQ	Government Communications Headquarters
GDP	gross domestic product
GFC	global financial crisis

ILO	International Labour Organization
IMF	International Monetary Fund
IO	international organization
IOM	International Organization for Migration
IPCC	Intergovernmental Panel on Climate Change
ITO	International Trade Organization
MMT	Modern Monetary Theory
NAFTA	North American Free Trade Agreement
NATO	North Atlantic Treaty Organization
NGEU	Next Generation European Union
NHS	National Health Service
NIEO	New International Economic Order
NRP	National Reform Programmes
NSA	National Security Agency
OECD	Organisation for Economic Co-operation and Development
P3	public–private partnership
PBO	Parliamentary Budget Office [Canada]
PRO Act	Protecting the Right to Organize Act
QE	quantitative easing
RBIO	rules-based international order
RCEP	(Asian) Regional Comprehensive Economic Partnership
SNP	Scottish National Party
TPP	Trans-Pacific Partnership
UKIP	UK Independence Party
UNCTAD	United Nations Conference on Trade and Development
USMCA	United States–Mexico–Canada Agreement
WEF	World Economic Forum
WEO	World Economic Outlook
WHO	World Health Organization
WTO	World Trade Organization

Acknowledgements

In preparing this volume I have benefited from the contributions of many people, through their research, ideas and suggestions, and providing feedback on various drafts. I would particularly like to thank Jan Keeton, Shona McBride, the anonymous reviewers, Stephen Wenham, Heather Whiteside, Joy Schnittker, Don Wells, Gary Teeple, John Gibb, Lily Eskin, John Young, Simon Lee and Nour Afara. Funding through the Canada Research Chairs Program is gratefully acknowledged. In many ways the book has its origins in two collaborative projects funded by the Social Sciences and Humanities Research Council of Canada (SSHRC): 'Varieties of austerity' (435-2016-0638), and 'Austerity and its alternatives' (890-2015-0025). The research collaborations and associated workshops and conferences created a stimulating intellectual environment that enriched my understanding of the political economy of neoliberal global capitalism and led directly to the current volume. My thanks to all the participants and partners in those earlier projects.

1

Introduction

Why 'dystopia'?

The word 'dystopia' translates as 'a bad place', and most definitions include a sense of further downward decline and catastrophic change to come. Discussing dystopian writings, Tom Moylan (2000, p xi) refers to them as being 'the product of the terrors of the twentieth century ... exploitation, repression, state violence, war, genocide, disease, famine, ecocide, depression, debt, and the steady depletion of humanity through the buying and selling of everyday life'. So far, the twenty-first century has lengthened rather than shortened the list (see Voigts and Boller, 2015).

Here are a few headlines randomly culled from various media sources over the past few months:

- 'Deadly flooding, heatwaves in Europe, highlight urgency of climate action'
- 'Brazil's Amazon: Deforestation "surges to 12 year high"'
- 'Global Austerity Alert: Looming budget cuts in 2021–25'
- 'American CEOs make 351 times more than workers ... In 1965 it was 15 to one'
- 'UK: Food banks outnumber McDonald's restaurants'
- 'Europe's brutal fourth wave shows we're just not ready for normal'
- 'Climate refugees – the world's forgotten victims'
- 'After the chaos in Kabul, is the American century over?'
- 'Deaths soar on perilous maritime migration routes to Europe'

The list could be extended indefinitely.

These media hits are by no means the most sensational. Calamity is a major theme in the news headlines. Descriptively they tell the story of the world we are living in – one of multiple crises and imminent dystopia. The word fits. That's where we are, or soon will be unless major changes are made. Modern life seems characterized by economic crisis, extremes of poverty and wealth, climate breakdown, a ravaging health pandemic, migrants drowning at sea in their desperation to escape dreadful living conditions in their home countries, interminable wars, and political failures.

Although the word 'crisis' can be overused it is commonly deployed to describe extremely difficult situations from which no easy exit seems to exist. Alternatively, it is used in the sense of a 'turning point' at which an untenable situation begins to change – either for better or for worse. And crises can be viewed as 'moments that reveal the fault lines in a system' (Castells, 2019, p 15), and thus focus attention on the need for alternatives.

What is needed to escape from this situation of multiple crises – economic, environmental, health, migration, conflict and security, inequality, and a crumbling international and political order? One issue that needs to be confronted is whether these crises are the result of 'external shocks' to the system, and hence uncontrollable except perhaps by way of adaption to their effects, or whether they are the product of a humanly constructed system, in which case more can be done in response. A related issue is whether the crises can be considered in isolation from each other or whether, and to what extent, they are interconnected. If isolated, responses can be specific and targeted. If interconnected, the solution needs to be more radical, comprehensive and drastic.

Of the various crises the one that looks most like it could be externally caused and isolated from the others is the health pandemic. Most likely it was caused zoonotically (that is, transmitted from animals to humans), and this could be regarded as an isolated, accidental event that was unpreventable and therefore uncontrollable. However, looked at more closely it appears to be linked in a number of ways to the environmental situation, globalization and the economic crisis. Human encroachment on the natural world has increased the likelihood of zoonotic transmission of diseases. Mike Davis (2020) has graphically described how the interconnections between global capitalism and the restructuring of animal production and destruction of smaller-scale fishing and agricultural practices in the developing world, combined with overcrowding (of animals and humans), create the conditions for interspecies transmission of diseases. Once unleashed, such viruses spread extremely rapidly due to the highly integrated global system, including the high rates of human travel. In the name of economic efficiency, states had made themselves reliant on global supply chains, the system of outsourcing production of goods and components to low-cost countries that, in moments of crisis, failed to deliver important products including medical equipment and vaccine manufacture. Finally, the capacity of states, including their public health agencies and health-care systems generally, had been undermined by years of austerity rationalized as a response to economic crises.

If the linkages between the pandemic and the other crises are noticeable, the connections between the others are clearer still. Rather than coming from 'outside the system' they are the logical product of neoliberal ideology and policies, and an associated global political economy, globalization. Neoliberalism can be viewed as an ideology that generates a package of approaches and policies towards economic, social and other issues. In principle, it emphasizes individualism over social or collective interests; the superiority of markets (in reality, the powerful actors that dominate them) over public decision-making; the rule of law; and the need for a minimal but strong state to defend private property rights and the capitalist system. Policies to put these principles into operation include: measures to ensure business confidence and profitability; privatization and deregulation; promotion of free trade and international capital mobility; preservation of the value of money (through anti-inflation measures); a limited and fiscally constrained state to keep taxes and expenditures low; flexible labour markets to empower capital; transfer of risk to individuals through designing programmes that make receipt of social benefits conditional on participation in or preparation for the labour force; and acceptance of market outcomes including inequality. Given variations over time and space, it can best be viewed as an ongoing process rather than a finished product.

My analysis of the multiple crises will make the case that the political economy of neoliberal global capitalism is deeply implicated in all of them. Sometimes this is as a direct cause, as in the case of unsustainable for-profit growth that imperils the environment and planet, produces extreme inequality and triggers regular financial and economic crises. At other times neoliberalism is an indirect but significant contributory factor, as in the way that austerity policies and neoliberal approaches more generally undermined public capacity to respond adequately to events such as the COVID-19 pandemic. Because the crises are interconnected and the product of the system itself, *Escaping Dystopia* argues that a radical transformation of the system itself is necessary. This means changing the economic and political arrangements integral to neoliberal globalism.

My purpose is not to draft a manifesto or provide a manual for activists of how to bring about radical change. These things will be worked out in practice. Rather, the purpose is to provide a logical account of what must be done if the root causes of the multiple crises are to be addressed. It is written in the dual hopes that it will improve academic understanding of the crisis we are in and that it can help those involved in the political process to maximize opportunities for change and avoid false turnings that lead nowhere or, perhaps more accurately, lead back to where we are now.

Overcoming these crises and forging alternatives to avoid a dystopian future is the most pressing and difficult issue of our times. Key questions are: What is to be done? How? And by whom?

The COVID-19 pandemic and associated economic crisis have focused attention on the state of the world and it is not a reassuring prospect. Options and alternatives are being advanced for the post-COVID future. Several alternative ideas and policies are already on the table. Einstein is reputed to have said that insanity is doing the same thing over and over again and expecting a different result. Some of the alternatives on offer fit that description. In fact, they will have the same results as they did before, and therefore offer no solution. Others look more promising but fall short. Radical transformation of existing structures and practices looks necessary. But is it achievable? Making any adequate response is made more difficult because of the condition of liberal democratic institutions. They are increasingly seen as both ineffective and lacking in legitimacy. This is the result of the deliberate hollowing-out of existing democratic institutions in the neoliberal era.

Representation of and accountability to the populace is poor (for example, see Gilens and Page, 2014; Pew, 2019).

Lack of democracy has unleashed poorly regulated economic liberalism. This has made the state and public authorities complicit in inequalities of wealth, income, opportunity and mobility through diminished social provision and solidarity. They have been inactive in the face of environmental degradation and have participated in regionalized warfare against weaker countries.

Existing political institutions fall into the category of 'obstacle' rather than spaces within which necessary changes can be engineered. To enable new policy priorities to succeed will require redesigning liberal democratic institutions to place them on foundations of popular sovereignty (literally the power of the people to determine what is to be done, and how it is to be done), an enhanced role for the state through a greater degree of intervention in economic and social affairs, and building a public domain, in the sense of expanding that sphere of life which is subject to collective determination by the population, rather than being under private ownership and control.

I will argue that institutional redesign to achieve democracy based on principles of popular sovereignty, initially at the national level, must be part of radical solutions. Such solutions will be radical because they need to privilege the social or collective over the individual, assert the primacy of the public over the private and of the state and public control over the market (and the capitalist class that dominates it). They will be at the national level because so far it is the highest level at which anything like popular sovereignty can be achieved. Of course, nation-states are far from equal in wealth and power, and the capacity to exercise sovereign decisions will vary. Changing the international order to reduce the privileges and rights enjoyed by capital, to recognize and ameliorate the historic injustices caused by colonialism, imperialism and neoliberal structural adjustment imperatives, and to permit greater national autonomy would greatly facilitate the process.

The liberal international order established in the aftermath of the Second World War is eroding (discussed more fully in Chapter 2). John Ikenberry (2011) has argued that an uneasy tension existed between the 'liberal' components – open markets, multilateral institutions, shared sovereignty, and the rule of law –

and the 'order' components, which placed more emphasis on state sovereignty. Over time its liberal elements grew, but the tensions remained and have arguably become more acute in recent years. Outside the Western bloc, many always viewed the liberal order as representing the imposition of rules favouring globally oriented capital (Kundnani, 2017). The rules were chosen and imposed by the United States and a cohort of close allies. Unsurprisingly, this rules-based international order (RBIO) worked to their advantage in a hierarchical system that consigned others to subordinate roles and constrained any measures they might take to develop nationally advantageous strategies.

The ongoing and developing disarray within the international liberal order creates both opportunities and all kinds of problems. These can be identified in the security sphere, where the risk of military conflict between major powers is growing, adding to the ongoing instability caused by limited wars. In the economy, conflicts over trade and investment, intellectual property rights and imposition of economic sanctions are a destabilizing element. There is a lack of coordinated action on issues like the environment, global health, wars and migration, as millions of people are dislocated and seek to move to better lives, often at unimaginable risk to themselves. If they manage to arrive at their destination, it is often to an unwelcoming reception where they are subject to abuse, discrimination, 'holding camps' and the rise of hostile political movements (Committee on Migration, Refugees and Displaced Persons, 2016).

Political institutions and political processes have not delivered effective responses to the multiple crises. Whole areas of policy-making are excluded from democratic input. Within the main institutions and mainstream political parties there is little debate or stomach for alternative perspectives. People's disaffection can take the form of withdrawal from the political process, as testified by low voter turnouts and declining membership of political parties (discussed in Chapter 3), or participation in anti-system politics of various types, including right-wing populism (discussed further in Chapter 4).

Whatever the obstacles, there is no shortage of discussion, but little certainty about how to envisage the future.

It is interesting how many observers look to the past either for inspiration or for warning. Previous periods of crisis in the 1920s,

1930s, World War II and the post-war years are regularly examined for lessons that might be applied in the current situation. The search for the underlying conditions that favoured some strategies and prevented others can pay dividends for today's analysts.

Today, what broad options or alternatives are under active discussion? Are any of them adequate to meet the challenges of the multiple crises that have been identified? Regardless of their likely effectiveness, what are their prospects of being adopted and implemented?

Three basic options are investigated in this book, together with some mention of anti-system politics, an untidy and contradictory bundle of processes that could either block or enable other alternatives.

First, there is an almost universal desire to get 'back to normal'. Not everyone sees this as desirable, considering that the multiple crises were in full flow even before the pandemic struck. But it is attractive rhetoric. Neoliberals wishing to restore some sort of pre-crises 'status quo' make good use of it. For the moment there are relatively few overt challenges to current policies of fiscal and monetary stimulus. However, one can detect opinion forming about restoring sustainable finances through future fiscal austerity. It is by no means a foregone conclusion that these ideas will prevail. There is a vibrant debate about alternative paradigms, including consideration of the ideas of Modern Monetary Theory (MMT), that suggest that under existing conditions an extended scope for fiscal deficits, and hence stimulus, can be financed by governmental money creation (Mitchell et al, 2019; Kelton, 2020).

Second, there are also mainstream alternatives that recognize that some significant reforms must be made. Centrist political leaders and organizations and some influential individuals believe that the worst effects of neoliberal globalism can be moderated while retaining the fundamentals of the system, especially its role for the private and profit-making sector.

Third, one can identify radical options that challenge the fundamentals of neoliberal capitalism and advocate its transformation. If the goal is something like a prosperous, relatively egalitarian economic system and society featuring full employment in secure and decent jobs, together with widely available public services to meet social needs such as health, education, ageing and housing, then it is far from utopian, except perhaps in contrast to existing reality. Environmentally, this economy would need to undergo rapid conversion to carbon neutrality and meet 'just transition' criteria. Internationally, a new economic order would need to allow for much greater nation-state autonomy and stipulate much more by way of controlling capital. This would encourage the expression of popular sovereignty at national and local levels. Unlike 'steady-state' or no-growth options, some growth would be necessary to enable crucial goals like the elimination of poverty to be achieved. This could be supplemented by redistribution from richer to poorer countries to assist with particular projects like the transition to a green economy. The destination is an international order composed of relatively prosperous, harmonious and environmentally sustainable societies coexisting together.

I argue that getting from here (impending dystopia) to there can be achieved only if the public domain is expanded at the expense of the private, and that the state, other public institutions and social forces working for change need to interact in new and democratic ways. Conflict with capital is inevitable as its current privileges are challenged. It is always possible that the process of radical transformation, like Keynesianism and the 1930s New Deal before it, might end up saving capitalism from itself. More likely, though, it would confine capitalism to a narrow sphere of activity. Either way there is no getting away from the fact that some degree of social conflict will be involved.

The process of constructing neoliberal globalization was a long and incremental one. It met a lot of resistance, and the neoliberal leopard was obliged to change its spots from time to time, though without changing its fundamental characteristics. One could anticipate a similar trajectory for radical transformation. Regardless of speed, however, undoing neoliberal globalization is a radical change with all the neoliberal components such as flexibilization, deregulation, privatization, the austerity state and international capital mobility being targeted. Intertwined and interconnected as these components are, the development of alternatives is rendered difficult. Still, it seems unduly pessimistic and passive to conclude that nothing can be done to avert the looming dystopia for which they are responsible.

To bring radical transformation about, new ideas and a new alignment of social forces are necessary. Neoliberalism has involved the removal of all kinds of important matters from the political process. In essence, it has involved the 'depoliticization of politics' (explored more fully in Chapter 3). A crucial aspect of radical transformation will be to reverse this process and change institutions to make them more representative of what people want, and to hold governments accountable. This has been a neglected item in radical thinking, which implicitly seems to rely on existing institutions to carry out a radical programme. This is a mistake because existing institutions are in themselves significant obstacles to radical change. Their reconstruction must be part of, not something separate from, exiting the multiple crises. The fact that these institutions are also unpopular will be useful to radicals. Targeting established elites and unresponsive institutions that are distrusted by significant sections of the population can help build coalitions for change and may potentially attract many to the cause of radical transformation.

In Chapter 2, I examine the multiple crises, their interconnections and causation. Chapter 3 focuses on the crisis in liberal democratic institutions, and Chapter 4 is a foray into various types of anti-system politics with an eye to what can be learned from this phenomenon. With that in mind, the broad alternatives that are the subject of debate among governments, organizations and citizens are outlined and can be evaluated, and the logic of the need for radical transformation established (Chapters 5–8). Obstacles and opportunities connected to bringing this about are presented in Chapters 9–10.

2

Trapped in Dystopia?

As of November 2021 there had been over 254 million confirmed cases of COVID-19 worldwide, including over 5.1 million deaths (WHO, 2021). The COVID-19 pandemic ranks as a health disaster. Even before the 2020 pandemic arrived, the world was enmeshed in a series of interconnected crises.

The International Monetary Fund (IMF) estimated that as a result of the health pandemic the global economy contracted by 4.4 per cent in 2020, the worst figure since the Great Depression of the 1930s.[1]

Economically there had been only a sluggish and incomplete recovery from the 2007–08 global financial crisis (GFC) and the austerity policies comprising fiscal consolidation (defined in terms of balanced budgets and ceilings on public debt), but also substantial restructuring of labour markets and the public sector, that followed (Blyth, 2013; Whiteside et al, 2021). The GFC itself was a more serious instance of the periodic economic upheavals and recessions that characterized the period since the adoption of neoliberalism in the 1970s.

Environmentally the situation remains dire, as a consensus among scientists projects the disastrous impact of global warming and loss of biodiversity (Ripple et al, 2017; IPCC, 2021).

Capitalism's focus on unlimited growth, cheap fossil-based energy and neoliberalism's priority for short-term profit maximization are deeply implicated in the climate crisis. The impact is already apparent and will worsen dramatically even if strong corrective measures are taken now. If they are not, then the future will be catastrophic.

The liberal international order is disintegrating. This is not necessarily a bad thing as it masked the imposition of rules chosen and imposed by the Unites States and its closest allies, and worked to their advantage and to that of globally oriented capital. The order is a hierarchical system that consigned other states and interests to subordinate roles. However, the problems in security, the economy, environment, global health, and migration, which are associated with its decline, have been noted.

Since neoliberal economic policies and support for a globalized capitalist economy have predominated for the last four decades, we can safely say that they are responsible for the multiple crises. The responsibility is direct in the case of the crises in the economy, liberal democratic institutions, environment and climate, and the international order, and is less direct, but still evident, in migration, security and global health. Neoliberal globalized capitalism is a system that has proved unstable, and it is unsustainable in the long run.

The multiple crises that beset the world are thus interconnected. Solutions are either not obvious or, if they are, will be difficult to achieve within the framework of existing political and economic systems. This is because neoliberal globalization has also produced a crisis in political institutions and political processes. Faced with economic, environmental and health security problems, people look to their political institutions to organize responses, only to discover another malfunctioning zone. Political institutions have been found wanting. At the national level their capacity has been weakened and their legitimacy undermined due to perceived lack of representation and accountability. Internationally, governance institutions are not democratic and are designed to constrain nation-state autonomy. There is a political crisis of liberal democracy that compounds the problems posed by the other crises. People suffering the consequences lack voice or power in addressing them.

In early 2020 these pre-existing crises were joined by the one in global health. Rumours and apprehensions of a new and deadly virus turned into reality. Major countries were found lacking in the most basic preparations for a pandemic. Recriminations between those countries and international organizations like the World Health Organization (WHO) contributed to a sense of panic that no one was in control. National strategies varied from the highly effective (China, Taiwan, New Zealand, South Korea) to the incompetent (the US, the UK, Brazil). Who can forget US President Trump's promotion of the unproven (in the context of COVID-19) hydroxychloroquine, Brazilian President Bolsonaro's dismissal of the disease as a "little flu", or the UK government's controversial 'herd immunity' strategy, adopted and then quickly dropped in spring 2020? Later, major countries acquired the lion's share of newly available vaccines and refused to provide a temporary waiver of intellectual property rights that were built into the liberal rules-based international order. A waiver would allow generic COVID-19 vaccines to be manufactured at low cost in the Global South. The Global Dashboard for Vaccine Equity estimated in November 2021 that around 65 per cent of people had been vaccinated with at least one dose in high-income countries, but only around 7.5 per cent in low-income countries.[2]

The magnitude of infections and hospitalizations exceeded the capacity of many health-care systems, and the number of deaths triggered emergency health measures, economic lockdowns, social distancing, travel restrictions and more. Under these conditions economies quickly moved into recession and a massive economic crisis joined the health-care one.

A growing number of issues receive the crisis designation – the increasing numbers of refugees, other types of migration, and various forms of insecurity such as personal safety, food and housing. These are linked to the economic, security and environmental challenges (see Figure 2.1).

Overcoming these crises and avoiding a dystopian future is an urgent priority. Moving ahead requires identification of alternatives and pathways to a more rational and sustainable future. To be able to do that first calls for an understanding of how the multiple crises we face intersect to bring us to this bad place. Then attention must turn to what is needed to break the links between them, and to open space for corrective action. It also requires us to identify in what spheres, public, private or mixed, and at what level(s) – global, national, or local – corrective action can best be applied.

For the past several decades the economic system can be characterized as a globalized variant of capitalism informed and organized by neoliberalism. That system is central to the development and/or continuation of the crises that have been identified. Long-term crises – of climate and environment, and the breakdown of the international security order – continued their development unabated during the neoliberal period that took shape in the 1970s and 1980s and continues to this day. There were periodic, serious, but limited economic crises. These have now been joined by events that threaten the survival of the global neoliberal economic order itself and, with that, the sustainability of capitalism – a challenge that last arose in the 1930s.

Fundamental features of the neoliberal global order have been exposed as deeply flawed. These include free trade and capital mobility which, among other things, promoted reliance on global just-in-time supply chains that are prone to disruption in times of emergency. The order is sustained by global governance through regional integration and trade agreements, although these seem unable either to prevent economic crises from arising or to deal effectively with them when they do. In this context market-based approaches are either deficient as a potential solution, or else are a contributory factor to the severity of the situation. Yet whether they will be abandoned, and if so, what may replace them, remains unclear. Political systems as presently configured seem unable to respond adequately.

Figure 2.1: Capitalism and its neoliberal global variant in crisis

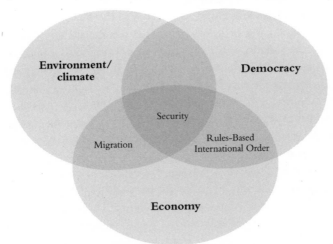

Crises of capitalism and neoliberalism

Capitalism itself is a crisis-prone system. After World War II there was a period of relative stability – variously referred to as the post-war compromise or settlement, the Keynesian era or the 'Thirty Golden Years'. In the neoliberal period instability has become normal. There were several major recessions and financial breakdowns prior to 2007–08 although they tended not to be global or system-wide. The GFC was a genuinely global financial crisis that transformed into a widespread economic recession. Recovery was very slow and, in many countries, incomplete at the time of the COVID-19 pandemic and a further massive economic downturn in 2020. The earlier crises were transparently internal to the system of neoliberalism. That is, they were caused by misplaced faith in market forces which, in the absence of state intervention to correct them, regularly fail.

Global neoliberalism from the 1970s was itself an attempt by the state and capital to fix capitalism's problems of the day, on terms demanded by capital. The problems included global overaccumulation of capital. This means that there was too much accumulated capital available, given a relative paucity of profitable investment opportunities. Opportunities needed to be created. In addition, a militant working class was able to exploit its bargaining power in conditions of relatively full employment. This challenge had to be defeated. Inflation was attributed to wage pressures, although other explanations connected to the 1970s oil crises, or the US financing of its Vietnam War were available. Measures to defeat inflation also diminished working-class power and restructured the 'post-war' settlement, including the welfare state.

Looking at the very long term, state policy has always sought to satisfy some combination of the accumulation needs of capital, and measures to legitimate or secure consent to an inherently unequal system. If legitimation fails, coercive measures designed to stabilize it can be imposed.[3]

Over time, the balance between these functions or activities may change. We saw this with the displacement of Keynesianism by neoliberalism in the late twentieth century. That transition led to a much stronger emphasis on the needs of capital accumulation and corporations' ability to make investments. This came at the expense of legitimation. As well, the means of achieving each was different. The Keynesian approach had conferred real benefits on the working class through its goal of full employment and an enhanced welfare state. It relied on a degree of national autonomy, and state coordination or light planning of the economy. National political economies were often depicted as 'mixed economies' with a relatively high percentage of the economy being publicly owned. State management of the economy was designed to sustain a high level of demand through private consumption, investment and public spending. This produced enough demand for labour to lead to full employment, made the welfare state affordable because enough people were working, and also provided profit-making opportunities to sustain capital accumulation.

Under neoliberalism, state-supported capital accumulation would rely much more on market mechanisms, free trade internationally, privatization and a restructured labour market with more conditional social benefits at home. The erosion of legitimation by way of concrete collective benefits (full employment and the welfare state) led to a greater emphasis on a mixture of ideological appeals and individualized incentives. As usual, in the background was the option of increased coercion, as in anti-trade union measures, and increased surveillance of general populations, and suspected radicals in particular.

The creation of a 'rules-based' international economic order governed by enforceable trade and investment agreements, and the disciplines of international organizations like the World Bank and the IMF, was a key element of the neoliberal package. Geographically, previously closed areas of the world were opened as investment opportunities and/or sources of cheap labour. This served as a spatial solution to the problem of overaccumulation of capital. David Harvey (2001, pp 241–2) has shown that this triggers a number of strategies, including expansion geographically into new regions, increasing foreign trade, exporting capital and in general expanding towards the creation of a global market.

There were also political benefits for capital. Once established, the rules served to 'depoliticize' key issues by removing them from the realm of domestic democratic political processes. Subjects covered by the rules were regarded as 'settled' and no longer open for discussion. Domestically, capital accumulation was served by privatization.

Privatization policies, in addition to the sale of state-owned assets, included public–private partnerships, marketization of intra-state activities, and outsourcing of publicly funded services to private providers. All these led to invented markets, and hence created profit-making opportunities, within what was previously the public domain.

Integrated into this approach was financialization, a process whereby financial markets, institutions and actors gained influence over economic policy and economic outcomes, initially at the expense of producers and distributors of real products (Sawyer, 2017). Later, these potentially conflicting interests within capital were reconciled by a process of fusion – finance became the common modus operandi. Financialization has been described as a systemic transformation of mature capitalist economies that involves three processes: first, large non-financial corporations reduce their reliance on bank loans and acquire independent financial capacities; second, banks expand their activities in financial markets, well beyond traditional functions of lending to households and businesses; third, households become increasingly involved in the realm of finance both as debtors and as asset holders. These developments have important implications for capitalist profit-making, and are linked to stagnating real wages (and extracting profit from wages and salaries), and increased lending to individuals as sources of profit for banks (Lapavitsas, 2011). Deregulation of the financial sector enabled another strategy to deal with overaccumulation issues. It involved a vast expansion of innovative financial products which could be traded and were prone to speculative transactions. It meant that those with liquid capital were able to expand markets in financial rather than real commodities, and to invent and trade in new instruments such as mortgage-backed securities, collateralized debt obligations (CDOs) and credit default swaps (CDS). Privately created and privately held debt expanded, distributed between households, corporations and the public sector. Indeed, some argue that the most important aspect of modern political economies is not that they are market oriented but that they are debt based (Di Muzio and Robbins, 2016). Interest-bearing debt is seen as the primary way in which economic inequality is generated as more money is redistributed to creditors. Debt instruments therefore divide society into debtors and creditors within a power structure that privileges the latter over the former.

These relationships are apparent in the transformation of state finances, depicted by Wolfgang Streeck (2014) as a transition from a 'tax state' to a 'debt state'. As a result of states' dependence on private creditors, whose claims are given precedence over others in the event of a crisis, the degree of accountability to citizens is diminished, and the extent of national sovereignty is undermined. Thus, financialization and debt, which are intrinsic to neoliberalism, are implicated in the crisis of democratic governance and in the erosion of the international order.

In the highly speculative economy, in which vast fortunes are made by those at the top, successive waves of neoliberal tax reform conferred benefits on wealthy individuals and on corporations. Meanwhile, wages and the social wage (social programmes and supports) were suppressed. Steadily increasing levels of inequality were one obvious result. One example is the financialization of housing. Residential properties are increasingly seen as financial assets – as investments rather than homes. Government policies have reinforced this through deregulating rental markets, withdrawing from social housing and promoting home ownership (see Doling and Ronald, 2010; August and Walks, 2018; Hawes and Grisdale, 2020). Housing costs and rents are outpacing income growth by increasingly wider margins (Fung et al, n.d.). Housing can also be traded globally, including through mortgage-backed securities (Walks, 2014; Dewilde, 2018). In the private rental sector, private equity firms (such as Blackstone or other real estate investment trusts) have accumulated single-family homes and apartment blocks, increasing rents while holding onto profitable, tangible assets (see Christophers, 2021).

Neoliberal deregulation of the financial sector and, more broadly, its liberation of corporations from controls that had previously governed their behaviour, led directly to the GFC. Neoliberal policies produced a lightly regulated economy dominated by finance, and the GFC was the end-product of the processes that it set in motion. The subsequent economic recessions were the most serious since the Great Depression of the 1930s. Recovery from the depths of the immediate recession in 2008–09, and from subsequent recessions after the introduction of austerity in 2010, was slow, fragile and incomplete. The crisis itself and the resort to stimulus, followed, very quickly, by austerity, fit a common pattern across most states in the Global North. Although there was a common strategy centred around austerity, normally defined as fiscal consolidation, including controls of budget deficits and public debt, but also including public sector restructuring and labour market restructuring, there was also considerable variety across global regions and nation-states, and within nation-states too (Whiteside et al, 2021).

Lessons that could have been learned from earlier crises were not learned. There had been no re-evaluation of the policy regime being implemented. The problems first became apparent with the collapse of a number of US investment banks and mortgage giants. Except for Lehman Brothers, which was allowed to fail, these were bailed out by the US government through massive debt purchasing schemes. The crisis was not confined to finance, narrowly defined. In November 2008 the S&P stock market index was down nearly 45 per cent compared to its 2007 high (Altman, 2009).

Unlike previous financial crises this one originated in the US, the centre of global capitalism and its ideological twin, neoliberalism, and soon spread out from there. What began as a US banking and financial market crisis spread particularly to countries with highly internationalized financial sectors, highly leveraged banks and high levels of exposure to the toxic assets associated with the US subprime mortgage market. Thus, a US financial crisis turned into a global economic crisis, leading to a global recession. The financial and banking sectors were affected first as a slumping housing market in late 2006 led, in 2007, to revelations of worthless financial assets associated with subprime lending markets.[4] Bailouts in these sectors did not lead to permanent ownership stakes in the companies involved. Reflecting the ideological tenor of the times, they were often described as 'pre-privatization' measures rather than the partial nationalizations that they could well have remained. They illustrate the state unconditionally rushing to rescue the private sector.

Given that interest rates were at already historical lows, monetary tools were initially deemed exhausted. So, in confronting the GFC and recession governments resorted to fiscal measures – stimulus spending in order to avoid complete economic collapse. This may have averted a deeper recession, but it did not represent a change of strategy on the part of dominant elites. In any case, it was dropped in favour of austerity policies within two years. To the extent stimulus policies continued, they took the form of rediscovered monetary policy – 'quantitative easing' (QE). QE creates money by the central bank taking on liabilities or debts from the private banks. It advances them funds that, it is assumed, they will lend to investors, thus stimulating the economy. The actual stimulus seems to have been limited (there were few profitable opportunities while demand remained sluggish), but the mechanism served to solidify the position of the corporate sector and the rich generally (Teeple, 2017).

Though truly global, the impact of the GFC did vary by region. An IMF report (Arias and Wen, 2015) noted that Europe and the Middle East were hardest hit in terms of gross domestic product (GDP) decline in 2008–09, with reductions ranging between 10 and 20 per cent. They were followed by Latin America, Oceania, North America and Africa. However, Asia's experience was one of slower growth rather than absolute decline. Similarly, in terms of recovery, some Asian countries – the Asian Tigers (Hong Kong, Singapore, South Korea and Taiwan), plus China and Japan – grew back quickly, with Europe as a whole lagging far behind. There was also variation among the countries of the Global North, though the common pattern was one of slow recovery. In the European Union (EU), for example, constant price GDP per capita was only 9 per cent higher in 2019 than it had been in 2010, and in the US it was 10 per cent higher. Annual increases in this important measure of income per head thus averaged only 1 per cent.

Such a grim experience is partly captured in various labour market statistics – rates of unemployment, youth unemployment and long-term (that is, more than one year) unemployment. Even where benefits exist for the unemployed, there are negative consequences for both individuals and society. It has long been known that higher unemployment increases poverty, and causes shifts in self-esteem, anxiety and stress, leading to increased alcoholism, drug use, domestic violence, suicides, admissions to mental hospitals and crime (McBride, 1992, pp 7–8). Societal costs include lost production, impaired productivity, lost revenues, and additional expenditures to cope with unemployment's collateral damage. The impact on many countries in the Global South, which lack even modest levels of social support, is correspondingly more severe.

The degree to which employment is precarious is another indicator of social and individual damage, as is the adequacy of the social security net underlying the labour market. The GFC and austerity meant high unemployment rates and, for particular groups – youth, and those who were out of work for a year or more – the impact was especially profound. The type and longevity of unemployment experienced has an impact over the life cycle through 'scarring' – long-term negative impacts on earnings and employment rates. In some countries, youth unemployment reached catastrophic heights. In Greece, in 2013, 54 per cent of young men and 64 per cent of young women aged 15–24 were without work[5] and, in 2019, the rate was still double what it had been when the crisis struck. Spain's experience was similar. In these and some other countries it is no exaggeration to speak of a 'lost generation'.

The labour-restructuring component of austerity meant controlling unit labour costs. This was rationalized as a means of increasing competitiveness. Measures were intended to weaken labour as a collective entity. They included decentralization of collective bargaining institutions, imposing outcomes on bargaining through wage freezes, and reducing or bypassing the influence of social dialogue institutions where they existed. Actions directed at individual workers reduced employment standards and labour protection and increased employers' flexibility. Through 'activation' measures to (re-)engage in labour market participation the unemployed and vulnerable persons were made responsible for their own situation and for exiting from it (see Farnsworth and Irving, 2015). For especially vulnerable sections of the working class, their already meagre insulation from market turbulence was much reduced. This can be observed in changes in household poverty and insecurity (personal debt), labour market precarity, housing insecurity and homelessness, food insecurity and hunger, and diminished voice (Whiteside et al, 2021, ch 6). There is a large constituency of people who justifiably consider that the system does not work for them. They provide one basis of support for anti-system politics (Castells, 2019).

The dominant narrative used to justify fiscal austerity was that governments were spending too much and incurring too much debt. This inaccurate account completely evades the question of why they were spending more after the crisis and who was responsible for it (see Blyth, 2013, pp 5–6). Ian Gough (2011, pp 53–8) argued convincingly that increased public spending and debt was the cost of governments' financial interventions to prevent collapse of the private, market economy in general, and of the banking and financial sector in particular.

In the orthodox accounts, balanced budgets were seen as necessary to restore business confidence. Even then, the ideological rather than scientific nature of policy choices was quite visible, though mostly ignored. If a balanced budget was required, it could logically be achieved by some mixture of tax increases or expenditure cuts. Cutting spending was the road most heavily travelled, with the reshaping of the welfare state through spending reductions and conditionalities on social supports being the chief instruments. On the other hand, some expenditures were greatly expanded. Firms, including banks, were bailed out or temporarily bought out. Bad debts were transferred from company books to the public accounts to be paid by the general taxpayer, and deficits and debt as a percentage of GDP grew accordingly. This fuelled demands for further austerity to deal with state 'profligacy', as the culpability of the private sector, especially its financial institutions, for the crisis was conveniently obscured amid rhetoric of shared sacrifice to save the economy. The world had hardly recovered from this debacle when the COVID-19 pandemic struck.

The economic fallout from the pandemic

Estimates of the economic costs of the health pandemic vary widely and it is not my purpose to try and reconcile them. They are, in any case, still unfolding. The following snapshots are intended merely as illustrations.

The April 2021 World Economic Outlook (WEO) by the IMF suggested that the global economy contracted by 3.3 per cent in 2020. The contraction was smaller than that projected in the October 2020 WEO, reflecting higher-than-expected growth in the second half of the year as lockdowns were eased and economies adapted to new ways of functioning.[6] In October 2021, the World Bank reported that the COVID-19 pandemic increased global government debt by 13 percentage points of GDP to a new record of 97 per cent of GDP (Kose et al, 2021, p 2). Advanced economies implemented fiscal support in the order of 20 per cent of GDP, while emerging economies implemented support in the order of 6 per cent of GDP (respectively, ten and four times the stimulus implemented after the 2007–08 GFC; Kose et al, 2021, p 8).

In October 2021, the International Labour Organization (ILO) reported that global working hours in 2021 are estimated to remain significantly below the level attained in the last quarter of 2019. Overall, during the third quarter of 2021, global hours worked were still 4.7 per cent below the level of the fourth quarter of 2019 (the pre-crisis benchmark), equivalent to the loss of 137 million full-time jobs. Analysis of labour force survey data from 23 countries also suggests that lower-wage workers have suffered disproportionately. Global employment declined more for women (who accounted for 38.9 per cent of total employment before COVID-19, but 47.6 per cent of employment losses in 2020), youth (13 per cent of total employment in 2019, but 34.2 per cent of the 2020 decline in employment in 2020) and medium- to low-skilled workers. The global recovery of employment continues to be fragile and uneven (ILO, 2021).

The World Bank estimated that the number of pandemic-induced global new poor was expected to increase by between 143 million and 163 million in 2021. Other estimates had the global new poor increasing from 175 million to 228 million from June 2020 to January 2021 (Lakner et al, 2021).

The COVID-19 crisis thus exacerbated pre-existing inequalities. Lack of social protection – for example among the world's two billion informal sector workers comprising self-employed persons, or employees of businesses that are not registered with or regulated or taxed by governments – means that pandemic-related work disruptions have had massive consequences for family incomes and livelihoods. The crisis has also hit women harder than men. As employment recovery unfolds it will be uneven, due to unequal vaccine access and the limited capacity of most developing and emerging economies to support much in the way of fiscal stimulus.

All countries suffered from diversion of health resources from other priorities, with both immediate and longer-term consequences. These included deaths among non-COVID patients who were unable to obtain timely treatment, deterioration of chronic conditions, huge backlogs of non-urgent but necessary surgeries, and so on. Similarly, other things being equal, school closures will have a long-run effect on productivity and lifetime earnings of individuals, and will produce even greater inequalities than those currently existing. Hunger and homelessness worsened, along with gender-based violence.

If these are common features of the impact of COVID-19, they are experienced more profoundly in less developed countries with already inadequate resources and which, additionally, are often indebted to unsustainable levels. This time, unlike the GFC, developing countries were hit hardest (Achcar, 2020). Unemployment soared, and in low-income and middle-income countries, where much of the employment and economic activity is in the informal sector and enjoys little or no social protection, the effect was intensified. Poverty alleviation was already under pressure because of climate change and ongoing military conflicts in countries like Syria, Yemen, and South Sudan. Reducing extreme poverty to 3 per cent by 2030, in line with UN Sustainable Development Goals, now seems impossible.

In the developed world, income and wealth inequality has risen over the past several decades, and COVID-19 has made this worse. The costs of the pandemic are being borne disproportionately by low-income populations which are both more exposed to the health risks and more likely to experience job losses and declines in well-being. These effects are concentrated in economically disadvantaged minorities (Qureshi, 2020).

Neoliberal global capitalism has produced societies that are highly unequal in both the conditions and the opportunities they provide to their citizens. Moreover, it is highly unstable and wracked by periodic crises. Devised to address particular problems that business was experiencing in the 1970s, it is long past its shelf life and has become the common factor in all these crises.

Climate capitalism

Capitalism is built on permanent expansion of economic activities and unlimited growth. Increasingly these are incompatible with environmental sustainability. Some authors have focused on the role of predatory, rich elites in driving a consumer culture of overconsumption (Kempf, 2007; see also Jackson, 2009; Kenner, 2019). As important as this may be, multiple factors interact to create the environmental problem. They include fossil-based energy usage in all stages of production and consumption, and transportation by air, shipping, private cars and trucks. The important thing they have in common is carbon emissions and this has become the focus of much of the action directed against global warming.

Taking aim at carbon emissions caused by reliance on fossil fuels, the United Nations Intergovernmental Panel on Climate Change (IPCC) has warned of environmental disaster unless annual carbon emissions are cut by half by 2030, and to zero by 2050. In a special report on global warming (IPCC, 2018) the panel presented a scientific consensus on the impacts of warming to 1.5°C and 2.0°C. Projected impacts included widespread temperature extremes with regionally diverse variations in precipitation – heavy in some areas with more frequent flooding, and drought and desertification in others. Sea levels were expected to rise, potentially by several metres in the very long-run if significant polar ice melts were experienced. The range of many forms of life – insects, birds, animals – was projected to decline. Other risks due to forest fires and the spread of invasive species were identified. Marine biodiversity, fisheries and ecosystems were all threatened by warming. Similarly, climate-related risks to health, livelihoods, food security, water supply, human security and economic growth were all projected to increase. These developments particularly affect vulnerable populations – indigenous peoples, coastal dwellers and the poor – but no one can escape the broader consequences. Measures to limit global warming to 1.5°C require unprecedented transitions in energy, land, urban, infrastructure and industrial systems. These conclusions were confirmed and amplified in a subsequent report (IPCC, 2021).

There is no shortage of material suggesting that the endless, unchecked growth characteristics of capitalism are responsible for the climate crisis. Angela Carter (2020, p 107) nicely summarizes this position in noting that capitalism is inherently 'eco-hostile' because of endless growth, commodification and extraction of natural resources (see also, for example, Daly, 1996). The environment is assigned a role as a storehouse of resources, and a dumping ground for by-products of production. All this is linked to multiple forms of social injustice (Carter, 2020, pp 107–9). Others, like Nicholas Stern, author of a 700-page report, *The Economics of Climate Change*, for the UK government, observed, 'climate change is a result of the greatest market failure the world has seen'.[7] Such accounts could point to the need for a radical and comprehensive change in our economic system to avert environmental catastrophe. However, Stern's own subsequent views stopped well short of radicalism (Stern, 2015, pp 97–8, 246). He proposed correction of market failure by methods like cap-and-trade systems and tax incentives to stimulate private research and development, and to facilitate private investment for 'green growth'. 'Cap-and-trade' describes a situation where upper limits (caps) on emissions are established by the state, and where firms that fail to use their full allowance can sell the balance to firms that are overproducing their limit (trade). The cost involved to the firm with greater emissions provides an incentive to convert to greener production methods, especially if the cap is reduced over time, hence rendering purchase of the right to pollute more and more expensive over time. Essentially these are modest reforms that continue to give primacy to the very market forces that are responsible for the crisis. The public or state role is to enable market solutions.

While these may be judged inadequate, it does not follow that capitalism will collapse in the face of a growing realization of this among the general public, or that capitalists lack options in resisting demands for comprehensive change (see Harvey, 2014, Part 3[8]). It is possible for business to pursue profit-making opportunities and a growth strategy under conditions of environmental deterioration or collapse, probably with greater reliance on coercion and authoritarianism rather than democratic politics.

Efforts to control climate change have, to date, proved disappointing. The Kyoto Protocol (in force from 2005) was the first legally binding climate treaty and required developed countries to reduce emissions. However, developing countries did not have to meet mandatory reductions. The US did not ratify the Protocol, and Canada withdrew from it in 2012. It is generally regarded as having been a failure. The Paris Agreement (adopted 2015) took a different approach. Countries offered voluntary pledges, but these are not legally binding. Advocates argue that this 'bottom-up' approach offers better prospects of success. More pessimistic accounts (cited in Clémençon, 2016) point to the lack of legally binding emission targets, lack of specific financial supports to assist developing countries in complying with their own targets, and the failure to confront the link between the environment and the capitalist economic system (seen as the fundamental problem), or the trade-off between control of climate on the one hand, and the global transactions encouraged by neoliberal international trade objectives on the other.

Although the Paris Agreement represented some progress towards controlling global warming it was insufficient to solving the long-term problem (Clémençon, 2016, p 13). Meeting the Agreement's goal was not helped by the Trump administration's withdrawal (subsequently reversed under President Biden). That said, however, most national governments face strong business opposition 'designed to keep the lucrative business-as-usual going for as long as possible' (Clémençon, 2016, p 20).

Referring to the main debates within international climate negotiations, Uddin (2017) notes that there is little indication that the industrialized countries are actually willing to give up their position of advantage. Climate change so far has been mostly felt by the South, and the region is dependent on the North to overcome the environmental challenges. Uddin notes that the North–South divide is at the core of global environmental politics. Countries that are more resilient to the effects of environmental degradation, mostly in the Global North, are not ready yet to take responsibility for carbon emissions. This stance reflects the hierarchies of power present in the international order.

The North–South divide has long been central to climate negotiations. In the Copenhagen Accord in 2009 high-income countries agreed on a concrete dollar pledge to be provided to developed countries. That Accord promised US$30 billion in 'fast-start finance' between 2010 and 2012, followed by a US$100 billion a year by 2020 (Bracking, 2015). The Paris Agreement, agreeing to limit global warming to 2°C, preferably 1.5°C, compared to pre-industrial levels also reinforced the US$100 billion pledge of climate finance annually (Romano et al, 2018).

That target has remained a bone of contention. Lack of political agreement surrounding what classifies as climate finance, or how the agreements should be interpreted and applied, has led to considerable discretion on behalf of donor countries (Streck and Chagas, 2011; Pickering et al, 2015). Inconsistency in methodologies has also allowed donor countries to count all financial instruments (grants versus loans) as the same, as well as failing to distinguish between funding reallocation (using overseas development aid for climate purposes), and increased, new and additional funding (Roberts et al, 2021). Failure to clarify methodologies led institutions such as the Organisation for Economic Co-operation and Development (OECD) to overstate climate finance. Oxfam reported in 2020 that public climate finance to developing countries was only one third of the OECD's estimates, as Oxfam states that, besides grants, only the benefit accrued from lending at below-market rates of loans should be counted (Oxfam, 2020b). With only 20 per cent of public climate finance reported as grants in a 2020 report (compared to 80 per cent in loans and non-grant instruments), overreporting may be an endemic issue (Oxfam, 2020b; 2021). Similarly, Care International (2021) reported that climate finance projects often bear no relation to climate adaptation efforts.

Break-up? The international order

Internationally, Western countries are committed to a liberal rules-based international order (RBIO). States proclaim adherence to a common set of values and, underpinning them, to a capitalist economic system that privileges private property rights. In practice, the rules are much more binding on states than on capital, and on weaker states than on stronger ones. In 1990 the RBIO became a unipolar order with one pre-eminent power, the United States. There are now unmistakable signs that this order is transitioning to a multipolar one (with several great powers, not one, some of which do not share important parts of the previous ideological consensus; see Wright, 2018). Two emergent or resurgent great powers, China and Russia, reject the US assertion that it is the single rule-maker and enforcer of the international order.

For realist scholars like John J. Mearsheimer (2019), this international order has been in decline since around 2005. He illustrates this by a number of examples from the security and economic spheres, and I have added one or two others. Important among these is the dissonance between the proclaimed values of the liberal order and its actual mode of operation (Losurdo and Elliott, 2011). The impact of this factor is little studied but almost certainly contributes to the malaise and disaffection felt by many citizens. It points to an ideological problem that blends into concerns about the decline of democracy and institutional and moral failures.

Political leaders in the United States have not been shy about proclaiming what they consider to be their right to determine global events. President Bush the younger said in his inaugural State of the Union address that the world now recognized 'one sole and pre-eminent power, the United States of America'.[9] And former US Secretary of State Madeleine Albright asserted that the US had become the 'indispensable nation'.[10] References to 'American exceptionalism' are widespread in political-historical discourse in that country.

The liberal values of the RBIO include (liberal) democracy, respect for human rights and fundamental political freedoms, competition, free trade, respect for private property rights, and the rule of law. Many states in the international community endorse and are attached to these values. Less often acknowledged, but still broadly accepted, is that it is a hierarchical order in which deference to US leadership or dominance in economic and, especially, security matters is the norm. The economically advanced countries are advantaged relative to the rest.

Mearsheimer (2019) has made explicit what adherence to this international order involves. Its defining features have led, in his view, to the system's crisis and ultimate failure. These include a desire to spread, and often impose, liberal democracy around the world, based on a belief in universal and superior values expressed in its principles, and that capital normally is best protected under such a political system. It is an order held together by consent from many participants but by selective coercion against others. Various pressures and sanctions used as instruments of US policy include political assassinations, such as that of Iranian General Qasem Soleimani, and military interventions to produce regime compliance or regime change in non-compliant states. These have led, especially since 9/11, to an almost constant state of war between the US and its allies on the one hand, and some unfortunate country on the other (Cockburn, 2021).

The degree to which US dominance of the liberal international order has relied on military supremacy is startling. The United States has nearly 800 military bases in more than 70 countries and territories abroad. The UK, France and Russia, by contrast, have about 30 foreign bases combined (Vine, 2015); China has one. Similarly, military spending by the US accounts for 38 per cent of all military spending globally – almost as much as the next ten spenders combined (Tian et al, 2020).

There is a long list of wars waged by the US, often involving allies in ad hoc 'coalitions of the willing' that are assembled more to provide political cover than for the necessity of any military contribution. These wars include that in Afghanistan and the second Iraq war, allegedly fought to destroy weapons of mass destruction, about the existence of which US President Bush and UK Prime Minister Blair blatantly lied. It produced regime change in Iraq and caused continuing violence and disorder on a massive scale. Bombing Libya also produced regime change. However, the failed state that followed the end of the Gaddafi regime has been wracked by civil war and became a transit route for migrants wanting to reach the EU. Attempted regime change in Syria did not succeed, but a vicious civil war with hundreds of thousands of deaths, millions of displaced people, and mass migrations inside and out of the country was the result. Attempts to shore up a regime deposed by internal opposition in the Yemen have produced the biggest humanitarian disaster in many years, with over 200,000 deaths. The rationale was that the Houthi rebels, who now occupy most of what used to be North Yemen, were instruments of an outside state regarded by the US as an enemy – Iran. Thus, the US gave carte blanche and assistance to its Saudi allies to launch murderous airstrikes against its opponents in Yemen. Studies of the Houthi movement (see Brandt, 2017) indicate that it is almost wholly an internally based movement, owing little to outside support, from Iran or anywhere else.

Potential military conflicts with China in the South China Sea, and with Russia in Eastern Europe (the result of NATO's and the EU's eastward expansion, according to Mearsheimer, 2019) complete the picture of a pre-eminent power now facing challenges to its influence from powers which, while by no means equal to it, are serious military actors which cannot be subdued by the methods used – with limited success, it must be said – in places like Afghanistan and Iraq.

Construction of international institutions that constrain or condition nation-state behaviour is a manifestation of the 'one size fits all' characteristics of a unipolar order. Over time, and when accompanied by more structural impacts of globalization that have negative effects on significant numbers of the population, it fuels internal opposition. Currently, although perhaps not in the long run, this has taken the form of anti-system politics, including right-wing populism. In addition to all of this, geopolitical developments such as Russia's partial recovery from its deep crisis of the 1990s and the ongoing rise of China mean that significant actors in the international system prize national sovereignty and are hostile to what they see as interference in their internal affairs. Key aspects of the RBIO are no longer accepted by some of the most powerful countries in the international system and they are no longer prepared to suffer indignities in silence.

Economic, environmental and the military/security situations all contribute to other crises such as the drive to migrate that has itself become a flashpoint in many countries – both those that are destinations and those that are sources (see Figure 2.2). According to OECD data on migration, flows to OECD countries increased from 3.85 million in 2000 to 7.06 million in 2016, with a temporary lull during the global financial crisis (IOM, 2020). Justice for Immigrants (2017) outlines several key factors and root causes of migration. First, safety factors, such as danger to individuals, can prompt them to migrate. Discrimination and persecution based on nationality, religion, race, political beliefs, or membership status in a particular social group such as LGBTQ+, can motivate people to move in search of a safer location. Fleeing danger also can result from war, including civil war, or a need to escape criminal gang activity (Bank et al, 2017; Justice for Immigrants, 2017). Refugees made up about 10 per cent of the migrant population. Second, economic migration is driven by people moving from poorer developing areas into richer areas where wages are higher, and more employment is available. Third, environmental factors are increasing involuntary migration. In part they are a product of the neoliberal growth model in agriculture and resource extraction. Crop failures and pollution of water, air, and soil create serious health risks to local inhabitants, forcing them to look for a better life elsewhere for themselves and their families. Natural disasters, such as earthquakes and hurricanes, flooding, and drought are important factors. Apart from migrants crossing international borders, the IOM (2021) reports that more than 50 million people are displaced within their own countries, uprooted by disasters, conflicts or violence.

Figure 2.2: Migration and the crises

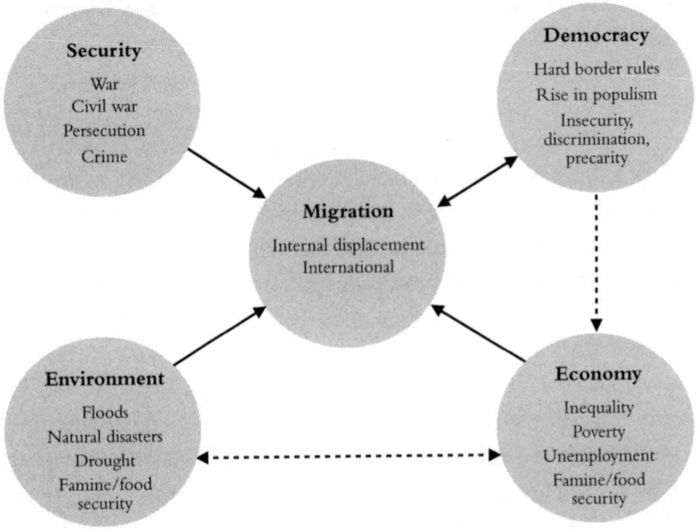

Coercion at home in the surveillance state

International security and militarization spill over into to the challenge to democracy, dealt with in the chapters to follow. The cases of Edward Snowden and Julian Assange and revelations about police and security services' infiltration of protest movements in the UK illustrate this, but they are really only the tip of a much bigger iceberg connected to the surveillance state, the acquisition of vast amounts of information and data about citizens and its deployment in the interests of social control. Similarly, surveillance capitalism involves private corporations obtaining such information for purposes of commodifying it (Zuboff, 2019).

Edward Snowden, a former technical assistant for the Central Intelligence Agency (CIA), and government contractor for the National Security Agency (NSA) leaked information showing that the NSA was collecting telephone records from tens of millions of Americans, and tapped directly into servers of nine internet firms, including Facebook, Microsoft, Google and Yahoo, to track online communication. The UK's electronic eavesdropping agency, GCHQ (Government Communication Headquarters), was also accused of gathering information on the online companies. Snowden revealed that several allied countries, embassies and EU offices were 'bugged'. Claims emerged that the NSA spied on the EU offices in the US and Europe, and on the EU internal computer network in Washington, and the 27-member bloc's UN office in New York. It electronically eavesdropped in Brussels, where the EU Council of Ministers and European Council are located, and on German Chancellor Angela Merkel's mobile phone, along with tapping millions of text messages and phone calls of ordinary German citizens. The reports also suggest that the NSA broke US privacy laws hundreds of times every year (West, 2015). To put this into perspective, Tom Engelhardt (2014) made the point that although Snowden's release of classified information was substantial, his files came from only one of 20 odd agencies and were a tiny percentage of the total files collected and stored. Under hot pursuit by the US government, Snowden eventually found refuge in Russia.

Julian Assange co-founded a website called Wikileaks, which published thousands of classified documents including exposure of US forces in Iraq and Afghanistan killing civilians. After a complex series of charges, the grant and subsequent withdrawal of political asylum, and ejection from an embassy where he had found refuge, Assange remains incarcerated in the UK and under threat of extradition to the US.

In the UK it is known that undercover police officers have infiltrated over one thousand British political groups (Woodman,

2018b). A number of unsavoury practices have been identified during their operations, including: the withholding of exculpatory evidence; the tricking of women (and men) into intimate or even sexual relationships with undercover agents; cohabitation/marriage and/or children with undercover agents; identity theft from dead children; and planning and participation in serious crimes, including arson (Lubbers, 2015; Evans, 2018). Left-wing protests received particular attention. The dissent which the 'political police' protect against is often – implicitly or explicitly – anti-capitalist (Bonino and Kaoullas, 2015; Woodman, 2018a). The special units shared deep connections with industry. In 2018, the Metropolitan Police admitted that the Special Branch forwarded information regarding political organizers to the Consulting Association, which established a blacklist of construction workers due to their union organizing and political affiliations (Casciani, 2018; IER, 2020). Former political police have also founded and/or joined private surveillance firms, using their former skills for commercial purposes.

These revelations of the activities of the secret state in liberal democracies could be added to at length. They are important because they show how little the population is trusted by the authorities and how vindictive these authorities are when their illegal acts are exposed. The discussion connects to more generalized concerns about the quality of contemporary democracy.

Conclusions

All these crises contribute to the approaching dystopia from which we need to escape. None stands alone. Rather they intersect in numerous ways, with global capitalism and the implementation of neoliberal ideas and practices bearing a principal responsibility for their negative and dangerous effects. Economically the system is unstable, produces undesirable results like extreme inequality, and is prone to punishing crises in which its beneficiaries are protected at the expense of the general population. Its focus on unlimited growth fuels the environmental crisis. While the pandemic is a separate crisis it is also a central component of the climate crisis narrative, being linked to zoonotic transmission of diseases, itself linked to declining fertility and arable land.

At the same time as being responsible for the situation, neoliberal ideas and interests block the development of alternatives and solutions. A repurposed set of national-level and international institutions has created an impasse in which stability is unsustainable but progressive change cannot be achieved easily.

3

The Three Ds: Disaffection, Disarray, Democracy

The unhappy convergence of crises already noted has been accompanied by a crisis of the institutions and democratic processes that are needed to deal with them. Liberal democratic political systems are often seen as elite driven, unresponsive to citizens and not as representative or accountable as would be suggested in democratic theory. If this is true at the national level, it is even more so in the cases of multilevel or global governance.

Global institutions are remote from democratic influence, except as brokered through their member states. Globally, economic governance institutions are more powerful than those addressing issues such as the environment or health. Because they privilege unlimited economic growth over other goals and diminish the capacity of nation-states to address issues of concern to their citizens, global institutions are part of the problem rather than part of any solution. They contribute to what, under neoliberalism, may been termed the 'depoliticization of politics' – the removal of crucially important issues from public control.

Essentially, neoliberalism has attempted to depoliticize important choices by embedding authority to deal with them in unrepresentative and unaccountable locations (at either international or national level) and by substituting, for democratic discourse and decision-making, adherence to pre-ordained rules. The result is that nation-states have been partially hollowed out from above, and internally their political processes are distrusted.

Concerns about the state of democracy are hardly new but they have changed their focus in recent decades. In the early 1970s, literature identifying a crisis of democracy began to emerge. It maintained that there was 'too much democracy'. Now it is more common to hear the complaint that there is not enough.

The earlier literature argued that Western electorates had rising expectations and were making demands far beyond the capacity of governments to meet. As a result, governments were subject to 'overload', and the gap between what they could provide and what their populations demanded could give rise to 'ungovernability' (Crozier, Huntington and Watanuki, 1975). Summarizing much of this literature, Crozier et al's report, prepared for the Trilateral Commission,[1] pointed to 'a breakdown of traditional means of social control, a delegitimation of political and other means of authority' as well as excessive demands (Crozier et al, 1975, p 8; see also Pilon, 2013, p 47). Critics noted that running through these analyses was a concern for the established order and authority, and apprehension about the dangers of excessive democracy (Chomsky, 1999). The period was one of vibrant political contestation in which, for a time, working-class organizations and left-wing movements and parties sought to consolidate and extend the achievements made over the Keynesian era. In this they were seen as expecting and demanding too much. Neoliberalism and its selective rolling-back of the state was the response that won the day.

Five decades later there are concerns about the state of democracy, often triggered by the rise of 'illiberal democracies' (Zakaria, 1997), citing cases like Hungary or Poland, and 'anti-system politics' (Hopkin, 2020), a more widespread phenomenon associated with the rise of right-wing populism in many countries. These discussions focus on populist rejection of democratic norms and, particularly, social liberal values, such as commitments to minority rights and non-discrimination. Economic liberalism is less challenged by these movements. Be that as it may, the picture drawn conflates the liberal and democratic components of liberal democracy and is often expressed as depicting an insufficiency of democracy rather than an excess of it. How did this happen?

It is partly because distrust of democracy is part of the neoliberal tradition itself and, as neoliberalism became the dominant ideology, that distrust found practical expression in changes to political structures. The result has been that the democratic element of the liberal democratic compromise, arguably always somewhat imbalanced and favouring the liberal component over the democratic one, has been further diminished. One consequence is that our institutions are widely seen as unresponsive to what people actually want, and are unfit to deal effectively with the multiple crises we face. Rather than the problem being one of illiberal democracy, it is one of increasingly undemocratic liberalism.

Liberal democracy has always represented an uneasy tension between liberalism (with a focus on individualism, private property rights, choice, and competition) and democracy (meaning rule of, for, and by the people). This tension was well captured by C.B. Macpherson (1965, pp 4–5) when he emphasized that liberal democracy was historically a system in which liberalism came first, and elements of democracy were grafted on later. For example, in most Western countries extension of the right to vote for substantial numbers of people came after a liberal, market society was already established. This meant that the type of democracy that was introduced was strongly influenced by the pre-existing liberal society. What emerged – liberal democracy – was a system of power in two senses. The first was the politics by which people are governed and 'made to do things they would not otherwise do and made to refrain from doing things they otherwise might do'. Second, though, this system was one in which 'liberal-democracy and capitalism go together. Liberal-democracy is found only in countries whose economic system is wholly or predominantly that of capitalist enterprise'. This defined the purpose of liberal democratic systems, which existed 'to uphold and enforce a certain kind of society, a certain set of relations between individuals, a certain set of rights and claims that people have on each other both directly, and indirectly through their rights to property' (Macpherson, 1965, p 4).

Tensions in the liberal democratic compromise arise from the combination of economic inequality, the inevitable outcome of a capitalist system, and the political equality implied by democracy. What happens if the people choose to use their political rights to curtail or abolish economic inequality? The tensions between the two are most easily managed when times are prosperous and when most people in capitalist societies can consider themselves winners – either in relation to others, if society is becoming more equal, or in relation to themselves over time, if living standards are rising. It has been some time since either of these conditions held true. Martin Wolfe (2016) argued in a *Financial Times* article that:

> Widely shared increases in real incomes played a vital part in legitimizing capitalism and stabilizing democracy. Today, however, capitalism is finding it far more difficult to generate such improvements in prosperity. On the contrary, the evidence is of growing inequality and slowing productivity growth. This poisonous brew makes democracy intolerant and capitalism illegitimate.

Classical liberal accounts tend to pay less attention to outcomes and focus instead on procedures and processes. For example, liberal democracy is 'a political system marked not only by free and fair elections but also by the rule of law, separation of powers, and the protection of basic liberties of speech, assembly, religion, and property' (Zakaria, 1997, p 22). If the processes are fair, so too must be the outcomes. Contained in the idea of free and fair elections is the notion that the governments established as a result of such processes must by these means represent the population and be accountable to it. The implication is also that most important issues will be decided by democratic procedures and that, albeit indirectly through representation, the people do rule. The modern device through which this might be achieved is a system of competitive political parties between which choices can be made (Mair, 2013).

Neoliberal distrust of democratic procedures and its consequences

Neoliberal democratic theory is narrower still than these classic liberal approaches. True representation and accountability are seen as unachievable and, instead, democracy is reduced to a choice between contenders for government office, within a context of constitutionally guaranteed liberal rights. Alternative conceptions would certainly include a choice of programmes – a choice of what is to be done and not just who is to do it. To forestall a broader version of democracy, which might focus on outcomes such as relative equality from gaining traction, neoliberals have considered that free markets must be protected from political interference. Institutional devices have been designed to prevent democratic politics from undermining essential features of capitalism (Sánchez-Cuenca, 2020). Neoliberalism involves a reduction of the state in some areas, especially provision of social supports, but also in terms of taking responsibility for economic management. That function is now left to the 'market'. Even there, however, state policies, including subsidies for fossil fuels and agriculture, and its overall macroeconomic stance, continue to have a major impact on markets. In other areas – security, and creating the legal-constitutional frameworks for defence of property rights – the state's role has expanded (Gill and Cutler, 2014).

Democracy is reduced to a set of procedures designed only to produce governments through popular elections. It can be used to choose who is in office, but not what they will do. At most, it can serve as a set of devices for non-violent replacement of rulers, and thus limit the concentration of power in the hands of any particular individual or team of leaders (Sánchez-Cuenca, 2020).

Depoliticization consists of replacing the idea of democratic policy-making, through representation of the voice of the people, by the application of rules designed and implemented by those considered to be experts. Another dimension of depoliticization is to transfer national or international decision-making authority to bodies where little, if any, accountability can be expected.

In summary, neoliberal institutional theory relies on two arguments. First, democracy in the sense of collective decision-making is not possible. In a more limited sense, democracy may serve as a safeguard against concentration of political power. Second, depoliticization offers a neutral and efficient alternative to realize and institute collective welfare (via the market) and leaves other decisions in the hands of technocrats or experts. In such a vision there is limited role for the representative and accountability functions that democratic theorists have traditionally regarded as central features of a liberal democratic system. Adoption and implementation of such a theoretical perspective has led one analyst to refer to a transition from liberal democracy to neoliberal democracy. By this Jonathan Hopkin meant a system in which open markets were no longer a matter for political debate or dispute, and in which important decisions had been removed entirely from the scope of electoral politics (Hopkin, 2020, p 5). Others, noting the increasing insulation of decision-makers from social or political challenges, refer to 'authoritarian neoliberalism' (Bruff, 2014), or, focusing on the ways the European Union has bypassed the division of competencies or powers between itself and the nation-states belonging to it and entrenched neoliberal doctrines beyond the reach of any popular control, as 'authoritarian constitutionalism' (Oberndorfer, 2014).

There is considerable public concern about a democratic deficit and disaffection with democracy within our liberal democratic systems. Partly disaffection is the result of the reduced public domain produced by depoliticization and relocation of decision-making to unaccountable bodies. Relocation can be spatial, as functions are transferred upwards to a regional or global level. It can also be organizational, as the state creates arm's-length bodies to handle major portfolios and marketizes its own activities. Similarly, it may be private, as various forms of private authority replace public authority (McBride, 2010; Wilks, 2013). In the areas that remain open to democratic politics the two other deficits, one of representation, the other of accountability, contribute to the overall democratic deficit. The combination of factors limiting democratic decision-making has led to various kinds of anti-system politics that are the subject of the next chapter.

In modern times, representation normally connotes a territorial dimension. Representatives serve the population of a given local area. Notionally, their actions reflect in some way the preferences of their constituents who live in that particular locality and to whom, in turn, they will be held accountable in a future election. Peter Mair (1992) has accurately depicted this as 'the ideology of local representation', because the reality is quite different. Few local constituencies constitute natural communities where a common interest might emerge and be reflected in the behaviour of a representative. And, in almost all liberal democracies, the vast majority of the people vote because of the party of their local candidates, not on the basis of their personal qualities (Pilon, 2007, pp 126–7, 140–3). Individual locality-based politicians may perform some services for constituents, helping with applications for social benefits or expediting passport applications, for instance, but their role and vote in the legislature is driven by the party they belong to, and voters' verdict on them is similarly determined.

In terms of fulfilling the liberal democratic principles of representation and accountability, therefore, a great deal hinges on how well political parties perform these functions. Their failure to do so, in combination with other trends in contemporary politics, is a significant part of the explanation for the democratic deficit that has led to disaffection and a search for alternatives. In the standard political-science literature of a generation ago, parties were depicted as offering a two-way communication function between leaders and the population, a choice between policies and, of course, a choice of leadership teams. Only the latter is really performed today, and even there it is a less of a choice between collective leaderships than it is a choice of who the head of government will be. Some indicators of the declining role of parties can be found in the lower turnout rates in elections noted in many jurisdictions, reports of declining party loyalty and, more directly, in declining membership of the parties themselves (Mair, 2013, pp 13–16; Crouch, 2020, pp 6–11).[2] Together these trends mean that the 'zone of engagement' between citizens and political leaders has shrunk and diminished in quality. Citizens have increasingly disengaged from politics. The distancing between people and elites is mutual (Mair, 2013, pp 76–7). Politicians and their staffs have become increasingly professionalized and disconnected from the citizenry, focused on office-seeking rather than the expression of interests or ideas, adept at public relations and polling designed to manipulate or manage public opinion, and prone to, or believed to be prone to, corruption.

As well, in policy terms, mainstream parties have become virtually indistinguishable in their defence of the fundamentals of the status quo. These are parties, as Tariq Ali (2015, p 15) puts it, of the 'extreme centre'. Jonathan Hopkin (2020, p 5) describes the parties as having converged ideologically around market liberalism so that they now resemble 'cartels' that offer a very limited range of policy options. The failure of these options, as evidenced by the multiple crises, means that the system is in disarray.

One result has been the rise of anti-system parties and movements. Much of the discussion of this phenomenon has focused on the rise of populism, but there are other variants of anti-system parties, such as those still calling for the abolition of capitalism and its replacement by some form of socialism, and minority nationalist formations calling for the dissolution of an existing nation-state.

In accounts of the rise of populism, loosely defined as a belief system that juxtaposes the interests of the 'people' on the one hand, and the 'elite' on the other (see Mudde and Rovira Kaltwasser, 2017), there is emphasis on the fact that, for significant numbers of voters, the political system as a whole neither reflects nor even talks about issues that are important to them. This applies to established political parties and, more generally, the political and media elites. In the development of such sentiments, lack of representation is part of the issue; the other, and connected part, is lack of accountability. This takes a number of forms – relocating decisions to geographically remote and unaccountable locations, and the way in which existing institutions, even if closer to home, actually operate.

Taken together these factors would seem to meet classic definitions of elite dominance (Birch, 2007, ch 4), which is reinforced by the rise of governance networks in many policy areas. Networks are comprised of governments and various stakeholders and are not well connected to official representative bodies. Network governance describes collaborative and negotiated decision-making between public and private entities which are relatively autonomous from each other. They are not positioned in any kind of hierarchy yet are interdependent and in need of each other's cooperation to make or implement policies – hence the motive to participate in the networks. Agreements and understandings reached in the networks may be difficult to unravel as one participant's failure to ratify imperils the whole agreement. Moreover, the longer the chain of delegation, the weaker the democratic accountability. This is particularly evident in multilevel governance situations. It has been argued that network forms of governance can be democratic, but it is little in evidence. Actually existing network activities are often deliberately obscure. The rationale is that compromises may better emerge outside the public eye. Given multiple actors and lack of transparency it is hard to identify who is responsible for what. The effectiveness of the democratic accountability is undermined if responsibility cannot be attributed to particular actors.

Governments implementing neoliberalism have aimed to insulate the economy from democratic politics. A (highly politicized) depoliticization of key institutions has been undertaken. Constitutional law or quasi-constitutional arrangements has been one method that has been implemented at both international and national levels (Clarkson, 1993; McBride, 2003; Gill and Cutler, 2014). Policy areas significantly removed from democratic pressures or control include monetary policy, trade and investment policy, and fiscal policy. Others, like labour relations and labour market policies, are also being targeted (Whiteside et al, 2021). In a wide range of very important spheres the reach of democratic processes is much reduced or, in some cases, wholly absent. One reason there is scepticism about democracy and disaffection from mainstream politics, and growth in support for anti-system movements, is that many important issues are decided in venues beyond democratic control.

Several varieties of this type of depoliticization through constitutionalization are identifiable. Nation-states have sacrificed control by assuming obligations to observe specified rules of international organizations or as part of binding and enforceable international treaties. Typically, trade and investment agreements or treaties constrain state activity in a number of areas. They also help to insure against the risk of 'defection' by individual states which might undergo a change of government. If a new government has different priorities from the one that originally signed or was in support of the agreement it will discover that binding and enforceable international treaties serve to lock in earlier commitments. This renders them immune from democratic pressures (Gruber, 2000). Significant components of these policies are predetermined by rules that are designed to be permanently insulated from democratic processes. Often, as with investor-state dispute settlement mechanisms in trade and investment agreements, adjudication over disputes is handed over to 'non-political' and essentially private forums such as tribunals staffed by commercial arbitrators (Van Harten, 2005).

The World Trade Organization administers a family of agreements that go well beyond traditional tariff issues and permit challenges to national policies or regulations in areas like consumer protection, health and safety, and environmental measures if these are viewed as impeding international trade in some way. It has been depicted as being focused on 'setting limits … on national state regulation' (Picciotto, 2003). A number of policies that could be the basis of industrial strategies, such as domestic content requirements on manufacturing (see McBride and Shields, 2013), or the use of state-owned enterprises for non-commercial purposes, are banned or made more difficult.

The North American Free Trade Agreement (NAFTA) limited state interference with foreign investment in a variety of ways, and the power of capital investors was enhanced vis-à-vis nation-states. In embracing NAFTA, Mexico changed its own constitution by making 30 amendments to bring it into compliance (Gill and Cutler, 2014, p 6, n 3). NAFTA Chapter 11 gave foreign investors from the other NAFTA signatories the right to launch cases against states and have them adjudicated, essentially under the rules of international private commercial arbitration. Such procedures have been widely criticized as inducing 'regulatory chill' on states (see Van Harten and Scott, 2016). Certain types of state regulation would attract international trade disputes and the possibility of sanctions and financial damages, outcomes that governments are anxious to avoid. NAFTA's objectives included the elimination of trade barriers, encouraging the cross-border movement of goods and services, increasing investment opportunities, protection of intellectual property rights, and reduction of national discretion to discriminate in favour of domestic industries. It prohibited a wide range of performance requirements that states might impose on foreign investors to guarantee they would receive benefits from the investment. For Canadian business, limits on the interventionist powers of the Canadian state were deemed a 'desirable loss of sovereignty' (Doern and Tomlin, 1991, p 258). They also, of course, limited popular sovereignty by reducing the scope within which democratic preferences could be implemented.

Given the continued commitment of Canada and Mexico to investor-state dispute settlement mechanisms in international agreements, one can conclude that the regulatory chill effect, deterring government regulation, is not unwelcome. Neoliberal governments can use international commitments as a means of avoiding domestic debates they do not want to have. In the negotiations that replaced NAFTA with the United States–Mexico–Canada Agreement (USMCA), the US pushed for the removal of the investor-state dispute provisions with Canada.

Canadian critics of investor-state dispute clauses had seen them as significant intrusions on Canadian sovereignty (McBride, 2006) so their removal, though not instigated by the Canadian government, represented a gain for those wishing to enhance the country's autonomy and policy capacity. However, other clauses in the USMCA offset their removal (McBride, 2020).

The EU–Canada Comprehensive Economic and Trade Agreement (CETA) requires subnational governments (that is, municipalities, provinces, and states) to open up procurement markets to each other's corporations. This precludes governments from favouring local companies and local economic development and reduces their ability to use public spending to achieve social, economic, or environmental goals (Barlow, 2015). Such market access commitments inhibit governments from creating new public monopolies (even regionally and locally), including in areas such as wastewater services, waste management services, and public health or automobile insurance. Canadian critics of the agreement have argued that governments are now constrained from expanding existing public services into new areas for fear of accumulating trade sanctions or disputes. This induces a 'policy chill', where penalties deter governments from acting in the public interest. Private interests are favoured through the 'ratchet effect', whereby future reforms are essentially stuck as, once foreign investors/service providers are established in previously socialized sectors, it is hard to reverse without incurring financial penalties. Investor-state dispute settlement is ensconced in the CETA (Sinclair, 2019).

There are also many national examples of attempts to remove issues from the democratic agenda. One is the adoption of balanced budget legislation. Depending on how this is done it can be more or less binding. In many state-level constitutions in the US, for example, balanced budgets are required. In some Westminster-style parliamentary systems, such as a number of Canadian provinces, legislation sets out the same goals. The fact that this was ordinary legislation in parliamentary systems, and could be easily rescinded or ignored, meant that these measures were partially of symbolic value (McBride and Whiteside, 2011). However, in the right circumstances they strengthen the negotiating position of finance ministers in internal governmental deliberations. Another example of depoliticization is the creation of arm's-length agencies to deliver public services without strict accountability to the public via legislatures. Frequent resort to public–private partnerships has much the same effect in accountability terms (Whiteside, 2015).

The European Union (EU), too, has significantly eroded the scope for democracy. In the EU case, this is both by inhibiting democracy at the member-state level, by imposing rules and thresholds limiting what decisions are possible, and by its own internally undemocratic procedures, which are so obscure and remote from popular input that they render effective representation and accountability impossible.

The European Fiscal Compact provides a good example. The Fiscal Compact was negotiated as part of an intergovernmental treaty between member states (the Treaty on Stability, Coordination and Governance in the Economic and Monetary Union; TSCG) that was technically outside the European Union. Nevertheless, under its rubric, states cede a lot of political power upwards to EU institutions, particularly the European Commission and the European Court of Justice (ECJ). The Fiscal Compact's design is intended to construct both international-level and national legal constraints on fiscal policy. States are required to implement these rules 'through provisions of binding force and permanent character, preferably constitutional' (TSCG, Art 3, para 2). Thus, the Fiscal Compact, signed in 2012 by 25 out of the then 27 EU members,[3] 'establishes a pervasive legal regime to tighten the budgetary policies ... with the goal of ensuring fiscal discipline in the member states as a pre-condition for financial stability in the entire Euro-zone' (Fabbrini, 2013, p 8). Many of the states subject to these rules have yet to constitutionalize them formally. However, the treaties that contain these measures partially constitutionalize them through binding their signatories, even if those with parliamentary-type systems under which, theoretically, no parliament can bind its successors. The rules reflect and 'lock in' neoliberal policy preferences. German Chancellor Angela Merkel's comment is particularly revealing: 'The Fiscal Pact is about inserting debt brakes permanently in the national legal systems. They shall possess a binding and eternal validity' (cited in Oberndorfer, 2012).

The Compact is incorporated into EU decision-making processes like the 'European Semester',[4] and so members must adhere to its conditions, submit 'every major economic policy reform it plans to implement', and participate in summits and annual meetings on budgetary policies and other issues in the Compact (Degryse, 2012, p 58). In the event of a deficit deemed excessive under the Compact, countries must submit national reform programmes with structural adjustment to the European Council and Commission. If these rules are not incorporated into national laws, the states could be taken to the ECJ and may receive financial sanctions (Degryse, 2012, p 58). This means member states are tightly integrated into a highly obscure political system in which lines of accountability are almost impossible to draw.

After the 2008 crisis, supranational policy responses have aimed at 'restoring competitiveness and sustainability' primarily through fiscal consolidation (austerity) but also through labour market restructuring. Three main policy interventions in areas related to wage policies (an area of national rather than EU jurisdiction) stemmed from the EU's view that the economic difficulties were the result of too much debt and too little competitiveness. The EU argued in favour of intense austerity policies in order to overcome the debt crisis (and this became more pronounced after the adoption of the Fiscal Pact in March 2012, which effectively constitutionalized austerity). Less competitive countries that belonged to the European Monetary Union (EMU) were subjected to 'a policy of internal devaluation', which involved increasing competitiveness by reducing labour costs, effectively functioning as a substitute for currency devaluation which membership in the eurozone had removed as an option (Myant et al, 2016).

Neoclassical economic arguments that sharp increases in unemployment are the result of 'institutional rigidities' in the labour market have taken root and have been pushed by the EU. Its 'Europe 2020' project sought to undertake reforms of pensions, social protection, health–care and education systems 'in order to achieve fiscal consolidation and long-term financial sustainability' (De La Porte and Pochet, 2014, p 289).

The situation with respect to monetary policy is even more striking. In the eurozone, of course, the independence of the European Central Bank (ECB) was secured by international agreements or treaties. Its own account shows its independence to be extremely robust, with little accountability other than transparency and explaining its actions.[5] Within the eurozone, the ECB has been assigned the primary goal of maintaining price stability, and its independence in pursuing this has been given constitutional status in the Statute of the European System of Central Banks and of the European Central Bank, and in the European Community Treaty itself. The focus on anti-inflationary policy fits the interests of finance capital in an era of deregulated financial markets and capital mobility, and the credibility of states in this area is enhanced by deflationary policies of fiscal austerity (Burnham, 1999). More generally, central banks, often by normal legislative or regulatory change, have been made more independent of governments and hence, even if indirectly, of the public. Over the 1989–2010 period there was a steady movement towards central bank independence (CBI) covering advanced countries, emerging economies and developing countries (Polillo and Guillen, 2005; Dincer and Eichengreen, 2014). Both at national and international levels there is long-standing literature suggesting that autonomous central banks will favour austerity and financial orthodoxy over policies of stimulus (Kurzer, 1988). Thus, neoliberal goals are advanced by making central banks independent. Its other effect is that it converts political debates about appropriate monetary policy into obscure, technical issues beyond the scope of public scrutiny (Hay, 2007, pp 116–17).

'Europe 2020' provides another example. It and subsequent agreements are integrated into the European Semester decision-making processes. 'Europe 2020' included the European Employment Strategy (EES), which provides a set of employment guidelines proposed by the European Commission, surveillance mechanisms, National Reform Programmes (NRPs) submitted by national governments to be reviewed by the Commission, and Country Reports and Country-Specific Recommendations (CSRs) published by the Commission (European Commission, 2016a). For member states, these processes are quasi-constitutional in nature and embed important labour market decisions in processes that are unconnected to public input, however notional.

Discussing key institutions within the EU, Perry Anderson (2021) notes that constitutionalism is ignored when doing so promotes supranationalism over the jurisdictional capacity of nation-states. The constitutional limits that have been discussed so far, then, should be understood as limits imposed on nation- or member states.[6] He points out, citing Horsley (2018), that the ECJ saw itself as the 'driving force of integration', although there was no basis for this in the founding treaties. Supreme or constitutional courts at the national level are always subject to a degree of protection against legislative 'correction' of their decisions. The ECJ's decisions are irreversible and not subject to any legislative amendment or overrule. Anderson (2021, p 27) comments that 'it would be difficult to conceive of a judicial institution in the West that … was purer of any trace of democratic accountability'. The European Commission, essentially the EU's executive branch that stands at the apex of the EU's large bureaucracy, wields great power within the EU. It is the primary target of some 30,000 registered lobbyists, 63 per cent of whom represent corporations, and it manages the complex regulations and rules on behalf of the EU. The *acquis communitaire*, the codification of EU regulations that new member states have to sign up to, and existing ones supposedly comply with, is now 90,000 pages long (Anderson, 2021, p 29). As already noted, the ECB enjoys near absolute independence (other than by treaty revision) and has the single objective of maintaining monetary stability (that is, inflation control). Referring to an earlier assessment by Fritz Scharpf, Anderson (2021, p 31) writes of these three institutions, the Court, Commission and Central Bank, that 'it is precisely those institutions which have the greatest impact on the daily life of most people that are furthest removed from democratic accountability'.

The most accountable EU institutions are the European Parliament, generally conceded to be of minimal practical significance in European governance, though its existence and the elections to it may supply a veneer of legitimacy, and the European Council. The latter is composed of heads of government and, since they occupy those positions as a result of elections, there are lines of accountability running from electorates, through national parliaments (or presidencies in case of directly elected presidential systems), to Brussels and the Council. However, a dictum advanced earlier in the chapter in a different context may be apposite here too: the longer the lines of delegation, the less representation and accountability apply.

For Anderson, however, basing his argument on that of Bickerton (2012), the situation is more serious than that. Bickerton argues that nation-states, which founded and joined the EU, have undergone a transition into member states. The distinction is a subtle one, and largely unnoticed. But its implications are hugely significant. What it amounts to is that horizontal ties between members of the (EU) club are more significant than vertical ties between (nation-state) governments and their own societies. The frame of reference has shifted. As a result,

> National governments commit to limit their own powers in order to contain the power of domestic populations. Instead of the people expressing themselves qua constituent power through this constitutional architecture, national governments seek to limit popular power by binding themselves through an external set of rules, procedures and norms. An internal working out of popular sovereignty that serves to unite state and society is replaced with an externalization of constraints to national power intended as a way of separating popular will from the policy-making process. (Bickerton, cited in Anderson, 2021, p 31)

The dense and layered network of supranational rules, surveillance, reporting and disciplinary mechanisms in the EU are a stark example of 'neoliberal democracy' through depoliticized and (top-down) constitutionalized governance. As its theorists intended, neoliberal democracy is a hollowed-out shell. In this context the power of capital, both internationally and nationally, is maximized. Some of the key relationships are shown in Figure 3.1.

The most important actor is capital or business. It has used its enormous power to create an international economic system in which its interests are protected by enforceable rules. Capital uses its power and influence to shape nation-state politics and behaviour. Simultaneously, nation-states are on the receiving end of a rules-based international order which constrains their activities in certain respects. In adopting neoliberal ideas and institutions nation-states cede authority to capital and also undermine their own democratic processes by acceding to depoliticization, but also by weakening potential sources of opposition, such as labour.

Figure 3.1: Power relationships

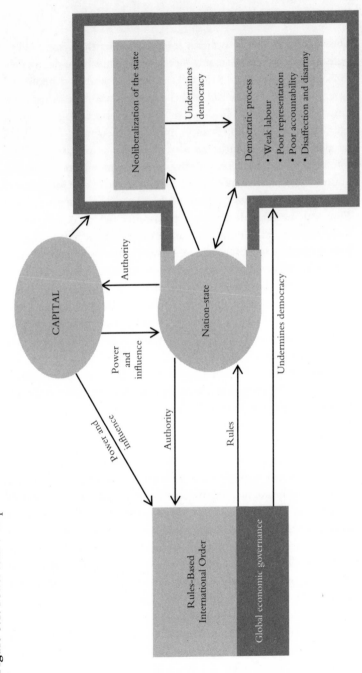

Democratic implications

Unsurprisingly, public policies emerging under this system fail to reflect the representation and accountability norms of democracy (Schäfer and Streeck, 2013, p 1). They also embed a neoliberal orientation to economic governance and crisis response that empowers capital and leads to an assault on the living standards, opportunities, and hopes and aspirations of workers. The EU's pandemic response indicates that the new constitutional rules intended to protect economically orthodox prescriptions did not entirely hold. And 'depoliticization' proved to have its limits in the sense that the process of deciding on coronavirus support in the European Union was intensely political. One aspect of political contention was about conditionalities related to accessing money. Clearly, at one level the jostling between groups of nation-states about the design of the rescue packages in Europe is anything but depoliticized. However, in terms of democratic participation it largely remains so (see also the descriptions of EU political processes in Gillingham, 2016). The type of politics on offer at the EU serves as a support to neoliberal constitutionalization rather than an alternative to it.

Complementing the argument about the realities of politics inside the EU is Wolfgang Streeck's (2014, pp 79–86) more generally applicable argument that states are increasingly accountable to two constituencies or 'peoples', often with divergent interests. These are the 'staatsvolk' (the nationally based general citizenry), and the 'marktvolk' (creditors with global rather than national interests). In this view, the emergence of finance 'marks a new stage in the relationship between capitalism and democracy, in which capital exercises its political influence not only indirectly (by investing or not investing in national economies) but also directly (by financing or not financing the state itself)' (Streeck, 2014, p 84).

By depoliticizing crucial spheres of policy-making that used, ultimately if imperfectly, to be in the hands of the public (Hay, 2007; Offe, 2013), the scope for the exercise of democratic politics is diminished. Policies continue to be made but, the outcomes having been fixed in certain respects, the need for public input is reduced as technical application of rules replaces debate about more fundamental questions. In reality, such rules are expressions of previous choices that are now institutionalized. So, in a very real sense the public is taken out of the policy process.

The crisis in our institutions is a problem because the nation-state and the state arguably offer the best prospects for confronting the multiple crises that represent our present dystopia. Yet the nation-state, considered as a vehicle in which action could be taken, has been hollowed out. And the state, in its other meaning of public institutions, has been drastically weakened by the long neoliberal hegemony. As states have been the architects both of globalization and of domestic neoliberalism, this weakening is largely a self-inflicted wound. One result is the rise of anti-system politics that is explored in the next chapter.

4

Breaking the Mould through Anti-System Politics?

Nation-states, the highest jurisdictional level at which anything resembling democracy is practised, have come under challenge from a variety of forces. Neoliberal ideology has promoted globalization and market-based solutions that have advantaged capital. State ability to regulate capital has been reduced. This has been reinforced by the impact of international trade and investment agreements and, for some states, by the conditionalities imposed by international organizations. In some areas, nation-states simply don't do as much as they used to. Their impotence or claimed impotence in the face of global challenges is noted and resented by some of their citizens. Efforts to reverse this situation have been made internationally; the anti-globalization movement of the 1990s and 2000s is an example. And national efforts have also been attempted to capture or recapture the state from the elites seen to be running it.

In combination these activities amount to the rise of anti-system politics (Hopkin, 2020). The movements involved may be unlikely themselves to engineer system change in the political economy of neoliberal globalization. However, in many cases they serve to destabilize the system, and their presence and activities could provide openings for system change.

Curiously, the formerly vibrant and mostly left-wing anti-globalization movement lost focus during the course of the 2000s. Both coercion and co-option played roles. State repression after 9/11 through antiterrorism laws, increased securitization of summit sites, and criminalization of protestors led to exhaustion (Ayres, 2004; Mertes, 2015; Conway, 2016). International economic organizations co-opted or diverted energies through the co-option of mainstream non-governmental organizations (NGOs) that saw communication as more effective than confrontation (Munck, 2006).

Tensions within the movement itself also existed, including those between the more traditional left-wing organizations and the 'newer' organizations; overemphasizing the Global North at the expense of the Global South (including through unequal access to the internet; Clark and Thermudo, 2006); and the failure to develop a common framing or common solution (Ayres, 2004). Originally on the political left, anti-globalization is often depicted as having switched from a left- to a right-wing issue (Horner et al, 2018; Slobodian, 2019). As they became neoliberalized, centre-left parties bought into globalization, and left the field open to movements expressing nationalist, and nativist, hostility to globalism.

The nature of the challenge posed by the earlier anti-globalization movement and some of the anti-system parties and movements discussed in this chapter clearly differs. At least in its initial stages the anti-globalization movement was anti-*neoliberal* globalization, and it therefore took on the central ingredient of the international economic system. The challenges of today's anti-system political movements vary quite a bit but are more focused on opposition to established elites and a claim to speak on behalf of 'the people'. In most cases it is more about perceived problems with democracy than with neoliberalism. Yet because of its hostility to globalism, it does ask questions about the role of international institutions and the need for greater autonomy at the nation-state level. Populism is one example, and this builds on a dichotomy between 'us' (the people) and 'them', sometimes in bizarre ways, as with the association between populism and various types of conspiracy theories (Castanho Silva et al, 2017), leading to the mobilization of such groups as wellness and alternative medicine circles, libertarians, poor and marginalized communities, united really only by a distrust of different kinds of elites. More generally, depending on how each part of the formula 'people versus elites' is defined, somewhat different politics ensue.

Disaffection with the political class or the establishment – elites in the economy, politics, society, religion and the media – is central to the populist version of anti-system politics. Typically, elites are portrayed as corrupt, self-interested and out of touch with the preferences and needs of ordinary people. In the context of minority nationalist movements, which are anti-system but may or may not be populist, the elite or establishment may be external to the nation. For Scottish nationalists it is London or Westminster; for those in Catalonia, Madrid; for the supporters of Brexit in the UK, it is Brussels and the EU. Here the anti-system goal focuses on 'taking back control' of the nation's affairs through separating from the existing political entity or achieving a radical reform within it. These movements may or may not be expressed in populist terms.

The concept of the 'nation' to which control should be returned varies widely. For the right populists nationalism is a cultural or sociological, even xenophobic, construction. Supporters wear the label 'nationalist' with pride in the characteristics claimed for the included people. Opponents use the same label to refer to its ethnocentric, racist and xenophobic tone.

On the left an alternative construction could take the form of a jurisdictional or political sense as rights belonging to the legal entity known as a nation-state, and to all who live within it as citizens (however constituted culturally or sociologically). The nation-state then becomes the entity or vehicle within which democratic politics can best be practised. This type of nationalism could be better expressed as 'nation-state-ism' since it simply advances the notion that democracy may be achieved most effectively at that jurisdictional level, rather than any higher one.

Notwithstanding the negative associations of nationalism in the right populist sense, that grouping might end up having done advocates of radical transformation a favour by rediscovering the potential of the nation-state. The nation-state may in fact be the best available vehicle to break the mould of neoliberal globalism and the liberal international order.

In this chapter, anti-system politics is surveyed through several lenses – left populism, right populism, minority nationalism, and its impact on established parties and politics. In the process the anti-elitism that these movements share is investigated, as well as the culture versus economics debate about the rise of anti-system politics, and the return, in some versions, to a focus on the nation-state. The purpose is to throw light on the issue of whether these anti-system political currents serve as an obstacle to radical transformation because of their divisiveness. Or do they, perhaps inadvertently, help to identify the vehicle that could drive radical transformation?

Anti-system parties and movements

Left populism

Left populist political movements such as Podemos in Spain, Syriza in Greece, and Sinn Fein in the Republic of Ireland, as well as dissidents within major centrist political parties like Jeremy Corbyn in the UK Labour Party[1] and Bernie Sanders in the US Democratic Party, represent one variety of anti-system politics. They posed challenges to the certainties of the neoliberal political consensus, especially around austerity in the post-GFC period. By no means successful in reversing austerity politics, they did, however, expose the emptiness of mainstream politics and contribute to the sense that democracy is in crisis. Liberal democratic institutions failed to respond adequately to the GFC or any other of the multiple crises they faced. As a result, traditional political organizations, the established political parties of the 'centre-right' and 'centre-left', have been widely discredited and their combined share of the vote has declined in some countries. These mainstream political formations have proved unable to identify real alternatives from which electorates can make choices and, once installed in office, produce only superficial, if any, change.

Spain provides examples of both left and right populism. On the left, Podemos was a new party, formed out of the social movement of the *Indignados* and 15-M anti-austerity protests. Podemos ('we can' in Spanish) made a breakthrough in the 2014 European elections when it gained 8 per cent of the popular vote. In the 2015 and 2016 national elections, both figures were at roughly 20 per cent. By April 2019, the total had declined to 14 per cent and fell one point further in the November 2019 election to 13 per cent. During its rise Podemos articulated two main themes – the need to make Spanish politics more democratic and the need to do things differently. The first theme tapped into the widespread disaffection and anti-establishment sentiments within the Spanish population that were exacerbated by the deep economic crisis (Lancaster, 2017, p 923; Sola and Rendueles, 2018). The second theme was opposition to the austerity policies pursued by both establishment parties in the wake of the crisis.

In Ireland, the 2020 Irish election saw the traditional Irish nationalist party, Sinn Fein, outdistance its centrist rivals, which had dominated the Irish state since its inception. The result has been referred to by Irish commentators as an 'earthquake', and as a 'seismic shift'. One analyst commented that, 'It took nine years and three elections, but the economic crash of 2008 has demolished the Irish party system' (Finn, 2020). Sinn Fein campaigned on working-class issues like housing affordability, and health. Exit polls showed that these were most important in voters' minds, and also that two thirds wanted public services investment to be prioritized over tax cuts (Finn, 2020), a clear rejection of the conventional wisdom of the austerity politics pursued since the crisis. The party was the overwhelming first choice of voters under 35 (Dolan, 2020). The exit polls also showed a class divide. Among upper- and middle-class voters Sinn Fein scored only 14 per cent, while among skilled workers and the working-class and non-working categories the party polled 33 to 35 per cent, a level almost equivalent to the combined Fine Gael/Fianna Fàil total of 39 per cent (Burtenshaw, 2020). This surge of apparently class-based politics is sometimes depicted as an example of left populism. However, Sinn Fein is a more complicated entity, being the nationalist party for a united Ireland. And, in Northern Ireland, the anti-austerity character of the party in the Republic has not been in evidence.

Right populism

Right-wing populism is the second variant of anti-system politics. This finds expression in movements or parties that challenge two elements of the neoliberal consensus.

First, right populists deviate from what has become the dominant feature of orthodox neoliberalism, which Nancy Fraser (2017) has depicted as 'progressive neoliberalism'. By this she means maintaining a neoliberal approach to economic issues that is especially responsive to the needs of finance, advanced technology and the entertainment/service industries, and combining it with a socially liberal stance on issues connected to race, gender, sexual orientation and cultural identity. This produces a politics which is feminist, anti-racist, pro-multicultural and pro-LGBTQ+ in the liberal sense, while being steadfastly neoliberal on economic issues.

In contrast to that social liberalism, right populists often exhibit xenophobic and nationalist attitudes and, in opposition to the cosmopolitan progressive neoliberal elites, they can be racist, misogynistic and homophobic. They may well still be neoliberal economically (except insofar as nation-state autonomy is preferred to globalism) but they stand on a socially conservative rather than liberal base. That base is often a rural, small-town one, or situated in declining industrial areas. Their 'us' versus 'them' imagery constitutes the national people in nativist, racial or ethnic terms and distinguishes between the true people and 'others'. The latter – migrants and minority racial or ethnic groups more generally – are considered as being outside the nation – an exclusion which leads to practical as well as symbolic consequences. The 'others' could be subject to various forms of discrimination: in employment, in housing, human rights discrimination, and ineligibility for social benefits of various kinds (Greven, 2016).

Such policies are often construed as appealing to the white working class, the old, the less educated, and those who feel left behind in the face of globalist modernity. The white working class has been singled out as representing a reactionary core for right populist movements. In such views it is depicted as racist, xenophobic and misogynist – as in Hillary Clinton's contemptuous metaphor of Trump supporters as a 'basket of deplorables'. More detailed investigations of white working-class culture in the US and the UK, and its intersections with race, reveal a more nuanced picture (McKenzie, 2015; Beider and Chahal, 2020).

Second, apart from their opposition to the social liberal component of progressive neoliberalism, right populists are opposed to the diminution of nation-states by global institutions. Those campaigning for the successful Brexit, or 'Leave', side in the 2016 UK referendum on membership of the EU provide an example. Other right populist parties, such as the National Front (FN) in France,[2] Alternative for Germany (AfD), and the Dutch

Freedom Party, similarly are either eurosceptic or opposed to membership of the EU. The governing right populist parties in Hungary and Poland are frequently hostile to EU directives and, in the US, Donald Trump's presidency was seen as disruptive to global institutions which Trump regarded as intruding on US sovereignty. In all these cases there is a strong appeal to the working class, particularly those employed in declining production and extractive industries that have been sidelined by globalization and whose living standards and security have been diminished. Appealing to those who believe they have been harmed by globalization has traction. Stirring racial and ethnic resentments has traction too but, unlike the first, it represents a diversion from the otherwise well-grounded discontents with globalization and neoliberalism.

Minority nationalism

Minority nationalist parties threaten the territorial integrity of some of the existing nation-states making up the international order. This is a third variety of anti-system politics. In cases of minority nationalisms, such as the Scottish National Party (SNP) in Scotland or the ideologically diverse proponents of an independent Catalonia in Spain, the politics around race and ethnicity were different from those of the right populists, but the disruptive impact on questioning the international system was similar. In essence, these movements also practised nation-state-ism, calling for the new states to be created to better service the interests of their peoples. In both these examples, however, continued membership in the EU was a part of the separatist agenda. Minority nationalists want their own nation-state, as opposed to the one in which they find themselves incorporated. But they also want to remain integrated into the world of global capital where, they calculate, they can do better than as sub-units in a state where they have little influence. Similarly, in the case of the left populist effort in Greece to escape the constraints of EU-imposed austerity, when push came to shove, the Syriza government opted to remain in the eurozone. That decision involved capitulation on its anti-austerity agenda, rather than follow-through on its successful referendum result that rejected the EU's terms.

In 2017, more than 2.25 million people turned out to vote for the independence referendum in Catalonia that the Spanish government branded as unconstitutional and illegal (Dewan, 2017). Although the Catalan regional government said 90 per cent of voters were in favour of a split from Madrid, the turnout was quite low. The Catalan authorities blamed the low turnout rate on the 'crackdown' on the vote which was initiated by the national government. Spain's highest court ruled the vote illegal under the Spanish constitution, and citing the judicial authority, Madrid flooded Catalonia with thousands of national police prior to the vote. Police seized millions of ballots and closed schools and other buildings that were to be used as polling sites (Dewan, 2017).

Less than two weeks before the referendum vote, Spanish police officers raided regional government offices in Catalonia, and arrested 14 senior officials (Jones, 2017). Carles Puigdemont, a centre-right politician and head of Catalonia's pro-sovereignty government, described the raids as a 'co-ordinated police assault' that showed that Madrid 'has de facto suspended self-government and applied a de facto state of emergency' in Catalonia (Jones, 2017). He and two of his ministers fled to Belgium in 2017 to avoid arrest for their role in organizing the independence referendum (Burgen, 2021). In 2019, nine Catalan separatist leaders were sentenced to between nine and 13 years in prison due to their role in the independence referendum (BBC, 2019). The longest sentence of 13 years was given to Oriol Junqueras, a member of the Republican Left (social democratic) party, former vice-president of Catalonia and the highest-ranking pro-independence leader on trial, for sedition and misuse of public funds (BBC, 2019).

In the rest of Spain, Catalan nationalism was used to trigger an assertive Spanish nationalism, including the development of a far-right, anti-immigrant, anti-Catalan independence party, Vox. It gained 15 per cent of the vote in November 2019. Before this the immigration/migrant issue had not featured prominently in Spanish politics. All establishment parties were opposed to holding referenda on Catalan independence, and the Podemos position, support for Catalonia's right to hold such a referendum while hoping for a result in favour of remaining in Spain, proved a difficult sell. Miley (2017) has argued that the main Catalan parties' defection from the constitutional order was instigated partly by the dynamics of austerity, but that it has rendered the country's constitutional framework, rather than its austerity regime, susceptible to collapse. Clearly, these national/regional factors, and therefore austerity indirectly, played a role in the complicated and finely balanced parliamentary situation that followed the November 2019 election.

The right populist Vox's arrival in Spain came as Spain's traditional two-party system, comprising the PSOE, the Partido Socialista Obrero Español (Spanish Socialist Workers' Party) and the PP, the Partido Popular (People's Party), came under pressure (Guy, 2019). Essentially Franco-ist, the ideology of conservative nationalism coupled with the Catalan crisis motivated this new political force. Vox is neoliberal on economic policy, with its position on taxes being 'the lower, the better' (Urra, 2018). Its main pitch is to a resurgent conservative Spanish nationalism and promises the suspension of the Catalan autonomy, the outlawing of subnational nationalist parties, and the maximum legal protection for the symbols of the nation such as the flag, the crown, and the anthem (Manzanaro and Rodriguez, 2019). Along with these promises, the party also suggests measures to curb irregular immigration, and rolling back legislation aimed at protecting women from gender violence, claiming that it discriminates against men (Hedgecoe, 2019; Manzanaro and Rodriguez, 2019).

Like the Catalan independence parties, but united into one organization, the Scottish nationalists are ideologically diverse. From the late 1970s to the 1990s the SNP was a self-proclaimed social democratic party. The party began advocating for full employment, government intervention in fuel, power and transport, a state bank to guide economic development, the expansion of cooperatives and credit unions, pensions adjusted to the costs of living, a minimum wage, and an improved National Health Service (NHS) (Lynch, 2009; Massetti, 2009). Alongside this, the party chose to advocate for lower business taxes (in an attempt to harness the oil and gas industry in Scotland) and defended this stance in social democratic terms by claiming that it would result in higher tax yields to fund progressive public services. The vision of an 'independent Scotland' thus included a tax-cutting agenda with a corporation tax as low as the Irish one (12.5 per cent) to give Scotland a comparative advantage over the rest of the UK and on the expectation of revenues from Scottish oil.

Following the GFC, from 2010, the SNP grew its anti-austerity reputation, rhetorically pitting itself against both the Labour and the Conservative-Liberal Democrat Westminster governments. The SNP advocated for counter-austerity measures to be implemented in an independent Scotland, including abolishing measures of the Welfare Reform Act 2012, boosting housing benefits, linking the minimum wage to inflation, renationalizing Royal Mail, and implementing steps to improve women's opportunities to join the workforce (Massetti, 2018). The SNP used a discourse of social justice to assemble public support for independence. Similarly, during this time the SNP employed narratives of social investment to further disseminate a new social democratic social welfare imaginary in Scotland. Social protection systems based on social investment were seen as a means to reduce unemployment and increase earning and spending power through investments in childcare, education, health and active labour market policies (Wiggan, 2017).

There was also an agenda that involved restructuring the whole Scottish economy to make Scottish workers and corporations 'competitive' in the global economy, through public sector efficiency reforms, building a skilled workforce, promoting the knowledge economy, and reducing government regulation on international trade of energy, goods, services, foreign investment and access to foreign corporations. This included a commitment to membership of international organizations (Paterson, 2014). The SNP government continue to argue that EU membership would serve Scottish interests through access to the EU's internal market. However, European economic integration diminishes the ability of member-state governments to promote domestic growth, redistribute wealth and address poverty through collective social-democratic principles, therefore subjecting Scotland to neoliberal policies. This generates questions as to whether the SNP is only rhetorically committed to social democratic principles (Paterson, 2015).

The SNP seems not to perceive any contradiction between achieving a globally competitive Scottish society and addressing structural inequalities in Scottish society. The idea of class is completely erased, with key drivers of poverty (profit-making, wealth accumulation and so on) still remaining in place

(Featherstone and Karaliotas, 2016, quoting Gerry Mooney), leaving the SNP committed to a form of social neoliberalism (Featherstone and Karaliotas, 2016, quoting Neil Davidson).

Impact on established system parties and politics

A survey of campaigns against the austerity policies implemented across the Western world after 2010 illustrates how failure to present real choice contributed to the already-in-progress decline of parties of the 'centre'. This was true even when opposition movements had only limited success. Opposition to austerity focused frequently on quite specific measures – welfare cuts, user charges, housing evictions – but sometimes evolved into general challenges to the overall strategy itself. Sometimes austerity opponents won on specific issues. Generally, they fell short of the goal of reversing austerity policies. Even so, there were destabilizing consequences in some countries. As mainstream governments of the centre-right or centre-left moved to implement austerity measures it was common for incumbents to be punished in subsequent elections. However, replacement governments tended to be as committed to austerity as the ones displaced. Expressions of public anger and manifestations of resistance did occur. But alternative political vehicles were either not available or, where parties advocating an alternative to austerity did exist, failed to attract sufficient support to reverse the policy direction. The Syriza government in Greece did mobilize majority support in a successful referendum against EU-imposed austerity measures. But the government then ignored the result, capitulated to the EU, and imposed the measures anyway.

In several cases – Ireland, Spain and the Canadian province of Quebec are examples – the vote share of established 'centre' political parties haemorrhaged. Typically, these parties were either two more or less indistinguishable right-of-centre parties, as in Ireland, or some version of neoliberalized social democracy, and a conservative party on the right, as in Spain and Quebec. Governmental change involving these options did not produce policy change. Hence, for those who hoped for an alternative, there was renewed disaffection. Some of this might be passive and measured by withdrawal, and some of it might be activated by populist movements, or by mobilizing around unanticipated opportunities to register discontent (as with the UK referendum on the EU).

In Ireland, the share of the vote going to the dominant parties, Fianna Fáil and Fine Gael, fell from around 69 per cent in 2007 to 43 per cent in 2020; in Spain, the share going to the PP and PSOE fell from 84 per cent in 2008 to under 50 per cent in 2019; and in Quebec, the Liberal Party and Parti Québécois portion declined from 75 per cent in 2007 to around 42 per cent in 2018. The loss of vote share does not necessarily imply political transformation, and certainly did not mean a reversal of policy priorities such as austerity. However, combined with other powerful factors in those societies, austerity has contributed to the erosion or decay of existing political arrangements. This is part of the malaise affecting the legitimacy of existing institutions and processes.

Apart from specific examples like those discussed above there is evidence of widespread dissatisfaction with the status quo political economy. A poll covering 27 countries (IPSOS, 2019) recorded significant disaffection with the established economic and political order in all of them. Taken as a whole, 70 per cent of respondents agreed that the economy was rigged in favour of the rich and powerful, 66 per cent felt the political system ignored them, and 54 per cent agreed with the statement that their country was 'broken'.

The concerns of anti-system politics

Left and right populists and minority nationalists are different currents within anti-system politics. They differ in their blending of the ingredients of anti-elitism and in their focus on cultural and economic issues. However, in different ways they have helped to undermine some of the foundations on which neoliberalism is built.

Anti-elitism

Much anti-system rhetoric focuses on the elites in charge of the system. Often used in sweeping general terms, potentially this critique can be extended from the individuals or classes of individuals comprising the elite to the system itself. Rather than focusing on the personnel occupying particular roles and positions within hierarchies of wealth, power, and influence, resentment of economic elites ('the rich') can blend into a critique of corporate power or of the markets themselves. After all, it is their functioning that enables growing inequality and emergence of the elite individuals in the first place.

In some cases, hostility to elites can be directed at their socially liberal values (right populists). Sometimes it may be directed at elite responsibility for economic decline, and the harm inflicted on working-class people is emphasized (potentially both left and right populism). Overcoming the power of external elites, either in supranational entities like the EU (right populists) or existing national authorities (the minority nationalist variant of anti-system politics) and reconstituting a new nation-state or a more autonomous one could involve various kinds of politics. Neoliberal policies could simply be adopted in a new national context or with a different and more conservative social base. Or, rejuvenated national authority could be accompanied by a different ideology and policy package.

Perceptions of corrupt, self-interested political elites can extend to the system of liberal democracy itself (Oliver and Rahn, 2016; Berman, 2019). Democratic institutions are viewed as: unrepresentative and unaccountable (McBride and Schnittker, 2021); opaque, because of multilevel governance operating through networks and technocratic governance processes; over-reliant on mistrusted experts; and often as enablers of corrupt or dishonest decision-making. If the processes are distrusted, so too are the results which have emanated from the system. Some of this is reflected in the rise of social movements opposed to the economic effects of neoliberal globalization. These include those opposed to austerity, and the Occupy movement that drew attention to the vast inequality between the top 1 per cent of the population and the other 99 per cent. Such insights and slogans have been well documented in more scientific studies which also drew attention to the growing income and wealth gaps in neoliberal democracies (Piketty, 2014). The imposition of harsh austerity policies inflicted severe harm on working-class citizens and anyone occupying a lower place in the social hierarchy (Mendoza, 2015). Those at the top, on the other hand, continued to amass wealth and power.

Right populists have more commonly targeted 'others' based on racial, religious, or cultural characteristics that, they hold, do not belong in the true 'people'. For this they have been rightly condemned and dismissed by those on the left. Quite apart from its often racist content it is an assertion that misidentifies the cause and is a distraction. It is true that globalization has left many behind by flexibilizing labour markets and conditions and removing social supports from many working-class people. Simultaneously, capitalist elites have been enriched, and a new middle class of high-skilled employees who are able to navigate the new speculative and financialized economy have done well. There have been losers as well as winners. And the voice of the losers has been marginalized within the institutions of the liberal democratic state. The erosion of democracy from above – the substitution of pre-determined international rules for national processes of debate and discussion – has impoverished democratic procedures. National politics is no longer of the same importance as it once was. An important part of the populist message, generally derided by cosmopolitan elites of both right and left, is to return decision-making to the nation-state level. Despite being contaminated by the racist baggage characteristic of these movements, one enduring contribution of right populism might be the rejuvenation of the nation-state as a site for democratic action.

Left populist movements ought to have a better, class-based answer to the question of why whole sections of the working class have been left behind. However, they seem conflicted on whether globalization is an issue. Ideologically they lean to ideas of internationalism and solidarity among peoples, and to horizontal rather than hierarchical power relations. This sometimes led to naïveté about what was possible at the global level, and a dismissal of nation-state options as being infected by 'nationalism'. Given the current alignment between international organizations and global capital this leaves few avenues open. However distasteful nationalism may be to some opponents of neoliberal capitalism, there is a case to be considered that the nation-state itself is the most likely venue in which its dismantling can begin. To decontextualize Mrs Thatcher, 'there is no alternative', or at least no obvious one.

Minority nationalist parties are correct to identify the nation-state as an important site of democracy, identity and control. They vary widely in what options might be pursued at that level. Certainly, in the Scottish and Catalan cases they see no contradiction in continuity of membership in entities like the EU. Whether they are overly optimistic on this point is an open question, but the calculation seems to be that having their own nation-state, rather than being subsumed in a bigger one, will be advantageous.

Anti-system parties and movements are not new. But they have become more prominent since the GFC and are increasingly referenced as threats to democracy, or as evidence that democracy is in crisis. There is an ongoing dispute about whether their rise has been driven by cultural or economic factors. On the right, globalization or globalism attracts the enmity of most of the right-wing anti-system or populist parties because of its impact on national communities and the living standards of those left out or left behind. On the left, neoliberalism, with its suppression of working-class living standards and privileging of private market power over public political power is similarly anathema. But the link to those movements based on national questions is more difficult to classify on this dimension. They are simultaneously in favour of breaking free of the centralized political power of a particular nation-state but are commonly wedded to the new independent country they seek remaining embedded in supranational entities such as the EU, with all the consequences in terms of democracy.

The culturalist diversion

Right populist parties have appealed to the traditional voter base of social democratic parties, which traditionally championed workers, the poor, the uneducated and those who felt disadvantaged. However, as the centre-left parties adopted neoliberal viewpoints, they lost connection with that base and increasingly targeted supporters based in an educated, urban, white-collar, middle-class segment of the population. Their failure to develop solutions to current economic and social challenges that have a major impact on those in their former social base has enabled the populist right to mobilize parts of traditional left constituencies around its own agenda, including scapegoating of immigrant and racial minorities.

In France, for example, the FN has advocated denying free access to basic health-care to illegal migrants, stripping dual citizens of their French nationality when convicted of links with jihadism, and making it impossible for illegal migrants to legalize their stay in France. Notably, proposals included reserving certain rights, like free education, only to French citizens. The central message of Marine Le Pen's 2017 campaign was to keep France for the French (Chrisafis, 2017) by promising to give priority to French people over non-nationals in jobs, housing and welfare, and she proposed a referendum to cement this policy into the Constitution (Chrisafis, 2017). Yet there had been a shift in FN policy which discursively became more critical of the European austerity agenda and somewhat moderated its racist pronouncements (Bieling, 2021).

In Austria, anti-immigration rhetoric is prominent within the Freedom Party, and many citizens see immigration as a threat to Austrian identity and culture. Immigration is framed as economically costly and as reducing the resources available to poorer Austrians (Hafez et al, 2019). The party has proposed improved health-care for elderly people funded by cutting spending on immigrants, asylum seekers, and refugees (Uldam, 2015), and financing a proposed tax reduction programme through savings on social benefits, especially for foreigners and migrants. The party wants to exclude asylum seekers from minimum welfare benefits, and reform child benefits for employees who work in Austria but have children in other EU countries.

Similar trends are evident in Hungary where, according to Prime Minister Viktor Orbán, the 2008 financial crisis proved that the Western-led liberal world was no longer able to protect people from economic harm, while the 2015 migration crisis demonstrated that Europe could not protect Christian cultural identity (Szelenyi, 2019). As well, the inequality resulting from globalization played a significant role in weakening liberal democracy because it eroded the social status of the middle class (Szelenyi, 2019). Based on these perceptions, refugees and migrants became enemies, along with those societal and political actors who help, organize, and bring them into Europe, such as NGOs, the EU, and George Soros (Krekó et al, 2019). Fidesz, or the Hungarian Civic Alliance, is a right-wing populist and national-conservative political party which has been able to keep immigration on the top of the agenda by continuing campaigns based on hate-inciting rhetoric, conspiracy theories and disinformation. Since 2015, it has simplified public discourse to the single issue of migration.

And in the UK, even before the Brexit referendum, studies of voters for the UK Independence Party (UKIP) showed that intense Euroscepticism was combined with strong hostility towards immigration, or hostility to politicians, or both. UKIP voters were consistently the most receptive to demands for the UK to pull out of the EU and to subscribe to a more restrictive conception of national identity, feeling anxious about immigration, and being excluded by a political class that they view as corrupt, out-of-touch and uncaring (Goodwin, 2014).

Reviewing the record of right-wing parties in Europe, Bieling (2021) reached the conclusion that the GFC had induced a selective and far from uniform reorientation in economic and social policy. Protectionism, more state intervention, and generous, but exclusive, social services became more prominent. This hardly added up to an anti-capitalist position. Rather, the parties show their origins as bourgeois formations by trying to shift the burden of austerity onto other countries (through imposing austerity on them) or, within national boundaries, by exclusionary welfare state and labour policies.

Return to the nation-state

In the UK the seminal event in the rise of populism was the referendum on membership of the EU in 2016. The choice presented was simple: Remain or Leave. And by a small but clear majority, the result was to leave (52 per cent to 48 per cent). Campaigning for the remain side was an impressive array of established elites and experts – banks, businesses, most trade union leaders, all the main political parties, and a range of economic experts. From time to time, international endorsements would be received from the likes of US President Obama and the IMF. The leave vote reflected long-term scepticism about EU membership but also provided a focal point for all those dissatisfied with neoliberalism and its effects, and nostalgic about British life before its perceived decline. This represents an unusual conjunction of the materially disadvantaged and the section of the economically more comfortable traditional middle class that is psychologically anchored in a national rather than a global context.

Was the Brexit result a cultural phenomenon based on xenophobic, racist, older, non-cosmopolitan individuals? Or was it primarily a function of the wreckage wrought by decades of neoliberalism, exacerbated by post-2010 austerity, and fuelled by resentments that important issues, including but not limited to immigration, were ignored by both national and EU elites?

Nearly half (49 per cent) of leave voters said the biggest single reason for wanting to leave the EU was 'the principle that decisions about the UK should be taken in the UK'. One third (33 per cent) said the main reason was that leaving 'offered the best chance for the UK to regain control over immigration and its own borders'; 13 per cent said remaining would mean having no choice 'about how the EU expanded its membership or its powers in the years ahead'. Just over 6 per cent said their main reason was that 'when it comes to trade and the economy, the UK would benefit more from being outside the EU than from being part of it'.

Using standard UK statistical categories, the AB social group – broadly speaking, professionals and managers – were the only social group among whom a majority voted to remain (57 per cent). The C1 group – supervisory, clerical and junior managerial, administrative, professional occupations – divided fairly evenly; nearly two thirds of C2DEs – those in skilled manual occupations and semi-skilled and unskilled manual occupations, unemployed persons and the lowest grade occupations – voted to leave the EU (64 per cent).[3] Clearly, Leave was the preference for working-class and poorer voters by a substantial majority, and Remain the preference for middle-class voters, also by substantial majority (Butcher, 2019).

The referendum result was the most important part of a series of destabilizing events in British politics. The election of a left leader of the UK Labour Party, Jeremy Corbyn, threatened for a time to make that party an opponent of the neoliberal consensus rather than, as under its previous leaders such as Tony Blair, an integral component of it. Corbyn was bitterly opposed within the party apparatus and the Parliamentary Labour Party, and his replacement by Sir Keir Starmer in 2020 signalled a return of the Labour Party to the political centre or right. Events and leadership struggles within the Conservative Party as it stumbled but eventually succeeded in delivering Brexit were also a sign of instability arrested, probably temporarily by Boris Johnson's accession to the office of Prime Minister, and the conclusion of an agreement with the EU bringing an end to UK membership. The closer-than-expected result of the Scottish independence referendum in 2014 (55 per cent to 45 per cent), the ongoing electoral success of the SNP, and post-Brexit polls showing the independence side could win a repeat referendum were also signs of potential national disintegration.

Despite their appeal to the victims of neoliberal policies, the 2017 manifesto of the right populist UKIP revealed no break from domestic neoliberalism. Their vision of post-Brexit Britain on the world market stage is one of a low-tax, low-regulation economy (UKIP, 2017). Tariffs would be reduced wherever possible, unless initiating anti-dumping measures. UKIP endorsed the World Trade Organization's (WTO) aim for trade to flow as freely and as smoothly as possible (UKIP, 2017), although the party opposed the establishment and continuance of protectionist customs unions, such as the EU (UKIP, 2017). Additionally, UKIP wanted the country to 'take back control' of important areas of economic policy which they had been forced to surrender to the EU. The UK could then resume full responsibility for taxation and have more room to plan its industrial and regional policy without worrying about the EU state aid rules (UKIP, 2017).

In the 2016 US presidential election, hostility to globalism featured in the right populist campaign of Donald Trump and the left populist challenge within the Democratic Party represented by Bernie Sanders' unsuccessful campaign to win the party nomination. From the left, Sanders opposed international trade agreements because of their harmful effects upon the US working class. These, for Sanders, could be mitigated by a more generous welfare state and by reforming the agreements to realize their potential to address human rights or labour rights issues.

From the right, Trump's rhetoric about the harmful effects on America's workers centred on the need to bring jobs back, by relocating American firms on US soil, by easing environmental regulation that was destroying jobs in industries like coal production and by controlling immigration to prevent jobs being 'taken away' from US nationals. This certainly struck a chord with those US workers left behind in the rust belts that were formerly the flagships of industry, who were now unable to sustain the 'middle-class' lifestyles that were formerly supported by working there. Traditionally, these were bastions of Democratic Party support. The Trump campaign slogan 'Make America Great Again' captured concern about relative decline both at the international level and internally in terms of living standards and economic security. Politically, in Trump's hands it also resonated with an anti-immigration position. He claimed that American jobs were being lost to illegal immigrants, and built on a potent tradition of racism in the US, with the primary targets in 2016 being Mexicans and Muslims.

Lying behind the rhetoric was an assessment that the multilateral international economic order was no longer working as strongly in US interests or in the interests of US business as had been the case in the past. In that context an alternative order based on the overt exercise of US power through bilateral agreements and trade wars against rivals, including allies, would work better. This strategy is an important difference in the US's attitude to the established order, although it is not necessarily an anti-globalization one. Rather, it represents a different method for the US to achieve economic and military superiority. The new method rests on the overt assertion of power within asymmetrical power structures (Yilmazkuda and Yilmazkuda, 2014). The calculation is that in most bilateral formats the US is the stronger partner and can thus extract greater benefits than it can in the multilateral ones it played a key part in creating. Its defection from these arrangements therefore created significant problems for its erstwhile partners and for the functioning of the global system.

In line with this approach the Trump administration quit the Trans-Pacific Partnership (TPP) (later the Comprehensive and Progressive Agreement for Trans-Pacific Partnership, CPTPP), insisted on a renegotiation of NAFTA (which became the USMCA), and obstructed the working of the WTO appellate body by blocking appointments, a stance that has not been altered by the incoming Biden administration. A series of other aggressive moves followed: within NATO; withdrawal from the Paris Climate Agreement, a move since reversed by Biden; and the undermining of the authority of the WHO.

Taken together, these changes do not destroy the pre-existing system but they do indicate an important shift. Significantly, the change in US strategy cannot be attributed entirely to the triumph of Trump's right-wing populism. Aspects of the change of strategy clearly reflect longer-standing US discontent with the operation of the international system and worries about relative decline, and continue to be implemented under the new President. The rules-based international order was always a bit of a fantasy if it was interpreted to mean fair rules applied on a level playing field. The rules were established by and most benefited the stronger players. But the move to an overtly power-based international order is a change and, notwithstanding softer rhetoric coming from President Biden, it remains to be seen to what extent it will be reversed.

In Europe, fear of globalization is one of the most important factors that pushes European citizens towards populist right-wing parties (Barkin, 2016). Given the penchant for deriving lessons from history, the 1930s and the rise of fascism in Europe is a reference point. Berman argues that the social and economic problems currently faced by Europe are not as dire as they were in the interwar period but concedes the EU may have undermined its own legitimacy through its role in causing or worsening the financial crisis. The EU was so focused on the importance of economic integration that it demonstrated that nationally elected governments no longer had economic sovereignty. Liberalization of markets took priority over social needs (Berman, 2019). Post-GFC and post-pandemic choices are often posed in terms of 'more Europe', or 'less Europe' with greater national autonomy. The EU's record after the GFC, and arguably in handling vaccine distribution during the pandemic, point to the latter alternative.

This was certainly the conclusion drawn by right populists. During a key election speech in 2016, Marine Le Pen repeatedly spoke of 'the people', who are seen as a French nation unprotected in the face of economic liberalism and multiculturalism imposed from abroad, especially the EU (Sandford, 2017). The message was repeated again at another speech, where Le Pen took world leaders to task over 'unregulated globalization' (Sandford, 2017). Le Pen argued economic globalism rejects all limits, all regulations, and consequently weakens the immune defences of the nation-state. She links lack of borders, lack of a national currency, and loss of national authority over laws and management of the economy to enabling another type of globalization to be born and grow – Islamist fundamentalism (Sandford, 2017). Le Pen's party thus blends economic, cultural and security themes. It emphasizes the terrorist threat, the refugee crisis, immigration, mass unemployment, deindustrialization, and voters who struggle to make ends meet (Chrisafis, 2017). Ironically, the left has largely vacated the anti-globalization field, leaving a vacuum that the right has entered.

More democracy or less inside the nation–state?

Populism is widely viewed as a symptom, or reflection, of growing dissatisfaction with democracy, and this dissatisfaction often emerges when citizens believe that parties, governments and elites are unwilling to respond to their needs and demands (Berman, 2019, p 657). Populist politicians work outside traditional institutions by discussing concerns that the institutional elites ignore. These appeals are not necessarily nationalist or xenophobic, and in the past environmental 'green' movements made similar appeals. Similarly, Oliver and Rahn (2016, p 190) state that populism is for the 'people', and against 'nefarious, parasitic elites who undermine rightful sovereign of the common folks'.

Concretely, the demand for more democracy is primarily focused on bringing decision-making home to the nation–state level. Once it is there, what proposals have right populists made for enhancing democratic decision-making? They are somewhat thin on the ground, but the Brexit Party 'contract', or manifesto (Brexit Party, 2019), in the UK provides some examples. These include electoral reform; subjecting MPs who switch parties to recall petitions; and provisions for citizens initiatives to call referendums. The last two of these express a preference for direct rather than indirect or representative democracy. So, plebiscites or referenda on specific issues are a popular instrument in these circles.

There have been a number of referenda in which the populist faith in their potential to repudiate elite opinion was justified. The classic elite response to such defeats is to depict the votes as a victory of popular ignorance and to work to ensure their reversal. The French and Dutch referendums on the European Constitution and the initial Irish votes rejecting the Nice Treaty 2001 dealing with eastern expansion of the EU, and the Lisbon Treaty, which made a series of centralizing institutional reforms, provide clear examples of this. These negative votes were subsequently reversed. Syriza's referendum on austerity also fits this profile, although the result was ignored rather than reversed. Yet others, Brexit being a notable example, have succeeded in breaking the mould. Considered in the context of enhancing democracy, 'referendums are useful tools for any outsider movement seeking to expose the divide between established, controlled, "tactical" political speech and mass opinion. Strategically, that is crucial, but that is also their limit' (Foley and Ramand, 2018).

Explaining the rise of anti-system politics

Primarily, the debate in explaining the rise of anti-system politics revolves around those who stress economic factors and those who stress social and cultural factors. Economic factors include the disruptive effects of globalization, neoliberalism and technological change. Additionally, increasing trade openness, the rise of non-Western economic powers, and growing automation that has made life more insecure for the working and middle classes play a role.

The other narrative stresses cultural social change, and emphasizes the growing numbers of foreign-born residents, particularly those of non-European background. Over the past few years, the foreign-born share of the population increased in many European countries. This narrative aims at the impacts of these changes, with many citizens, particularly white males (conceived as a previously dominant group, without regard to social class), who feel like strangers in their own countries. Social change has led to citizen dissatisfaction with liberal democracy for allowing the decline of national cultures, traditions and sovereignty. However, there is an economic dimension to this too. Without conceding credibility to the explanations for hardship proffered by right populists, such as 'migrants take "our" jobs', it remains the case that real wages have been largely stagnant, precarious employment and insecurity have increased and social supports have diminished for broad swathes of the population. Can the two views be re-ordered to take advantage of anti-elitist and anti-globalization sentiments? For those committed to a radical transformation of neoliberal politics it is a pressing issue of whether, and how, a common class politics can be constructed in a way that overcomes the divisions in society that are exploited by right populists.

The rise of anti-system politics threatens aspects of the political order that has characterized Western societies since, at least, the end of the Cold War. Left populism has mounted a challenge to economic orthodoxy in the form of anti-austerity movements since the GFC. For the most part they have proved insufficiently powerful to force a reversal in that policy regime. Nevertheless, they may have contributed to a re-examination of neoliberal political economy that has developed since the COVID-19 pandemic and associated economic crisis struck in 2020.

Right populism has undermined, and in some countries replaced, the progressive neoliberal paradigm that Nancy Fraser (2017) described by neoliberalism with a socially conservative face and an alternative social base. However, it also challenged the primacy of the global or supranational economy, over the politics of national autonomy or choice.

In fact, anti-system movements based on national issues can take two forms. The first, and that most associated with the right populist version of hostility to foreign influences and foreign control, advocates dismantling the global order. Thus, in Europe, anti-EU sentiments are prevalent among right populist parties and achieved their highest stage of development in the successful Brexit campaign in the UK. In May 2021, EU expansion received another setback when the Swiss government citing 'substantial differences' broke off a seven-year-long negotiation with the EU to replace over 120 bilateral treaties with an overarching one that would move Switzerland into closer conformity with EU norms on salary protection, state aid rules and the access of EU citizens to Swiss social security benefits. And in a different sequence of events, in June 2021, Belarus, under heavy sanctions by the EU, suspended its participation in the EU's Eastern Partnership, an initiative aimed to deepen the EU's ties with neighbouring former communist countries.

In the US, the administration of Donald Trump waged a campaign against what it considered the unfair international trading system and, more broadly the architecture of global governance, depicted as reducing the sovereign right of the US to make its own decisions and exercise its 'right' to leadership at the world level. Thus, NAFTA was renegotiated, the US withdrew from the TPP/CPTPP, WHO and the Paris climate agreements, disrupted the functioning of the WTO, and waged tariff wars against China. It also resorted to unilateral imposition of sanctions, sometimes on economic, sometimes on security grounds, against a variety of countries including close allies.

Conclusions

There is no doubt that the rise of anti-system politics has been associated with a state of malaise and disaffection in many liberal democracies. Ingo Schmidt (2021) refers to a resulting crisis of legitimacy. Yet the situation is one where the new right and populists are not large enough to form a new hegemonic bloc themselves but are sufficiently large to obstruct the formation of an alternative bloc. This is hardly helpful from the point of view of those working for system change to overcome the various crises.

Yet their focus on taking back control, even if there is confusion about who it is to be taken from, and the possibilities of a (democratized) nation-state can be positives drawn from the dead-end of right-wing populism. For too long the political left, ideologically neoliberalized and detached from its original social base, has committed to idealistic internationalism or cosmopolitanism. Ignoring the possibilities at the nation-state level has been a major mistake, one that, oddly, right-wing populists and, separately and in a different way, minority nationalist movements have put back on the agenda.

5

What Is to Be Done?
Alternative Strategies

Faced with multiple, deep and interconnected crises, and a deficit in the scope and operation of democratic government, there is a tendency to look for similar situations in the past in an effort to draw lessons that could help chart our future. History seems increasingly a reference point and possible guide.

In the United States, Roosevelt's New Deal often serves as an inspiration. Especially when linked to environmental issues, it has given rise to calls for a Green New Deal to lead to economic recovery and renewal based on a 'just transition'. Economic activity and jobs would be transferred from the old, carbon-producing economy to a new one in which green jobs and green energy would be defining characteristics. Similar proposals have been advanced in the UK (Pettifor, 2020) and have also found reflection in various EU and OECD policies and documents (European Commission, 2019; OECD, 2021a; 2021b). In Canada, Seth Klein (2020) has invoked the example of World War II, an existential crisis that led to unprecedented and united mobilization of governments and the whole of society in pursuit of war aims. This time, he argues, the war needs to be against climate change, but similar levels of mobilization are needed, directed to creating jobs and reducing inequality on the basis of a green economy.

Efforts to draw lessons from history can either serve as inspiration or warning. Some periods, such as that between 1914 and 1945, offer both. The 1920s decade is often singled out as a period of failed response to the upheaval of World War I and its aftermath.

Failed attempts to restore the pre-war status quo led in turn to greater upheaval and disintegration, culminating in World War II. The interwar period also saw the development and popularization of alternatives to the pre-World War I orthodoxy. Some that achieved prominence during the 1930s served as building blocs of the post-World War II global order. The post-World War II period has been designated the '30 golden years'[1] of the Keynesian mixed economy, economic growth and full employment in the Western world. In the Eastern world, Soviet-style socialism or communism was in effect. There was relative international stability between the two rival ideological and economic systems embodied in the 'Cold War'. Old empires were dismantled in a process of decolonization and national liberation, and many new states emerged. Newly decolonized countries in the Third World, much later known as the Global South, enjoyed some ability to play off Western capitalism and Eastern socialism against one another, and achieved a modicum of autonomy, notwithstanding problems of underdevelopment and colonial legacies.

In the 1970s the underpinnings of the Western system eroded. Keynesian ideas that had informed policy, and which had a greater tolerance for national variation, were replaced by neoliberalism and globalization. Other alternatives had been advanced during the 1970s. They included expansion of the state's role in controlling markets. One example was the Alternative Economic Strategy proposed by Tony Benn in the British Labour Party. Benn (1989, p 302) described it as a policy of 'saving jobs, a vigorous micro-investment programme, import controls, control of the banks and insurance companies, control of export of capital, higher taxation of the rich, and Britain leaving the Common Market [later the European Union]'.

Internationally, the Group of 77 advocated a New International Economic Order (NIEO) to improve the situation of developing countries within the existing hierarchical international order. The group originally comprised 77 member states of the UN, when it was founded in 1964, and subsequently expanded its membership to well over a hundred. By the 1980s, however, it was clear that the social and political forces supporting such positions had been defeated and neoliberalism, expressed by politicians like Ronald Reagan in the US and Margaret Thatcher in the UK, the development of the Washington Consensus in international political economy, and the prioritization of market forces in the EU through the Single European Act 1986 had prevailed. Furthermore, in the 1990s the Eastern Bloc was to collapse entirely, and most states there underwent a rapid process of conversion to capitalist economies. At the time, the victory of Western-style capitalism seemed so complete that the 'end of history' was proclaimed (Fukuyama, 1992). All the big issues had been settled and the world could look forward to peace, prosperity and evolutionary rather than drastic change. The hubris that such views entailed was noted at the time. And, in retrospect, things didn't quite turn out that way.

Apart from ongoing and developing crises like that of global warming, the system of neoliberal globalization was prone to repeated economic dislocations culminating in the GFC of 2007–08, and the years of renewed austerity that followed it. States and international organizations competed in applying orthodox nostrums to the difficulties they faced, trying to roll the clock back to the pre-crisis status quo, and showing in the process that they had learned little from history, and especially from past policy mistakes (Blyth, 2013). Others considered that the death knell of neoliberal globalization might have been sounded by the GFC, the erosion, if not breakdown, of the international order, and the failure of austerity to resolve underlying issues. The subsequent arrival of the COVID-19 pandemic and associated economic downturn intensified discussion on these points.

Reviewing historical trends certainly reminds us that the long-run context is one of continuous and, sometimes, sudden change. Rarely, structural factors seemingly beyond human control may drive the change. But, for the most part, human agency will be involved. To paraphrase Marx's well-known aphorism: people do make their own history, but not under conditions chosen by themselves. But there is little certainty in the moment as to the direction change will take. Can forces committed to the continuation of neoliberalism succeed? Can an alternative prevail? If neoliberalism is to be displaced, what will replace it? Can any alternative meet the existential challenges posed by climate change and future energy provisioning, and the pandemic?

Looking back at previous crises in just a bit more detail, what can we learn? Relatedly, what do we mean by that much overused word 'crisis'? On the second point, Kahler and Lake (2013, pp 10–11) proposed two meanings. One is a situation that poses extreme danger or difficulty. Obviously, given the multiple crises already outlined, we are in such a situation. The second is the notion of a 'turning point', in which a fundamental change of direction takes place. Crisis (in meaning one) may, but does not necessarily, lead to a crisis (in meaning two). Sometimes an extremely dangerous and difficult situation may simply lead to 'doubling down' on existing practices, and a restoration of orthodoxy. Although it is likely that this will lead merely to postponement of a future turning point rather than its avoidance, depending on the alignment of political, economic and social forces this may be an acceptable short-term result for some players. In other cases, major and fundamental change may occur after an interregnum in which the future remains unclear and obscure. A key question, therefore, is: where do we sit as far as a potential turning point is concerned – restoration of orthodoxy, or a transition away from it? Our very brief review of historical instances yields both types of example.

Given the situation in 2021, the coterminous development in the 1920s of a health pandemic (Spanish flu) and economic upheaval has made it a popular destination in lesson-learning forays into the past. Then, too, there was a sense of multiple crises looming over society and, with the benefit of hindsight, we know that this did not end well. Politics in the 1920s reeled because of the devastation produced by World War I, the collapse of the pre-war economic and political order, the health pandemic and social upheaval, including the Russian Revolution and various revolutionary attempts in Western Europe.[2] In his effort to retrieve or rehabilitate historical analysis within international political economy, Randall Germain (2019) divides the interwar period in two, roughly coinciding with the two decades. In the 1920s, unsuccessful attempts were made to restore the pre-existing 'golden age' of the Gold Standard, fiscal conservatism and free trade. The Gold Standard meant automatic adjustments to trade imbalances which, because of the fixed nature of the currency exchange against gold, had to come at the expense of domestic cost factors such as wages. The 1930s were defined by economic collapse and depression, the rise of fascism, and by the inexorable drift to war.

Karl Polanyi (1944) characterized the 1920s as 'deeply conservative' and founded on the belief that only a return to the pre-1914 order could produce peace and prosperity. It was the utter failure of this endeavour that paved the way for the 'revolutionary' 1930s, once the experience of the Great Depression had begun to take effect. For Polanyi (1944, pp 29–30) the root cause of these failures and their dangerous consequences was the self-regulating market. Similarly, Louis Pauly tracked the efforts of the League of Nations to reconstitute the liberal international order. It succeeded in developing an expert consensus around some key ideas. But it was a classic case of failing to draw the correct lessons from the past. As Pauly notes (1996, p 22), given the Great Crash and ensuing depression, the League's 'blind faith in market solutions ... is truly breathtaking'. Growing recognition of systemic market failure in turn opened the path for radical change. Indeed, Eric Hobsbawm (1995, pp 94–5) noted that the slump 'destroyed economic liberalism for half a century'. Hobsbawm's characterization of the whole period between 1914 and 1945 is 'the Age of Catastrophe' in which the capitalist economic order was on the verge of collapse.

During the 1930s a series of options emerged, some of which were institutionalized in the post-World War II period. For Hobsbawm, there were three broad alternatives: communism; a reformed capitalism on social democratic lines (these would include varieties such as Roosevelt's New Deal in the United States, and the 'Middle Way' approach of Sweden); and fascism. The first two continued robustly into the post-war era. The latter, due to the defeat of Nazi Germany and its allies, was confined to outliers like Spain and Portugal. Peter Gourevitch (1986, ch 2) presented an overlapping but more elaborate schema, developed to show the choices available in three historic periods of crisis (the 1870s, the 1930s, and the 1970/1980s). Five were identified. These were: neoclassical liberalism (the primacy of the market); socialization of ownership and planning (socialism/communism); protectionism; demand stimulus (Keynesianism); and mercantilism (in the sense of the state aiding specific sectors or firms within its economy). Support for these broad options has waxed and waned over time but all remain on the table in some form or other.

In the context of the early 2020s, what broad options or alternatives are under active discussion? To what extent are each of them adequate to meet the challenges of the multiple crises that have been identified? Regardless of their likely effectiveness, what are their prospects of being adopted and implemented?

In the remainder of this chapter, three broad types of alternatives are sketched. They will be developed more fully in Chapters 6 through 8. Here, the intention is to outline them schematically in simplified 'ideal type' form. In the real world there are overlaps and intersections between them. Yet, if the real world is messier than discussion of ideal types suggests, it remains the case that potential solutions tend to crystallize around one or other of the possibilities identified here.

The first option consists of 'back to normal' perspectives advocated by neoliberals wishing to restore some sort of pre-crises 'status quo'. As the pandemic crisis drags on, so far there are relatively few open challenges to current policies of fiscal and monetary stimulus. However, the positioning of opinion about restoring sustainable finances through future fiscal austerity is already apparent. Second, there are modest but significant reforms put forward by centrist political organizations and individuals that believe the worst effects of neoliberal globalism can be moderated, while retaining the fundamentals of the system. Third, there are radical options challenging the fabric of neoliberal capitalism, and advocating its transformation.

Restoring the pre-crisis 'normal'

Looking back at the GFC and the period since then, we see the following pattern. Faced with the prospect of a complete financial and economic collapse, most states and international organizations turned to economic stimulus on a scale unprecedented in the neoliberal years. Initially, this was heralded as a sign that 'Keynes is back' but, in addition to being misleading in that respect (see Blyth, 2013; McBride and Evans, 2017, pp 5–7), it was short-lived. As economic stabilization returned, most states declared austerity (in the sense of deficit and debt reduction) to be a policy priority. As well as fiscal consolidation, they continued, albeit with variations, with associated austerity policies of public sector restructuring and labour flexibility (Whiteside et al, 2021). The severity of the 2007–08 GFC made a return to pre-crisis normality seem unlikely to many at the time. Yet that is what occurred, and those events could serve as a marker for policy elites once the immediate crisis caused by the pandemic is judged to have waned.

Response to the GFC rested on a reallocation of blame or responsibility from the private financial sector to the state. In reality, the existing financial private sector debts were transferred to the public accounts. Once the state assumed that role and advanced the money to stabilize the system (often on the grounds that whole sectors, or large firms within them, were 'too big to fail'), it assumed liability. To stabilize its own finances, according to the prevailing economic orthodoxy, it was necessary to practise austerity. The effect was to impose the costs of rectifying the crisis onto working-class people, in their roles either as taxpayers, recipients of (reduced) public services, or targets of labour reforms, enabling precarity to flourish in the labour market with reduced labour costs (and therefore reduced working-class incomes).

Thus, the three main domestic components of the post-2008 return to normal were: fiscal austerity via spending restraint concentrated in social policy portfolios; privatization and marketization of the public sector, including by way of public–private partnerships (P3s); and making the labour market still more 'flexible'. Internationally, the system comprised trade liberalization, promoting capital mobility, and protection of corporate power through state actions and expanded private authority. Despite this 'restoration', some of these components were already crumbling in the pre-Covid period, and others such as fiscal restraint seem now to have been brushed aside, at least temporarily. Still, restoring the pre-crisis normal means putting as much as possible of this architecture back in place.

Fiscal and monetary stimulus on a major scale has characterized the pandemic crisis response. But warning voices are already audible that the impact of such measures on the public finances is unsustainable. The prevailing neoliberal ideas may be under challenge but remain deeply embedded within ruling institutions at both international and national levels. Within organizations like the IMF and World Bank, dissident or heterodox views can be found in research departments and reports, but less commonly in their operational wings. For example, emergency pandemic loans to developing countries still contain the condition that governments 'remain fully committed to macroeconomic stability and ... fiscal consolidation' (ActionAid, 2020). Contradictory tendencies are at work in the international trading system – protectionism and defections from some arrangements (Trumpism in the US, Brexit in the UK), together with continued expansion of trade agreements such as the CPTPP and the Asian Regional Comprehensive Economic Partnership (RCEP). The WTO remains unwilling to relax intellectual property protections that might enable the supply of COVID-19 vaccines to be expanded in developing countries. Domestically and internationally, beneficiaries of the pre-crisis normal may be expected to push for its restoration. In the environmental portfolio, for example, Koch (2011) concluded that measures to mitigate climate change are politically difficult to achieve and their failure may lead to an authoritarian future in which rich nations of the Global North defend their way of life.

However, there is more evidence than formerly of significant divisions within policy elites. A key element in these developments, as in the post-2008 situation, will be the battle for control of the narrative between different factions of capital, and critical voices in civil society. The outcome of a similar battle after 2008 was clear – are there grounds for thinking this time will be different?

Saving the system: modest but significant reforms

This option consists of proposals at both national and international levels that would significantly reform the neoliberal model. Such reforms recognize (a) that things cannot return to exactly what they were, and (b) that multiple crises provide opportunities to transition to private and profitable adaptation strategies, possibly at public expense.

A range of possibilities exists and there is a continuum of measures ranging from the minor adjustments typical of the 'back to normal' option, to more significant ones. Judging how modest or significant these measures are, is certainly subjective. But the subjective judgements should be based on answers to the real questions behind this exercise. Do the measures taken or promised in this category have the capacity to solve the multiple crises? Or are they likely to provide some amelioration without coming to grips with fundamental causes of the crises? Some possible examples are provided below. Taken together they could be construed as an attempt to re-vision Keynesian approaches and adapt them to twenty-first-century crises and realities, including global rather than national capitalism.

National governments could adopt a more active role in the economy and position public services as investments rather than liabilities. The precarious labour market could be reformed and made less insecure. Proposals for a Universal Basic Income or, alternatively, a Job Guarantee are already in circulation and might achieve greater prominence. Increased taxes (especially wealth taxes, excess-profit taxes, closure of tax havens) could serve to increase governments' revenues and potential for action, and to contribute to redistribution and reduced inequality. Health systems could be built up and the role of profit in services such as long-term care re-examined. Trade could be modified to permit industrial policy to escape supply chains in important goods, such as those medical ones found to be in short supply during the pandemic. Even sizeable and affluent states like Canada were found to lack the capacity to manufacture essential medical goods and vaccines. Some versions of a Green New Deal idea might be associated with more spending and regulation. Other versions might have more radical impact.

Internationally, the EU could discover a more active role through initiatives such as the Recovery Fund and other changes to enable a more interventionist European-level state. In a significant departure from past practice, the EU has begun to issue 'social bonds' to finance short-term employment programmes. Such initiatives would build on previous examples of achieving tighter integration in periods of crisis. Importantly, although extending the EU role in fiscal policy may be a type of integration through crisis, there is no reason to be confident that the expansion happening now is an indicator of a more progressive fiscal stance emerging in the longer run. Fiscal rules in the EU have been only *temporarily* suspended (until 2022). The monetary and fiscal rules have not been revised and could return in the future. There are signs that the neoliberal certainties that have gripped international organizations (IOs) like the IMF are under challenge, at least theoretically, inside those organizations. Other, admittedly more marginal, IOs such as United Nations Conference on Trade and Development (UNCTAD) have advanced more radical proposals calling for permanently expanded government expenditures linked to industrial strategies to promote green energy, sustainable transport systems and enhanced social protection. The World Economic Forum (WEF) has floated the idea of a Great Reset, improving the economic system to achieve 'responsible capitalism'. Similarly, Mark Carney (2021), former governor of the Bank of Canada and of the Bank of England, has questioned the role of markets and called for new values, including solidarity, fairness, responsibility and compassion, to be embodied in business institutions that should also practise stakeholder capitalism and socially motivated investing, and put purpose before profit.

From this perspective, the economic recovery must put the world on a path to sustainability through initiatives like carbon pricing, and technological innovations to enhance the profitability of green solutions, and fairer outcomes of a system still primarily driven by the private sector. An optimistic conclusion, but still one requiring far-reaching change and perhaps creating a new 'middle way' between modest and radical change, was reached by Tooze's (2021) analysis of a number of European reports on pathways to a new zero-carbon future. Stopping short of the elimination of capitalism, Tooze's readings of the reports indicated that measures to reach the targets for 2050 (zero emissions) would involve major public subsidies to stimulate private investments on the required scale, and tighter regulations. All this would be very costly, but not impossibly so.

Modifications to the international trading system and taxation and spending levels at the national level, initiatives such as universal basic income schemes, new international accommodations, together with regulatory changes to improve labour markets, all have their advocates. A possible result of the pandemic's economic impact is that several of them could be implemented, to considerable public benefit. Whether the internal contradictions between them can be overcome is another question. And whether the multiple crises can be overcome without transforming the fundamentals of the system is yet another.

Transforming the system: radical options

Considered as ends in themselves by their supporters, the enactment of modest reforms could instead serve as stages or stepping stones on the way to more radical change. A precondition for such an escalation is the mobilization of social organizations and movements unwilling to accept initial reforms as endpoints but, rather, regarding their achievement as moments from which subsequent and more radical measures can be advanced. In fact, that is by far the most likely way that we can imagine radical change coming about. What would radical change look like?

Many commentators have invoked past traumatic events and the policy responses to them. Thus, there are calls for a new Marshall Plan, for a radical Green New Deal, for a return to the wartime mode of mobilizing the population to fight the common enemy, climate change, and planning the economy in the public interest to pursue pressing priorities such as reduction of inequality. These types of proposals place the public authorities in the driver's seat and require the subordination of private interests to the public interest through state planning. Specific proposals include: nationalization of banks and financial interests, making bailouts contingent on public acquisition of equity in firms; enhanced power for trade unions and drastic reforms to labour markets to enhance security of the workforce; major reform of the global trading system to enhance national capacity to respond to domestic demands; and, increasingly, substitution of economic planning for market determination. Initially resembling a version of 'left' Keynesianism, in the minds of proponents these measures have the potential to go beyond the goal of stabilizing capitalism and take the necessary next step of replacing it with some form of socialism (though this is not always labelled as such).

The intersection of the economic with the environmental crisis reinforces this conclusion. A number of economists specializing in the environment have pointed to the link between capitalist dynamics, the pressure to grow and the impact of consumerism. Consumerism is a value and practice spread widely throughout more affluent societies. Although the very rich reinvest most of their money into continuing accumulation, some authors have drawn attention to the scale and nature of their consumption and pointed to its role in sustaining the perpetual economic growth model, at major environmental cost (see Kempf, 2007; Di Muzio, 2015a).

In that context of unconstrained consumerism, it is difficult, if not impossible, to manage carbon emissions on the scale necessary to bring climate change and warming under control (Jackson and Victor, 2011). If so, only radical change will do. Under capitalism there is a constant drive for greater efficiency derived from increased productivity (more value produced from fewer or cheaper inputs such as labour, raw materials, or energy). Yet, as long as the increased product can be absorbed (enter consumerism), there may be greater rather than less use of these inputs. Hence, workers may support growth strategies on the grounds they may create more jobs. Similarly, enhancing productivity may require more energy inputs than previously. Even if decarbonization policies and green energy initiatives through new technologies are in effect, this may still produce an increase in total energy inputs. This is especially true in a transitional period where new technologies are being deployed, since their production and deployment may themselves increase emissions (Tanuro, 2013). The only way to break this vicious cycle is to roll back, if not eliminate, capitalist market relations and replace them by some form of economy based on production for social need rather than private profit.

Conclusions

Three broad types of alternatives are outlined in the chapter and the interconnections between them are provided in Figure 5.1.

Glancing at the figure highlights that the main options or alternatives differ along several dimensions: the degree to which they rely on global versus national autonomy (and within that difference whether binding global rules or international cooperation between more autonomous nation-states is preferable); the degree to which they rely on public solutions (including a permanently expanded role for the state) versus private ones; and the degree to which they involve less or more democracy.

The alternatives discussed will be developed more fully in the next three chapters. Here the intention has been to outline them schematically in simplified 'ideal type' form. In the real world there are overlaps and possibly sequencing of alternatives, as one may be perceived to fail and be augmented by components of the others. Yet, potential solutions tend to crystallize around one or other of the possibilities identified.

Figure 5.1: Alternatives

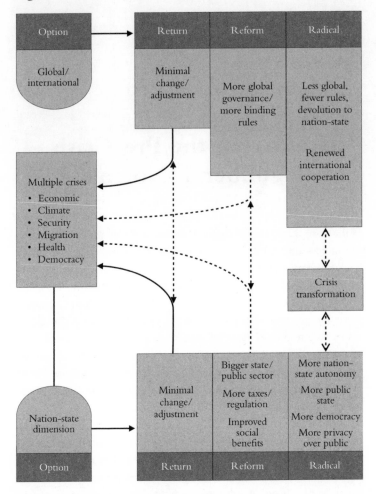

6

Restoring the Pre-Crisis Neoliberal 'Normal'

Will the multiple crises trigger a massive rethink and reorientation of our economic and political systems? Or will the voices of getting back to normal prevail, at least until there is further intensification of the crises? What can we learn from the recent past?

There is always room for a debate about how much change a particular crisis did or did not produce. Recalling the GFC, initial state responses included special measures to stimulate national economies and a degree of international coordination through the G20 to accomplish the same at the global level. Seen as necessary to avert a global economic collapse, these initiatives signalled a reversal of, or at least deviation from, decades of fiscal restraint.

At the time, some thought this meant a return to the Keynesianism of the post-war period. In the event this resort to stimulus was never more than a short-term panic reaction by political and financial elites. Neither fiscal policy nor monetary policy was focused on the restoration of full employment. Rather, the goal was to stabilize economic activity at a level consistent with low inflation and unemployment at what was believed to be its natural and non-inflationary level. That rate would be lower than would obtain during the crisis but would still be far from full employment in the Keynesian sense (McBride and Evans, 2017, pp 5–7).

Even this was to be short-lived. From 2010 austerity was adopted. It was clear that returning things to the pre-crisis neoliberal normal was the order of the day. Little had changed, at least as far as the policy stance implemented by states and international organizations was concerned. The approach being implemented was consistent with pre-crisis norms. The basic ideas about how to run the international economy and national economies remained fixed within the neoliberal paradigm.

Similar debates about how to deal with the pandemic economic crisis and its aftermath are under way now. A variety of options, including returning as far as possible to neoliberal normality, can be detected.

In assessing this debate about the ability of interests, ideas, institutions and underlying structural forces to resume continuity in the face of crisis it will be helpful to examine neoliberalism a little more closely. One distinction, common in the public policy literature on broad paradigms like neoliberalism, is between goals and the means or methods employed to achieve them or, in one classic and slightly more elaborate schema (Hall, 1993), between goals, instruments and settings. Methods or instruments may change while remaining true to the ultimate ends or goals. Alternatively, changes in methods or instruments sometimes may signify that more fundamental changes are under way.

And if we push the threshold for 'goals' high enough, the elastic nature of broad policy approaches or paradigms may suggest more continuity even in the midst of change. For example, the displacement of Keynesian approaches (predicated on state managed full employment) by neoliberalism (with the goal of inflation control and market liberalization) is rightly considered an example of a fundamental shift. The immediate goals and methods of achieving them were so distinct and had so much influence on the lived experience of people that it makes sense to speak of two eras – one Keynesian, one neoliberal. Yet, at a different level of analysis, it is worth recalling that Keynes' intention was always to save capitalism not to replace it. In that sense there is continuity between the two eras and approaches. Neoliberalism was implemented to rescue capitalism from the inflation of the 1970s and, more particularly, from an overaccumulation of capital in relation to profitable investment opportunities. Keynesianism was designed to save 1930s capitalism from a different set of problems: mass unemployment and underconsumption, and the political fall-out from them, including the challenge of communism on the left, and fascism on the right.

Before we rush to judgement on whether neoliberalism is likely to be jettisoned it is worthwhile also to consider its ideational flexibility, not to mention the array of interests and institutions lined up for its defence or restoration. Neoliberals have been:

> rethinking policies according to context and showing both a capacity for improvisation and an attitude of flexible response. If the end goal remains constant – safeguarding what neoliberals call a competitive order and exposing humanity ever more to the compulsions of adjustment according to the price mechanism – the means of arriving at this goal shift with time and place. (Plehwe et al, 2020, p 6)

Reasons for anticipating continuity or restoration of the 'normal' include cognitive and attitudinal lock-in on the part of elite decision-makers whose education and working lives have been defined by neoliberalism. They have a lot invested in the 'conventional wisdom'. Even with the best will in the world, they would find it hard to think outside that box. Clearly too, an array of powerful interests have benefited from these policies and will shift their preferences, if at all, reluctantly. Finally, the institutional architecture constructed during the neoliberal era was explicitly designed to make those policies proof against future change. On the other hand, the severity of the crisis has revealed massive failures in, for example, austerity-conditioned health-care systems. Such examples, in combination with the still evolving crises of the environment, security, and migration, might intensify the pressures for change.

Given the economic shock inflicted by the COVID-19 pandemic most governments, international organizations, and mainstream media commentators support the unprecedented degree of stimulus. It is seen as necessary ... at least for now. Whether such a stimulus, provided through spending and monetary quantitative easing, leads, as some hope and others fear, to a permanent expansion of the public sector and a rethinking of neoliberalism is an important question. Here, the focus is on early examples of discourse or advocacy seeking to restore the pre-crisis normal and its institutional context, and some examples of measures and policies, such as budgets, implemented by states.

The key area to be addressed in this chapter is the expansion of the state's role as expressed by fiscal means, with some attention to the role of monetary policy. In the other areas of interest – continued restructuring of the public sector and continued restructuring and flexibilization of labour – few changes intended to be permanent have been recorded since the pandemic. In that sense, restoring the pre-crisis status quo is unnecessary. So far, it remains in place. Similarly, the status of the RBIO, where signs of erosion and consolidation were apparent both before and during the pandemic, will not be dealt with here but will be picked up elsewhere in the book.

Getting fiscal and monetary policy right

What have international organizations, think tanks, financial media, and national governments had to say about exiting from the crisis and returning to normal? As we shall see, the debate is far from over. Both sides of the argument – 'we must get back to normal as soon as possible', and 'there can be no going back' – continue to be expressed.

From the beginning of the COVID-19 pandemic, the IMF has been telling member states to continue to spend and ignore the damage that support packages will cause public finances, and not to pull support too early (Elliot, 2020; IMF, 2020a). In April 2020, Kristalina Georgieva, the fund's managing director, stated that countries should spend what they can but to keep the receipts, with the intent to maintain accountability, transparency and legitimacy. Bloggers from the IMF's Fiscal Affairs Department made the additional point that if governments delivered on these ingredients it would not only serve 'managing the crisis but also managing the exit from the crisis and reverting to a sustainable long-term fiscal path'.[1] Even so, Georgieva's public arguments seem more tolerant of an expanded role for the public sector than the IMF has traditionally advanced: 'even after the global community's efforts to alleviate … financing constraints, these countries will need to reprioritise expenditure toward the health sector while safeguarding key public services (transport, energy, communications) and social protection' (Elliot, 2020). Regarding premature withdrawal of support policies, Georgieva argues that it is critical to continue 'lifelines' across the economy such as tax deferrals, credit guarantees, cash transfers and wage subsidies. Georgieva states that if these lifelines are cut too soon, then 'the Long Ascent becomes a precipitous fall' (Georgieva, 2020).

For post-COVID-19 recovery and resilience plans, the IMF (2020c) had advocated green transformation, digitalization and closing the gender gap. These themes echo those expressed by liberal reformers that are discussed in the next chapter. Within green transformation, there was an emphasis on a broad-based movement towards greater sustainability through credible, consistent and high-impact climate policies, the purpose of which would be to aid private companies in accelerating the green transition. Unsurprisingly, then, this is a publicly assisted or funded strategy based on the private sector and, as such, represents continuity in approach. For digitalization, the IMF stressed the need to provide digital access to households globally, with anticipated positive impacts on the quality of life through enhanced access to health-care and education. Lastly, the IMF positioned green policies and digitalization as a way of creating jobs and reducing inequalities. Georgieva reiterated that governments should avoid early withdrawal of support and target stimulus toward economic transformation (IMF, 2020b).

This reassuring rhetoric aside, it seems that in practice the IMF has failed to transcend the pre-crisis status quo. A review conducted by the European Network on Debt and Development (Eurodad) revealed IMF conditionalities locking a large number of countries into debt and austerity. Critical analysts viewed the main findings of the review as aggressively insisting on austerity measures, shifting the burden on to the vulnerable, slashing public services, and making no commitment to sustainable development (Munevar, 2020). This is similar to an Oxfam evaluation that concludes that the IMF is paving the way to a new era of austerity post-COVID-19 (Oxfam, 2020a). In response, the IMF has offered reassurances that countries have their support during COVID-19, and stresses that this is not the old IMF (Shenoy, 2020). Bhumika Muchala, senior researcher at the Third World Network, has argued that lenders should cancel countries' debt, and in response Gerry Rice, IMF communications director, states that the IMF is advocating this, although, he says, 'the IMF knows it has to be cautious about when to call for belt-tightening for countries receiving loans' (Shenoy, 2020).

In OECD documents, ideas of a return to austerity are not prominent, although they do occur. For example, in a report regarding the territorial impact of COVID-19, austerity was used as an example of what governments could do as a long-term solution. Specifically, the report (OECD, 2020d) stated that central government transfers will most likely be cut to rebalance public budgets and restore fiscal stability, and this could be done through future austerity measures. Furthermore, it warned that subnational governments need to prepare for the recovery phase after the crisis, and possible consolidation plans.

However, on the OECD website, that motif is less evident. Five key areas of focus are identified: inclusive recovery, resilient health-care, social challenges, green recovery, and global economy. The path to recovery is anticipated to be long and involves strengthening public health policies, supporting people, supporting businesses and supporting children (OECD, 2020b) There is a lot of discussion of future investment within critical areas, such as public and private investment in health, education and infrastructure. The report holds that 'enhanced resilience is also about investing in people skills, ensuring better education and labour market outcomes, and ultimately higher trend growth and wellbeing' (OECD, 2020c, p 8). To achieve this, the OECD notes the need for more and better-targeted resources for early years of education, better paid and trained education staff, and better lifelong training support. It notes that previous crises have resulted in lower investment and lasting infrastructure gaps, and that this needs to change (Boone, 2020).

None of these points are particularly new from the OECD. However, there are some signs of a change of emphasis. Laurence Boone, the OECD's chief economist, argued that countries should ditch short-term numeric targets for public deficit debts, and instead embrace long-term sustainability goals, which would include accepting public debt burdens until economies return closer to normal (Giles, 2021). She noted that the mistake during the GFC was not lack of stimulus in 2009, but instead what occurred in 2010–11 and afterwards (that is, austerity). Therefore, the first lesson is to ensure governments are not tightening in the one to two years following the pandemic trough of GDP (Giles, 2021). Boone also called on countries to continue using fiscal policy, such as higher public spending and lower taxes, to help economies recover and get unemployment down as the impact of the pandemic eases (Giles, 2021). Additionally, countries 'should get out of the mindset that we have one-size-fits-all fiscal rules to get debt back to a target' (Giles, 2021).

In a number of OECD countries, though, there are certainly signs of familiar arguments being recycled in preparation for the day some kind of recovery can be proclaimed. One of the key mechanisms traditionally used by earlier austerity advocates was weaponizing deficit hysteria. Some news headlines from around the world have portrayed the growing government debt and deficits in apocalyptic terms as: 'The Challenge of Our Lifetime' (Aiello, 2020); causing the 'Largest Recession in History' (Aguado and Pinedo, 2020; ESRI, 2020); and the 'The Worst Slump since 1706' (Pylas, 2020); a 'Peacetime Record' (Atkinson, 2020a); 'Explosive Debt Levels' (Chan, 2020) and, of course, how it 'isn't sustainable' potentially triggering 'a level of taxation that has not been seen for generations ...' (Press, 2020). In Canada, Andrew Coyne (a columnist at the Toronto *Globe and Mail*), criticized the federal government's 2020 Economic and Fiscal Snapshot as 'misleading'. He stated that the 'eye-popping' deficit and debt estimates, of $343 billion and $1.06 trillion respectively, were actually optimistic and understated the true amounts (Coyne, 2020).

This discourse may serve to mobilize anxiety surrounding national finances. Persuading voters something must be done about national finances could allow politicians to push for spending cuts and repeat the austerity agendas that have followed crises of the past (*Guardian*, 2020). The COVID-19 pandemic also fits into the mainstream narrative of crises caused by 'external shocks', which could further devolve responsibility away from the structure and functioning of the economy itself and, in the name of shared sacrifice, onto the backs of the population (Szymborska, 2020).

As a result, the austerity agenda is far from dead. A number of economists and politicians from across the OECD have argued that government deficits are unsustainable and unaffordable. Predictably, George Osborne (UK Chancellor of the Exchequer from 2010 to 2016 and labelled the 'architect of UK austerity') has called for a period of retrenchment post-crisis in order to bring down public sector debt (Atkinson, 2020b). In Canada, former prime minister Stephen Harper published an article in the *Wall*

Street Journal, calling the post-pandemic public sector balance sheets in Canada an 'unholy mess', while warning of an inevitable fiscal reckoning. He criticized leftists' visions of an expanded government, calling current fiscal measures unsustainable and unable to substitute for private sector wealth creation. Failing to practise 'mild austerity' proactively would result in debt crises of both national and subnational governments, thus necessitating a more brutal austerity later on (Harper, 2020; Yakabuski, 2020). Pay and pension differentials between public sector and private sector workers, and the vulnerability of private sector workers to lay-off and short working-time during the pandemic in comparison to the 'privileged' public sector, also feature in this discourse, particularly in terms of how, inevitably, taxpayers shoulder the costs. This leads to proposals for governments to be more business-like cost-cutters, with federal civil service pay cuts considered a good start. A permanent 20 per cent reduction in public sector wage bills has been proposed in order to lower the federal deficit and redress the imbalance favouring employees over taxpayers (Cross, 2020).

In the United States and Canada, the political right – Republicans and Conservatives, respectively – have stated that emergency relief benefits (including unemployment cheques in the US, or Canada Emergency Response Benefit [CERB] in Canada) provide a 'disincentive' to work, by paying people not to work and also providing them with more money than wages would (Sevastopulo, 2020; Wherry, 2020). This idea, instead of criticizing the over-reliance on the low-wage economy, portrays benefit recipients as lazy or opportunists, and is an old and discredited argument from the early neoliberal period (see McBride, 1992, pp 181–4).

On the other side of the debate, some leading newspapers and journals have published critiques of earlier uses of austerity, its disastrous outcomes and the need for strong, prosperous economic growth in dealing with the pandemic. A *Guardian* editorial (July 2020) called austerity a grotesque failure that must not be revived. In part its position was based on research showing that those who were hit hardest by austerity tended to support the Leave vote in the 2016 Brexit referendum (Editorial, 2020). The editorial argued that more cuts in the economy would make the UK's democracy even less stable. In a similar tone, the *Financial Times* announced that the death of austerity should not be mourned but argued that government should outline how they plan to reduce spending once economies return to full strength (Editorial Board, 2020). The Toronto *Globe and Mail* echoed similar thoughts, stating that austerity was not the right path prior to the pandemic, and it should not be the road chosen after because the future most Canadians aspire to does not include decades of cutbacks (*Globe and Mail*, 2020). Rather, Canadians want better health-care, schools, facilities, public transit and a cleaner environment.

Business groups seemed ready to countenance more government spending. In July 2020, the US Business Roundtable noted that states and local governments will need significant additional support to maintain their vital services and continue public sector employment. As well, they emphasized the digital implications of the pandemic, and called for improved access, usability and affordability of broadband (Bolton, 2020). However, the Roundtable also emphasized points of continuity, signifying a desire for a return to normal, rather than its reform. Thus, it recommended Congress should keep markets open, trade moving and supply chains resilient to support American jobs. By sustaining transportation and delivery networks, the report indicated business operations would be preserved and families well supplied (Bolton, 2020). Within the generalities there were strong preferences for measures which would lead to economic growth. These included a federal COVID-19 economic relief package (83 per cent of CEOs were in favour), and investments in infrastructure, such as roads and bridges, were seen as 'most' or 'very' important by 77 per cent of CEOs (Business Roundtable, 2020).

Clearly the debate continues. There are voices warning that the current stimulus will be unsustainable and that familiar measures of restraint, which will substantively be the same as austerity, but probably not be labelled that way, will be necessary in future. For those business interests and mainstream media tolerant of higher public spending it is a priority to ensure that much of it flows to investments than can either enhance productivity in the private sector and/or help it to finance a transition towards a greener economy and a more digitalized one.

In responding to the pandemic, as was also the case with the GFC, monetary policy has played a very important role. Central banks have done two main things. First, they have kept interest rates at extremely low levels. This makes private consumption or investment spending, using borrowed money, more attractive than saving or hoarding. Of course, it also permits or even encourages speculative spending, since the cost of borrowing is minimal. It may therefore fuel real estate or other bubbles that do not contribute to the real economy. On the other hand, it also enables public spending, in the form of government deficits and accumulation of debt, which is relatively easy to service as long as interest rates stay low. This low-interest environment, which central banks have signalled they intend to sustain, can stimulate the economy through these types of spending. There is, however, some debate about whether monetary policies of this type are capable of delivering sufficient stimulus to produce significant economic growth. Empirically, years of low interest rates by the European Central Bank and the US Federal Reserve Bank have failed to move the economies beyond weak growth. This can be attributed to their failure to trigger investment spending when expected returns are low, and consumer spending, when conditions are uncertain and insecure (Thornton, 2019).

Second, central banks have engaged in quantitative easing (QE) policies. Essentially, QE creates money, not through physically printing it, but by means of the central bank purchasing assets, often government or corporate bonds, from private banks and financial institutions. With the money they receive it is expected that private banks will lend to consumers or firms, thus theoretically triggering spending on their part and, in the process, providing an economic stimulus.

The amounts of money created by these methods by the US Federal Reserve Bank, the Bank of England, the European Central Bank, and others like the Bank of Canada are massive and unprecedented. Two examples will suffice. In November 2020 the Bank of England estimated that its QE activities amounted to 40 per cent of GDP.[2] US estimates show QE at around 44 per cent of GDP (Bachman, 2021).

Providing stimulus in this way is a preferable option for business, compared to government spending. It leaves control of how much to lend, how much to spend, and what to spend it on in the hands of the private sector. However, the mandates of central banks commonly target inflation control as an exclusive goal, or privilege it over other goals such as employment. Central banks' mandates have not changed, and some comments of bank leaders have shown that commitment to the continuation of expansionary policies is conditional. Paul Beaudry, Deputy Governor of the Bank of Canada, reminded the public that: 'our asset purchases are guided by the need to reach our 2 per cent inflation target. Low, stable and predictable inflation is the Bank of Canada's prime mission.' If inflation beyond the target rate threatens, then the bank could increase interest rates or stop or reverse asset purchases (Bank of Canada, 2020). Similarly, the Bank of England operates with a 2 per cent inflation target, and its Monetary Policy Report (Bank of England, 2021) kept its low interest and QE operations in place as inflation was well below target. The implication, though, is that if inflation returns to its 2 per cent level for any length of time, monetary policy will also return to normal. Similarly, a European Central Bank strategy review adopted a slightly more flexible approach to inflation targeting, averaging around 2 per cent over the medium term, but seemed, in the view of a former member of the German Council of Economic experts, to be speaking more to financial markets than to citizens (Bofinger, 2021).

A third option (discussed briefly in Chapter 7) is put forward by proponents of Modern Monetary Theory (MMT), which involves much greater increases in the money supply.

Reading the tea leaves: 2021 budgets and plans

Returning to fiscal policy, what can be gleaned from existing and projected budgets? In the immediate post-GFC period there was an expectation, or perhaps hope, that deficit spending by governments signalled a departure from neoliberal norms, and their replacement by ones more consistent with the earlier Keynesian era. These would have included full employment, restoration of the welfare state, greater social solidarity and enhanced rights for labour, and greater equality achieved through government social spending and a restructured tax system.

Such hopes or expectations were dashed after 2010, and most governments returned, voluntarily or under duress, to the neoliberal formula of achieving balanced budgets, controlling public debt, mostly by expenditure cuts but also including continued public sector restructuring through various forms of privatization, and attacks on working-class living standards though labour market reforms. Will this time be different?

The analysis here focuses on fiscal policy. Some commentary on the Biden recovery plans and proposed budget will be provided, despite continuing uncertainty of how an evenly divided US Senate will proceed. The general conclusion about the advanced countries, including the United States, is that current spending, impressive as it is compared to neoliberal normality, represents only a temporary deviation from it.

IMF data (see Table 6.1) indicated the similar pattern of spending and debt across advanced economies, emerging market economies, and low-income developing countries.

If the projections through to 2025 prove accurate, then the advanced economies will be spending a little more as a percentage of GDP than they did in the pre-pandemic year of 2015, and roughly the same as they did in 2000. Emerging and middle-income countries will be spending about the same as in 2015, and low-income developing countries will be spending less as a percentage of GDP in 2025 than they did in 2015.

It does not seem that increased emergency spending due to the pandemic will translate into structural change, any more than did the post-GFC peak in public spending. Of course, the volume of additional spending has led to increased public debt and these figures will persist for some time as shown in Table 6.2.

Table 6.1: Government expenditure as % of GDP, selected years, 1995 to projected 2025

	1995	2000	2005	2010	2015	2020	2025
Advanced economies	42.53	39.7	37.95	42.29	38.71	47.39	39.15
Emerging market and middle-income economies	22.23	24.99	26.4	29.96	31.6	35.04	31.71
Low-income developing countries	15.58	17.8	18.19	19.2	18.64	19.18	17.88

Source: IMF Fiscal Monitor (April 2021)

Table 6.2: General government gross debt as % of GDP, selected years

General government gross debt (% of GDP)	Advanced economies	Emerging market and developing economies	European Union
2007	71.1	35.7	62.1
2012	105.6	36.7	86.4
2017	103.1	50	83.3
2022 est.	121.6	66	91.6
2026 est.	121.1	71.2	86.9

Source: https://www.imf.org/external/datamapper/GGXWDN_G01_GDP_PT @FM/OEMDC/EU/MAE/ADVEC

If debt servicing costs rise due to unexpected increases in interest rates, then pressures to reduce government expenditures can be expected. Most commentators predict continued low interest rates and these are built into government projections. However, it is possible that inflationary pressures could trigger higher interest rates, notwithstanding central banks' desire to keep rates low to encourage economic recovery (Pittis, 2021). Hopes that rapid growth will enable the GDP ratio to diminish may founder because of sluggish growth, once the initial bounce-back from the pandemic is over. Then, pressures for a return to austerity can be anticipated. In the emerging and developing countries debt to GDP is lower, and so is the capacity to service it, especially if their recovery is impeded by lack of access to vaccines (the result of vaccine hoarding by the advanced economies and their refusal so far to waive WTO-protected intellectual property rights to enable vaccine production in developing countries).

Table 6.3 indicates that slow rather than rapid growth is expected after an initial period in which economies bounce back more vigorously.

Do the averages conceal a different story at the national level or regional levels? We briefly deal in turn with the US, the EU, the UK and Canada.

In the US, President Joe Biden sought to spend a record $6 trillion for the 2022 federal budget. This would be the highest sustained level of federal spending since World War II. The Committee for a Responsible Federal Budget (2021) estimated that debt would

Table 6.3: Real GDP growth (annual % change), selected years

Real GDP growth (annual % change)	Advanced economies	Emerging market and developing economies	European Union
2007	2.7	8.4	3.4
2012	1.2	5.4	−0.7
2017	2.5	4.8	3
2022 est.	3.6	5	3.9
2026 est.	1.5	4.4	1.6

Source: IMF https://www.imf.org/external/datamapper/NGDP_RPCH@WEO/
OEMDC/EU/MAE/ADVEC

rise from 100 per cent of GDP at the end of 2020 to 107.5 per cent by the end of 2031, possibly reaching as high as 117 per cent, depending on legislative outcomes. Budget deficits would total $14.5 trillion (5.1 per cent of GDP) over the next decade.[3]

Reflecting the strength of the Republican Party in the US Senate, and two dissident Democrat senators, some provisions were rolled back. The most notable changes include reducing the number of people who qualify for the $1,400 stimulus cheque, dropping the provision to gradually increase the minimum wage to $15 per hour, and reducing the federal unemployment payments. The $15 minimum wage was dropped after the Parliamentarian (Elizabeth MacDonough) determined it did not meet the standards legislation must meet to pass with a simple majority (Adamczyk, 2021).[4] The Senate version of the Bill also reduced federal unemployment insurance payments from the projected $400 per week to $300 per week (Sprunt, 2021).

On 15 November 2021, President Biden signed a $1 trillion infrastructure Bill into law. This fell short of Biden's initial $2.3 trillion proposal in March that year. Compromises were seen as necessary to secure a large group of Senate Republicans (Lobosco and Luhby, 2021; Tankersley, 2021).

In late October 2021, Biden announced plans for a $1.85 trillion social spending Bill (originally set to cost $3.5 trillion) to expand the social safety net and address climate change.[5] This Bill passed the US House of Representatives on 19 November. Missing from the framework are major priorities including dental and vision care, and measures to lower the cost of prescription drugs (Snell and Naylor, 2021; Sanger-Katz, 2021). Moreover, climate change provisions were scaled back. The Clean Energy Performance Program (formerly known as the Clean Electricity Standard, which aimed to provide incentives for utility companies to transition to greener technologies and fine those who didn't) was dropped (Walsh and Snell, 2021).

Some legislation, such as the American Rescue Plan, has been coined the 'most economically liberal in decades'. It removed work requirements, the sensitivity to risk of inflation and other 'centrist' concerns (Lemann, 2021). While a major improvement compared to its Obama-era equivalent, Trump's $2.2 trillion Coronavirus Aid, Relief, and Economic Security (or CARES) Act was slightly larger, and its anti-poverty impact is believed to be roughly the same. As the measures under this legislation are temporary, it does not really transform anything in the long run (Ackerman, 2021).

As for industrial policy, the Biden administration has proposed the American Jobs Plan, aimed at upgrading and repairing US infrastructure, investing in manufacturing, research and development, and expanding long-term health-care services. It included a number of tax increases on corporations – raising the corporate rate (to 28 per cent from 21 per cent), raising the minimum tax rate on the foreign income of US corporations (from 10.5 per cent to 21 per cent), and imposing a new corporate minimum tax (Committee for a Responsible Federal Budget, 2021; Ewall-Wice, 2021a). Biden's initial tax plans also included increasing the top income tax bracket from 37 per cent to 39.6 per cent, and tax on capital gains for the richest Americans the same as on income. Those were dropped (Ewall-Wice, 2021b). Biden has also stated that infrastructure is a key pillar of his climate plan (Waldman, 2021).

As of November 2021, Biden had failed to deliver the increased corporate income tax rate. Instead, his framework calls for two new 15 per cent minimum taxes – one on income American companies earn abroad and one on the profits that large corporations report on their shareholders (read: the G7 global minimum tax) (Tankersley and Rappeport, 2021).

Biden's initial proposals contained the most pro-union provisions, the Protecting the Right to Organize (or PRO) Act, since the National Labour Relations Act of 1935. The PRO Act would limit employers' ability to intervene in union election campaigns, impose steeper penalties for employers who break the law, legalize currently outlawed forms of union solidarity such as secondary boycotts, make it more difficult to misclassify workers as 'independent contractors' and forbid 'right to work' laws (Eidlin, 2021). As a result, this would potentially represent a transformative change (Savage, 2021). The social spending Bill faced significant hurdles from both parties, and a revised framework was presented as the 'Build Back Better Act'. This new Bill vastly reduced the proposed pro-labour provisions and still requires majority support in both chambers to become law (Porzio et al, 2021). It is unclear whether this Act will be passed by the Senate.

Alongside the infrastructure plan, President Biden has also taken executive actions to tackle the climate crisis, by taking a 'whole-of-government' approach through the Justice40 Initiative. The goals are to achieve a carbon-pollution-free power sector by 2035, and a net-zero economy by 2050. Net-zero is defined in formal terms as a situation in which the greenhouse gas emissions going into the atmosphere are balanced by removals out of the atmosphere.

Biden's climate plan aims at delivering 40 per cent of the overall benefits from federal investments in climate and clean energy to disadvantaged communities. His climate plan remains the most progressive climate plan of any US president in history, but it is still less ambitious than proposals from the Green New Deal. One of these proposals was to achieve net-zero greenhouse gas emissions by 2030 (rather than Biden's 2050). Moreover, he has not pledged to ban fracking (Snaith, 2021). Biden's clean electricity standard (CES), since dropped, was hailed the most aggressive initiative to shut down dirty power plants in American history. Nonetheless, it was criticized as a 'half-measure', promoting false climate solutions such as natural gas, nuclear and biomass power plants. Critics called for stricter renewable electricity standards limited to wind, solar and geothermal. Some feared it would be a complex technical scheme designed to avoid radical transitions (Grunwald, 2021). Advocates of the Green New Deal conceded that it was a step in the right direction but found the size and scale to be considerably lacking (Kurtzleben, 2021).

Watkins (2021) queries whether the large and unprecedented increases in expenditures really amounts to a 'seismic shift' as some have claimed. She points out that much of the expenditure, which is undoubtedly far greater than that undertaken in Europe, represents a 'catching-up' to European levels of infrastructure and social support. It may be transformative in the US context but, rather than bursting the boundaries of neoliberalism, simply represents a significant adjustment of the policy settings within it, instead of something more radical. In this context, many of the payments to individuals and families, and extensions to unemployment insurance, while reducing poverty and conferring real benefits, are 'one-off or temporary payments that leave the systemic reproduction of inequality unchanged' (Watkins, 2021, p 14).

Other elements of the packages may be longer-lasting. There is broad recognition that the US suffers from an infrastructure deficit, the result of decades of neoliberal neglect. In the 2019 World Economic Forum survey of competitiveness the US ranked thirteenth in the world for its infrastructure quality. In 2002 it had ranked fifth. The Council on Foreign Relations (2021, p 1) concluded that US infrastructure is 'both dangerously overstretched and lagging behind that of its economic competitors, particularly China'.

Apart from the increased spending, Biden's proposals imply a change of course on taxation – notably, increased corporate taxes at home and a global initiative to establish minimum rates of corporate taxes and thus lessen the danger of avoidance by corporations declaring incomes in overseas low-tax jurisdictions. However, in other areas there is little evidence of change. Calls for expansion of a federal infrastructure bank are linked to increased use of public–private partnerships, a central element of neoliberalism. So, while significant, the change so far seems largely one in the settings of policy rather than in the methods or instruments to be applied. This may be particularly true at the subnational level, notwithstanding some additional resources under Biden's recovery packages. In the US, every state but Vermont has either statutory or constitutional balanced budget legislation (NCSL, 2010) which is legally binding and has restrictive mechanisms which apply to all stages of the budget cycle (Hou and Smith, 2009, p 659). The ability of states to engage in stimulus-led recovery will therefore depend on voters' willingness to raise taxes and/or on federal largesse. Under the previous administration, cash-strapped states planned to cut spending on education and government services even in the midst of the pandemic (Myers, 2020; Walsh, 2020).

In Europe, the erosion of European Social Model aspirations (see Hermann and Mahnkopf, 2010) and national welfare state capacity over decades of neoliberalism made the impact of the pandemic worse than it might have been. As a response to its economic effects, the European Commission proposed EU funding to protect jobs and support investments in a green, digital, inclusive society and economy. The Commission also activated the general escape clause of the Stability and Growth Pact to allow member states to respond through increased spending and deficits. That said, activation of the general escape clause has its limits. It stipulates that its application must not endanger fiscal sustainability, and that deviations from the requirements are to be temporary in nature (European Commission, 2020a).

In another development, the Multiannual Financial Framework and NGEU provides grants and loans to member states and empowers the Commission to cover and effectively increase its budget by borrowing. This departure from past practice may represent a case of the 'integration by crisis' that has been part of the EU's historical evolution. The package has been criticized for falling short of the necessary levels of support (UNCTAD, 2021, p 8). Key programmes like the Recovery and Resilience Facility are firmly embedded in the EU's budgetary management and control systems (European Commission, 2020b). About 58 per cent of EU funds are to be spent on digital and green initiatives, and member states must create recovery and resilience plans which will be assessed by Directorate-General for Economic and Financial Affairs within the European Commission (ECFIN). If they do not conform to the Commission's structural reform objectives, typically involving pension and unemployment insurance cuts, and reductions in public sector employment, they may be rejected. Under the eurozone's rescue plan, the extension of the European Stability Mechanism (ESM) to fund health systems has also been criticized because of the austere conditionalities imposed on Greece, Ireland, and other EU countries post-GFC (Vergine, 2020). It is these processes, of course, that have locked in place neoliberal economic policy within the EU, and led Watkins to extrapolate about current and future developments that, 'As far as popular-democratic influence on economic policy is concerned, the end of the of the neoliberal era is farther away than ever in Europe' (Watkins, 2021, p 17).

Still, the EU response, in comparison to its own previous record, is designed to recover some of the legitimacy it lost because of its austerity policies after 2008. If successful, this greater flexibility on the part of the EU may enable it to achieve further integration. This might include transferring more authority over fiscal policy from the national to the supranational level. Centre-left proponents of 'more Europe' hope that post-pandemic spending will promote greater fiscal flexibility in the EU and undermine the fiscal and monetary neoliberalism that has characterized it. Whether the pandemic will trigger such a result or pave the way to a reassertion of neoliberalism through integration-through-crisis (ITC) remains unclear, although the latter is the more likely.

While one cannot generalize from a single case, developments in Italian politics tend to show that the restoration of neoliberalism is by no means unlikely. Despite the election of anti-system parties in that country, coalition governments have collapsed and been replaced by a government of technocrats, headed by Mario Draghi, the former head of the European Central Bank. The new government has enjoyed the parliamentary support of parties across the political spectrum. Draghi made it clear that funds from the Next Generation EU initiative would be used selectively and in conformity with the EU's ideas about efficiency. They would be allocated to firms with the capacity to compete and innovate. For workers and households, active labour market policies, in the neoliberal sense of activation and training for re-attachment to the labour force, would be the main mechanisms. The end result, according to Stefano Palombarini (2021, p 7), is that if not an exact return to the pre-pandemic status quo, this represents a case of never letting a good crisis go to waste. If the policy instruments are somewhat different, the policy goals of neoliberalism certainly seem unchanged.

Expanded public spending was a feature of the UK's 2021 Budget. This was a response to a 9.9 per cent decrease in GDP in 2020, apparently the largest one-year drop in 300 years. According to the 2021 Budget, government spending represented 39.8 per cent of GDP in 2019–20 and was projected to rise to 54.4 per cent before gradually dropping to 41.9 per cent by 2023–24. To provide some historical context (HM Treasury, 2021, p 37), this figure had been below 39 per cent from the 1980s until the GFC, after which it rose to around 46 per cent before declining again. The increase in the early 2020s is therefore significant but does not necessarily point to a permanently expanded role for the state: 'once the economic recovery is durably underway, the public finances must be restored to a sustainable path following a period of record peacetime borrowing' (HM Treasury, 2021, p 1).

The increase in public indebtedness as a result of this pandemic is significant – from 84.4 per cent of GDP to a projected 109.7 per cent by 2023–44, with a decline to 103.8 per cent by 2025–26. If the principle of fiscal sustainability is applied, then this debt might be reduced through either taxation or spending cuts. In other policy areas, pursuit of neoliberal ideology continues unabated. The government has used the pandemic as a means to transfer key public health duties of the NHS and other state bodies to the private sector without proper scrutiny (Garside and Neate, 2020). In health-care, functions that have been contracted out include testing centres, contact tracing, lab tests, purchase of personal protective equipment, and the building of and providing security for temporary COVID care hospitals. Similarly, Chancellor Rishi Sunak has warned of new squeezes on public sector workers' pay and has called for government departments to find 'cost savings' as a result of the pandemic (Partington, 2020).

In Canada the Parliamentary Budget Office (PBO, 2021, p 12) offered the projections shown in Table 6.4. Perhaps most importantly, the size of government, measured by its spending, would in this scenario be less in 2025 than it was before the pandemic – hardly an indicator of a radical change in economic policy.

Table 6.4: Canada: fiscal outlook (% of GDP)

	2019 /20	2020 /21	2021 /22	2022 /23	2023 /24	2024 /25	2025 /26
Total (program) spending	15.7	28.9	18.7	15.6	15.7	15.4	15.4
Budget balance	−1.7	−16.5	−5.0	−1.5	−1.3	−0.7	−0.7
Debt (federal)	31.2	49.3	49.8	48.6	47.8	46.8	45.8

Source: PBO, 2021

Real GDP was projected to reach its pre-crisis level by late 2021, due to improved commodity prices and availability of vaccines, and all ground lost in the labour market to be recovered in 2021/22. Yet influential voices, including those of former leading public servants, called for fiscal rules to be established, phasing out temporary income support programmes, shifting expenditures to investments in physical and digital infrastructure to enhance future productivity. Similarly, there were demands for spending on items such as childcare to be rationalized in terms of its contribution to economic growth and productivity, and for any further stimulus to be tightly targeted and temporary (Dodge and Horgan, 2021; Lynch and Deegan, 2021).

Provincially, the situation is similar. In Canada's largest provinces, Ontario and Quebec, major increases in public spending are intended to gradually return to balance and normality over the next few years. In Ontario, Doug Ford's Conservative government passed legislation to override collective agreements and take away rights from nurses and health-care professionals, and simultaneously watered down health and safety and environmental protections (ONA, 2020). In the COVID-19 outbreaks, the Ontario long-term care (LTC) sector came under public scrutiny. The incidence of infections and deaths in these largely private facilities (over 50 per cent are 'for profit') far exceeded the OECD average. Death rates in the 'for-profit' component of the sector greatly exceeded those in public or not-for-profit facilities. In some cases, the Canadian military had to be deployed as conditions inside facilities collapsed. What the soldiers found were horrific scenes of neglect, indignity and abuse, mismanagement, violation of standards of care, understaffing, and poor labour relations (Ritt, 2020), and deaths due to dehydration and malnutrition.

One governmental response was indicative of its continued commitment to the private sector. This was legislation to limit the liability of the operators responsible. Another was to establish a commission to report on the sector. The Commission's recommendations included increased staffing and funding, upgraded standards of care, more frequent and thorough inspections, and other measures to improve conditions. However, it did not confront the issue of privatization, and a continued role for the 'for-profit' component of the system is foreseen despite its deplorable record.

The use of P3s (public–private partnerships) is recommended in the construction of new facilities, despite this being a more expensive option than having infrastructure built publicly. Overall, this seems a response that repairs some of the damage found in private LTC facilities, but also an exercise in publicly financed damage limitation that leaves the fundamentals of the system intact, including its discredited for-profit components.

Other provinces also provide examples. In Newfoundland and Labrador, a major report with a mandate to identify a path out of the province's fiscal crisis recommended steep cuts to government spending (25 per cent in the health envelope, and 30 per cent in operating grants to post-secondary education institutions), increasing taxes and privatizing and opening up provincially owned assets to P3s (Mercer, 2021). In Manitoba, the Premier called for reducing employment and wages of public sector workers and implementing 'spending control mechanisms' with the aim of making cuts to services provided by government departments (Hajer and Fernandez, 2020).

No sign of new thinking in these provinces. In fact, in none of these cases is there much sign of a permanent expansion of the state's role, or of deviation from its prioritization of market forces. Despite the 'necessity' of current deficits, the OECD has also warned that subnational governments must prepare for the recovery phase after the pandemic, which may include possible consolidation plans and future austerity to restore fiscal stability (OECD, 2020b).

Conclusions

Thus, the post-pandemic economic outlook understandably remains uncertain. One useful survey of the world's main regions by UNCTAD noted promising developments in East Asia but concluded that in Latin America the economic growth trajectory was uncertain, partly because of accumulated debt from the GFC which hindered the necessary investments in both public and private sectors. In Europe the measures taken so far were judged inadequate to lead to a full economic recovery, and more likely to lead to the slow growth performance that existed before the COVID-19 pandemic struck (UNCTAD, 2021, p 14). Its overall assessment of risks can serve as a warning of what to expect unless a new and more dynamic political context emerges. The risks included:

> A misguided return to austerity after a deep and destructive recession is the main risk to our global outlook, especially in the context of fractured labour markets and deregulated financial markets. Together with the erosion of states' institutional capacity and policy space, these trends undermine the resilience of the global economy to all shocks. (UNCTAD, 2021, p 12)

Voices for change and reform are certainly predominant in current discussions, and ambitious proposals for change receive attention in the following chapters. But it is also evident that there are few signs of a radical rethink by governments in office, or international agencies in operation mode. Practices such as the conditionalities attached to IMF loans, and the actual projections of the future level of government spending, indicate that 'return to normal' may be the ultimate goal, at least for some actors. However disastrous and temporary that might prove, it is certainly a possible outcome. While conservatives highlight the 'necessity' of stimulus packages to mitigate the immediate effects of the pandemic, the austerity discourses used for decades appear to be cycling back as the preferred way to deal with the long-term effects of the pandemic. And, of course, that orientation does nothing to address the continuing saga represented by the other crises.

Saving the System by Building Back Better? Liberal Reform

Whether efforts to return to a pre-pandemic normal succeed or not remains to be seen. If the return to normal becomes the dominant policy push and has an impact, then the multiple crises we have identified will continue and intensify, possibly with short periods of remission in which their urgency fades until the next episode or outbreak. If the 'return to normal' imperative does not prevail, either discursively or in practice, then reform would be the next preferred option for its adherents, because significant adjustments would still be seen as preferable to measures that would be transformative.

In settling for reform, probably as modest as they can make it, advocates of a return to neoliberal normality will join together with those who favour more substantial reform on its own terms. The latter are actors, shaken by the incidence of one or more of the identified crises, who are more committed to serious changes which ameliorate the observable effects of the crises, and restrain the system's worst excesses. They do not challenge the fundamentals of the system itself. Their intentions are comparable to those of Keynes, in the 1930s, who theorized and wrote not to bury capitalism but to save it.

This chapter identifies the components of liberal reform (see Figure 7.1). Mostly the interconnectedness of the multiple crises is recognized. If the crises are interconnected so too must be the remedies. The profile of liberal reform presented here is constructed from analyses and recommendations, both pre- and post-pandemic, by international organizations like the OECD, think tanks, private and non-governmental actors, and influential individuals. It also pays attention to initial measures taken internationally and at the level of some of the bigger nation-states. Many of the measures are 'in progress' at best, but their content can be taken as indicative of what is to come, and what the possibilities and limits of liberal reform are likely to be.

The components include proposals and measures addressing the global security and economic governance context. Other elements aim to restore growth through economic recovery measures that accomplish a number of other ends. First, recovery should assist the transformation to a digitalized and green economy. Digitalization is directed at productivity enhancement and technological innovation and supports competitiveness and capital accumulation through new means. Achieving a green economy also may stimulate technological innovation while addressing the longer-term challenges posed by climate change and other environmental issues (such as loss of biodiversity). Second, recovery should be achieved in an 'inclusive' way. Inclusiveness, often operationally defined as reducing various forms of inequality, is intended to restore trust in or reduce alienation from political and economic institutions. This is important because lack of trust is seen as a threat to the liberal democratic values and institutions which are the preferred political shell for capitalist economies.

Being liberal reforms, these are compatible with and designed to restore the health and vibrancy of capitalism. In the present context this means a number of important shifts. Most important is the move away from the short-termism characteristic of liberal market economies to longer-term calculations of what is necessary for sustainability. In all of this, the role of the state may evolve from its role in neoliberalism, although the precise relationship between state and market, and between public and private sectors, remains vague in many of the reform discussions so far.

Figure 7.1: The virtuous cycle of liberal reform

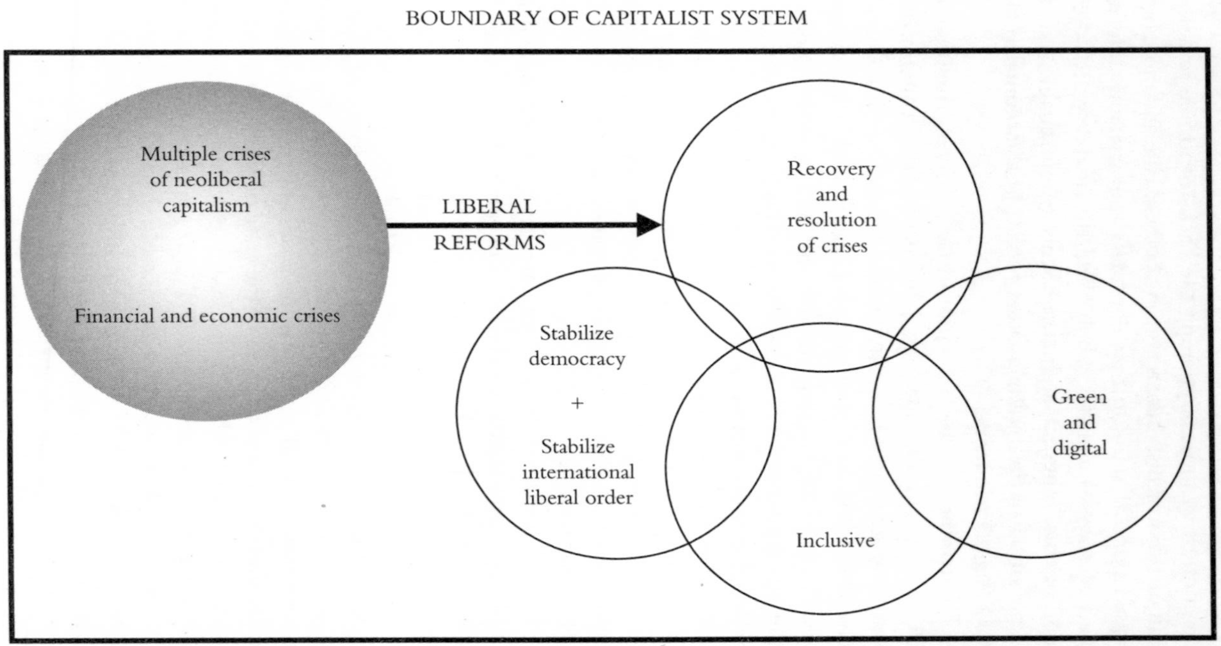

BOUNDARY OF CAPITALIST SYSTEM

Green and digital

Recovery and resolution of crises

Inclusive

Stabilize democracy

+

Stabilize international liberal order

LIBERAL REFORMS

Multiple crises of neoliberal capitalism

Financial and economic crises

Liberal reform

In contrast to those advocating the back-to-normal option with minor adjustments, there is a strong body of elite and more broadly based popular opinion that considers more serious reforms to be necessary to achieve stability and sustainability. If successful, proponents believe that such reforms would enable exit from some or all of the multiple crises revealed or accentuated by the COVID-19 pandemic.

Returning to economic prosperity involves 'Building Back Better'. That means addressing deficiencies of the economic system that have generated inequality, while simultaneously meeting the challenges posed by environmental disasters and climate change, and the need for ongoing technological and economic innovation through digitalization. The democracy crisis is generally depicted as based on poor results from or outputs of the existing system. This has undermined its legitimacy and fuelled distrust of institutions and elites. Fairer economic and greener environmental results could address the populist and nationalist (or alternatively, perhaps, nation-state-*ist*) challenges to liberal democracy and its rules-based international order.

Liberal reform measures are mostly at the discussion stage although some are beginning to be implemented. They often build on longer-run options that have achieved higher prominence due to the pandemic or the earlier GFC. The survey of reform measures and proposals will necessarily be selective,[1] but the intention is to identify the major themes, rather than every nuance of detail.

Existing economic reforms have focused on the short-term imperative to avoid economic collapse and are not intended to permanently expand the role of the state or public sector, at least as measured by spending. Under existing projections, government spending as a percentage of GDP will return to pre-crisis levels within a few years. The expansion embodied in monetary policy is also not intended to be permanent, although it is hoped that key elements of the policy such as low interest rates continue into the indefinite future. This means that dealing with the increased public debt resulting from emergency spending is a much easier task for governments. Even so, there are some concerns that inflationary pressures could alter the calculation about interest rates. If rates rose, then carrying costs of deficits and debts would be less sustainable than in current understandings.

If little substantive change in the state's role is seen in the 'back to normal' scenario, are things different in the reform packages? If the state's role is greater, how will this be defined and implemented? So far, there are few clear answers to these questions. Addressing inequality might involve changes to the legislated capital–labour relationship to increase the power of the latter, and thus its ability to extract improvements in wages and other working conditions. There are no indications that such measures are under active consideration. Tax reforms could reverse the distribution of wealth and income that the existing taxation system creates, with beneficial effects for more equal distribution, and for the total revenues available to governments. Or new social programmes might be implemented in some countries. In Canada, for example, childcare is often identified as a sector where changes could achieve both economic objectives (increase female labour-force participation) and social objectives (empower women; reduce the unequal burden of childcare). Provision of universal basic income is under discussion in many jurisdictions, and other measures like increased minimum wages, legislation to extend benefits to those in precarious employment, and ending discrimination in employment that afflicts racialized and migrant workers, are conceivable.

Investments to facilitate a private-sector-led transition to a green economy and to help the transition to a digitalized economy, including increased deployment of artificial intelligence (AI), are high priorities. Essentially, this would represent public subsidization of the adoption of new technologies by capital. Switching to a digitalized economy will have a major impact on existing labour markets, and the state's role in managing these dislocations. There are few details on these key issues in liberal reform proposals.

Generalizations rather than specifics abound in discussions of climate issues. Investments in green technology are key elements to exit a carbon-dependent production system and quickly transition to a carbon-neutral one (now generally referred to as net-zero). What the price will be in terms of finance and changed lifestyles, and who will pay it, remains unarticulated. Indeed, the hope that technology can render the transition painless and unobtrusive to citizens in affluent countries is palpable. President Biden's 'climate envoy' John Kerry, in offering the reassurance that the transition would have little impact on existing lifestyles, also stated that achieving the US's emission goals by 2050 depends to a large extent on technologies not yet invented (Harrabin, 2021).

There is already scientific scepticism about whether net-zero can be achieved using foreseeable methods:

> Current net zero policies will not keep warming to within 1.5°C because they were never intended to. They were and still are driven by a need to protect business as usual, not the climate. If we want to keep people safe then large and sustained cuts to carbon emissions need to happen now. (Dyke et al, 2021)

And the IPCC (2021) concluded that without a drastic cut in emissions immediately the 1.5° figure would be reached by 2040 at the latest (McGrath, 2021a).

The extent to which a strong state role is necessary compared to leaving control of the process in the hands of a suitably incentivized private sector is potentially a line of division within the reform camp. Many argue that to consolidate a political coalition behind the necessary transformations also requires policies for a 'just transition' in which workers (and businesses) in old sectors are compensated for or receive help in adjusting themselves to the new type of economy. All this has the potential to be very expensive.

Building back better: towards a digital and a green future

Definitions of what the digital economy is are numerous and not always consistent. However, at its core, the digital economy is the global network of economic activities, commercial transactions and professional interactions that are enabled by information and communications technologies. It includes online shopping platforms like Amazon, accommodation booking services like Airbnb, entertainment provision (for example, Netflix) and so on. But more fundamentally it includes the use of technologies currently found in many industries to execute tasks better, faster and differently than before, and also the use of new technologies to execute tasks and engage in activities that were not possible in the past. It includes artificial intelligence applications, driverless vehicles, and much more in the e-business and e-commerce areas.

Adapting to the new digital economy will require major investments, with proponents arguing that those countries which fail to make them will be left behind on productivity and efficiency metrics. Major investment in workforce skills, or reskilling existing workers, is also needed to avoid them being left behind (and thus fuelling further erosion of trust, and disaffection). One estimate (McKinsey Global Institute, 2021, p 18) is that 45 per cent of full-time-equivalent work can be automated using already existing technologies. While hardly definitive, such estimates do hint at the magnitude of the effort that will be required.

The OECD (2020a) notes that as policy-makers deal with the economy they will need to take a new look at the labour market structures and regulations, while working to make sure that displaced workers are not left behind. At this stage, few details are available about how this will happen.

Optimistic accounts stress the positive impacts of digitalization and automation that can lead to the creation of new jobs, skills enhancement, and increased entrepreneurialism and flexibility in the labour market. There may be a proliferation in new high-tech jobs as well as jobs in vocational education and training (Berger and Frey, 2016; Arntz et al, 2016). Similarly, increasing the use of robots, machines and algorithms could lead to occupational upgrading and specialization of workers, and work flexibility based on individual/family needs could help create a better work/life balance. Flexible work might also create an entrepreneurial worker, who uses their knowledge and experience to create competitiveness of the firm, at the same time enhancing their own marketability through ongoing learning, job networking and preparedness for alternate employment opportunities (MacEachen et al, 2008).

However, the bulk of academic research focuses on negative expectations about digitalization and automation, emphasizing the heightened asymmetry of power between firms and workers. Through 'creative destruction', technology will destroy jobs, business and/or entire sectors. Jobs may be created elsewhere, although this will likely contribute to 'job polarization' through a growing gap between complex, high-skilled jobs and simpler, low-skilled jobs. This gap will be accompanied by a dramatic decline of middle-skilled jobs as technology complements, or substitutes and devalues particular kinds of labour (Lovergine and Pellero, 2018). New well-paying jobs will be confined to high-skilled workers with STEM and bachelor's degrees, and income will be more unevenly distributed, forcing lower-skilled labour to assume more flexible, competitive and precarious positions (Sorgner, 2017). Much of the literature demonstrates that the rise of digitalization and automation and the platform economy will increase the labour supply but erode the standards-of-work arrangements, creating a huge gap between those with the knowledge and experience to succeed and those who must continually battle for sub-standard work (Vallas, 2019). In this scenario there will be increased segmentation in the labour market, leading to more inequality and raising more democratic deficit issues due to entrenched power differentials in an unequal society.

If this labour market dystopia prevails, 'micro-labour' will flourish. Micro-labour allows firms to recruit very temporary workers for specific tasks, and provides an algorithm to hire, place, set prices/ collect bids, and electronically pay people from around the world. This enables the outsourcing of work to independent contractors in order to minimize risk for the company, gaining inspiration, innovation and labour from workers quickly and at a fraction of the cost of formal employees (Bergvall-Kareborn and Howcroft, 2014; Irani, 2015). Liberal reform programmes barely touch on these issues. The tacit assumption seems to be that the optimistic scenario, supplemented by some skills training, will prevail.

New initiatives in the EU, both in the long-term EU budget and the Next Generation European Union (NGEU), reflect the objectives of making Europe greener, more digital, and more resilient. A mix of grants and loans in the NGEU is to be concentrated with minimum expenditure benchmarks of 37 per cent for climate and 20 per cent for digitalization. Although it is too soon to judge the NGEU, the assessment of earlier recovery strategies does point to problems in integrating multiple objectives. According to the OECD, green recovery measures represented only a small component of overall stimulus packages and were unlikely to have the transformational effects needed to address the climate crisis while building back the economy.

Harvey and Rankin (2020) provided some analysis of cost distribution in the EU's Green Deal proposals to transform Europe from a high- to low-carbon economy. Using a mixture of legislation and regulation to set targets, spending, and incentives to lever private sector investment, about €1 trillion would be involved, of which €279 billion would come thorough private sector spending induced by loan guarantees provided by the European Investment Bank, and the remainder from public moneys (€503 billion from the EU budget; €114 in participating funds from national governments). In addition, the EU promised a €100 billion Just Transition Fund. The amounts are impressive. Even so, and assuming the necessary political will to put it into effect, Harvey and Rankin cite one think tank as arguing that this is only about a third of the actual sums necessary.

In July 2021 the EU upped its game in the environmental area. Its proposals will require domestic companies to pay for the gases they release into the atmosphere and included an enhanced carbon tax to increase its price. From 2035 only sales of vehicles with zero emissions would be permitted.

An important departure from the international free-trade architecture was for a new tariff, the 'Carbon Border Adjustment Mechanism', to be imposed on imported products from countries with less strict emission policies. This could well fall foul of WTO rules on protectionist measures, being contrary to the 'like products' doctrines adhered to by the WTO. Hitherto, the trade organization has insisted that products be treated as the same, regardless of how they were produced. That is, different labour or environmental standards have not been grounds for subjecting similar goods to tariff restrictions. Other provisions in 'Fit for 55', a package of measures to put the EU on track for a 55 per cent reduction in carbon emissions by 2030, and net-zero emissions by 2050, call for increased use of carbon sinks such as forests and farmlands.

Apart from overseas opposition through the WTO if the measures are enacted, there are significant internal obstacles to approval within the EU. France and Germany are on record as being opposed to phasing out combustion engine cars by 2035 and instead calling for a longer period for plug-in hybrid cars. And some countries, like Poland, are still heavily reliant on fossil fuels like coal to generate most of their power (Ray, 2021). In addition, the reliance on the price mechanism is likely to have adverse effects on equality because it will hit low-income households hardest, as fuel and transport costs represent a higher share of disposable income in poorer households than in more affluent ones (Galgoczi, 2021). The poor also have less capacity to take advantage of energy-efficient alternatives like electric cars or to install solar panels. Disparities between member states are also likely to increase and the measure intended to offset these effects, the Climate Social Fund, is judged inadequate to the task, not only because the funding is too low, but also because some of it is dedicated to support initiatives such as charging stations for electric cars, which benefit the more affluent. Similarly, the formula for distributing funds to member states may not be sufficiently sensitive to inequalities.

Reviewing liberal reformers' proposals as a whole, there is a need for better alignment between short-term objectives of boosting jobs, income and growth, while reducing inequality, and long-term environmental commitments, such as net-zero emissions goals, and enhancing resilience. Current results raise concerns that such alignment is missing, and measures are largely having the effect of locking in existing industrial structures or going back to 'business-as-usual'. Overcoming this situation is part of the challenge facing liberal reformers. Failing to do so would make it resemble a public relations exercise or window-dressing rather than serious reform. It would fail to deliver the changes necessary to rescue the system from its own crises.

Building back better: inclusiveness

In both the economic and environmental spheres, the reformers' mantra is 'Building Back Better'. The term nicely encapsulates the objectives – 'building back' meaning recovery (with a hint of normality), but 'better' implying a different and superior range of methods and outcomes.

The OECD has highlighted the need to focus on a just transition. The OECD argues that stimulus measures typically have a central objective of creating jobs in the near future to help unemployment. In the longer run, recovery measures aimed at achieving environmental objectives, including confronting climate change, need to have a strong focus on creating quality, lasting jobs.

As such, this requires measures to support, retrain and relocate workers in sectors and industries that will likely be negatively impacted, to ensure a 'just transition'.

Reforms to bring about economic recovery either imply or explicitly include provisions to reduce inequality and insecurity. By these means they are intended to address inclusiveness, and arguably the democratic crisis that is rooted in poor outcomes for many people. OECD publications subsequent to the pandemic (for example OECD, 2020b) have stressed the need for recovery strategies to incorporate well-being and inclusiveness (partly to increase resilience to anticipated future shocks) and also to align with measures to alleviate climate impacts. The interconnectedness of globalism based on short-term economic growth and efficiency considerations, precarious global value chains and social inequality, combined with environmental degradation driven by the economic system, led the OECD to two conclusions. First, there was a need to shift to long-term thinking. Second, initial recovery measures fell well short of these goals (OECD, 2020b, p 4).

OECD recommendations were expressed in terms of a 'people-centred' recovery focused on well-being, more inclusion and less inequality. These would be part of environmentally focused objectives as well. Ideas here included progressive taxes that were beneficial to the most vulnerable. Preparing the workforce for a 'Just Transition' to a green economy was another central theme. Public spending initiatives could be designed to meet several goals at the same time. This would include initiatives to induce or leverage private sector finance to invest in environmentally sustainable projects in areas like renewable energy, retrofits of housing stock, scrappage schemes for obsolete cars and other equipment, electrification of transport including private cars, and the like. Increased use of digital technology to increase productivity and reduce emissions was advocated, a process which government could support by attaching conditions to stimulus packages.

Whatever the prospects for such policies in the Global North there is little ground for optimism about them in the Global South. In surveys of the World Economic Outlook, the World Bank Global Economic Prospects Reports for 2020 and 2021 noted the negative impact of the pandemic on investment and human capital development in the Global South. In a context of limited fiscal capacity and high debt loads, goals such as poverty reduction in emerging and developing countries are threatened. To counter this gloomy prospect, it considered that measures would be needed to secure core public services, maintain the private sector, and stimulate the economy by getting money into the hands of the people. Few details were provided.

In a similar exercise, the Economist Intelligence Unit (2021) focused on the developed countries and predicted a number of policy trends, including some significant reforms, that would be enacted in a context of high public debt and low economic growth. These included a revival of industrial policy targeted on the green economy, labour reforms to enhance social welfare and improve job security for both permanent and temporary workers, and tax reforms aimed at capital in general, or polluting industries in particular. This would help to finance state activities while also addressing both environmental and social challenges. Given anticipated low rates of growth and of inflation, monetary policies would need to be supportive of fiscal stimulus.

Facing declining populations and an ageing population, with attendant problems – a smaller labour force, productivity declines and high spending on the elderly (pensions and health-care) – states are challenged but do have various options. They can increase immigration levels to augment labour supply at various skill levels and/or they can institute labour market and innovation policy reforms to boost productivity and intensify usage of existing labour supply. Pension reforms might lengthen the working life of existing workers by extending retirement ages. Using the example of labour supply, we can see that whatever option is chosen it runs the risk of triggering opposition. Immigration has been one factor in the rise of right populism and the attack on liberal values. Changing the terms of retirement could also cause unrest as it alters the social contract when retirement ages are increased or pension rates adjusted. Given the nature of the exercise, the study provided few details, and, in fairness, the reforms might range from limited in some jurisdictions, to more comprehensive in others.

Such themes and tensions can be observed in ideas to reorient pre-pandemic labour policies towards greater social equity and inclusion. In 2018 the OECD launched a new version of its Jobs Strategy (originally established in 1994). The OECD claimed it represented a major shift from earlier neoliberal versions (see McBride and Williams, 2001; McBride and Watson, 2019). Some of the rationale for the new strategy focused on problems of democracy and the international order. The OECD defended the achievements of global integration and cooperation (OECD, 2018, p 2) but noted 'a rising backlash against globalization and rapid erosion of the trust in the multilateral system and institutions underpinning it' (OECD, 2018, p 4). Some factors connected to the eroding of trust were related to conditions in the labour market. Together with the effects of the 2008 financial and economic crisis – low growth, high unemployment, growing inequalities of income and opportunity – and the impact of other crises, such as climate change, global crime and terrorism, there was 'the fact that many people feel left behind by globalization and excluded from the benefits generated by greater interconnectedness and collaboration across borders' (OECD, 2018, p 2).

The Jobs Strategy was intended to play a key role in a paradigm shift towards integration of the labour market goals with other OECD initiatives on Inclusive Growth, New Approaches to Economic Challenges, Better Life and Green Growth. This would develop a better narrative that combined growth, inclusivity and sustainability. Thus, the new Jobs Strategy, rather than being a stand-alone labour market initiative, is explicitly embedded in a broader strategic vision aimed at defending the multilateral global order against its challengers.

Measures were recommended to encourage social mobility, improve access to quality jobs, promote equality of opportunity, increase minimum wages and redistribute income through the tax and benefits system. These had the laudable goal of reducing inequality. But can the chosen means deliver? Here, important caveats may limit effectiveness – such measures should not be implemented at such a level that they might impede economic growth, and those benefiting from redistribution should be subject to activation policies. Some recommendations stand firmly in the flexibility mode favoured by previous Jobs Strategies. For example, there is advocacy of flexible working hours and reductions in non-wage labour costs. On the other hand, there are calls to adopt a balance in employment protection legislation: it should not be overly restrictive and should allow for predictable dismissal costs, while protecting workers against possible abuses. Similarly, there is mention of establishing a moderate statutory minimum wage and promoting collective bargaining. But where the balance should be struck is indeterminate. Part of the older labour flexibilization approach remained embedded in the new reform agenda. Pointing to the two narratives uneasily combined in the new Jobs Strategy, Janssen (2019, p 227) called for trade union vigilance to ensure that the new narrative (based on inclusivity and fairer distribution) prevailed over the old one (based on flexibility).The OECD's new approach might well lead to some useful reforms but its self-portrayal as having undergone a paradigm shift is exaggerated,[2] and its ultimate resolution a matter of class conflict.

Building back better? The limits of liberal reform

Many of the components of liberal reform proposals are not well aligned with each other. To give just one example: transforming the economy through digitalization and investing in new technologies to accomplish green objectives are necessary to accomplish different goals such as increasing productivity and slowing global warming. But, whatever the potential long-term benefits, the costs tend to be up-front and have a greater impact on people on lower incomes. This exacerbates the inequality that has undermined social cohesion and political consent and contributed to the crisis of democracy. Whether, or to what extent, future job creation will offset potential losses remains unknown. To be consistent with climate goals, new jobs would need to be in the green economy and would require considerable reskilling of the existing workforce.

Anticipated improvements in democracy rest for the most part on results or output-based criteria. The expectation is that improved inclusiveness will siphon off discontent without the need for fundamental reforms in liberal democratic institutions.

Democratic and global context

For the moment, liberal reforms will occur within an eroding rules-based international order (RBIO). This lends them an air of unpredictability. That order was partially constructed with neoliberal capitalism in mind, and has provided the essential foundation for neoliberal globalization. According to Mearsheimer (2019, p 9), an international order comprises 'an organized group of international institutions that helps govern the interactions among member states'. Institutions, in turn, are defined as 'rules that the great powers devise and agree to follow, because they believe that obeying these rules is in their interest. The rules prescribe unacceptable forms of behaviour'. Normally, the rules operate to the benefit of the great powers that devised them. Even so, they can be disregarded by the dominant states when they deem it necessary, and so the rules are considerably more binding on the weaker states within the order.

The challenges to the post-Cold War, US-dominated, international liberal order comes from various sources, including the US itself in some areas. These challenges have undermined the major elements of the normality to which many long to return. Solving the multiple crises would be helped by more international cooperation. But efforts to rebuild the existing order are likely to cause conflicts rather than aid cooperation. Already the order has been challenged externally – notably by states like Russia, China and Iran. Russia and China both are explicit about being challengers of that order as they defend their national sovereignty not to comply with rules they consider as being ultimately defined by and imposed by the US. At the same time, internal challenges have come from the rise of right-wing populism in several nation-states, and from the Trump administration's hostility.

The 2020 US presidential election removed Donald Trump. His successor, Joe Biden, was widely welcomed among America's allies as rectifying one of the challenges to the existing order. Rhetorically, at least, Biden was quick to occupy the space created by Trump's departure and asserted that America was back and was prepared to lead again. Some concrete actions accompanied the rhetoric. Thus, the US rejoined the WHO and the Paris Agreement on Climate Change, and orchestrated a Leader's Summit on Climate Change in April 2021, and re-engaged with the Iran nuclear agreement, formally known as the Joint Comprehensive Plan of Action (JCPOA).

Clearly there was a considerable change of tone from the pronouncements of the previous administration, but there were many items of continuity suggesting that the challenge posed by Trump had deeper roots than that president's often bizarre behaviour. Anthony Blinken (2021), Secretary of State in the Biden administration, emphasized protection of American jobs, depiction of China as a long-term geopolitical rival capable of achieving international hegemony unless prevented, a determination to stop what the US considers theft of intellectual property, and trade losses due to currency manipulation. Similarly, although Blinken averred a preference for diplomatic solutions, he was quite explicit that this should be backed by maintaining 'the world's most powerful armed forces. Our ability to be effective diplomats depends in no small measure on the strength of our military'. The impact on its allies of the US defeat after 20 years of war in Afghanistan and its chaotic withdrawal from that country remains to be seen. Despite trillions of dollars spent, and thousands of lives lost, the mission failed to establish a strong, democratic state. Afghanistan has one of the largest displaced populations in the world, with over five million people being internally displaced or taking refuge outside the country (BBC, 2021). Several of America's European allies complained about Biden's withdrawal from Afghanistan, including over the incompetence with which it was carried out and the lack of meaningful consultation with NATO allies that also had over 10,000 troops in Afghanistan (Seligman, 2021).

Maintaining or returning to the status quo could be indicated by resumption of multilateral initiatives on climate change and in the global health area, with the US returning to the fold. In the vaccine response to COVID-19, the US has been accused of 'vaccine nationalism' due to hoarding supplies. It is not alone in this, however; the world's richer countries have been unrelenting in favouring access to the vaccines for their own populations and have taken few steps to make them available in developing countries. In denying developing countries access to vaccines before they attend to their own populations, they have practised what could be called 'vaccine imperialism' rather than vaccine nationalism. One instance is the refusal of major players to waive intellectual property rights to enable developing countries to produce COVID-19 vaccines. The US has indicated it favours a waiver, though narrower in scope than that proposed by South Africa and India. For the rest, however, maintaining the property rights protections even in the face of a catastrophic pandemic shows a determination to maintain key elements of the neoliberal architecture.

Similarly, most recently negotiated trade and investment agreements, such as CETA and the CPTPP, embed provisions such as investor-state dispute settlement mechanisms, thus continuing the policy of empowering capital in its relations with states. There is one notable exception. At American insistence, citing sovereignty concerns, the USMCA dropped investor-state dispute settlement provisions as they affected Canada and the US. Other clauses in the USMCA more than offset their removal and indicated a US commitment to making use of its power differential in bilateral, or in this case trilateral, agreements.

Under USMCA, notice must be given of intention to negotiate a free trade agreement with a non-market economy (widely interpreted to mean China). The USMCA member must supply all details of the negotiations and the final full text of the agreement to its partners who have the right to terminate the USMCA if not satisfied. Essentially, it gives other members a veto power. Paul Evans found it 'astonishing ... a severe restriction on Canadian independence and capability' as well as putting Canada into the American camp in its trade war with China.[3] China is Canada's second-largest export market; however, Canada's latitude to build on that connection is significantly reduced by the clause.

Of course, the subsequent deterioration of relations between Canada and China renders such an agreement unlikely. In December 2018, Meng Wanzhou, chief financial officer of the Chinese telecom firm Huawei, was arrested in Canada at the request of the United States and faced extradition to the US on fraud charges. Subsequently, two Canadians were arrested in China where they faced espionage charges. In September 2021, the US dropped its extradition warrant, enabling Canada to authorize Meng's return to China and, shortly afterwards, the two Canadians were released and returned to Canada. Relations between the two countries remained strained.

USMCA aside, the broader agreements also weaken the use which states, including their subnational entities, might make of government procurement as an instrument of industrial policy and extend limitations on the use of state-owned enterprises to function in non-commercial ways. Moreover, evidence that the benefit of such agreements is exaggerated are routinely ignored (see

Kohler and Storm, 2016). This suggests a theory-driven, or private interest-driven, explanation for the continued state enthusiasm about the agreements. Again, this is evidence of continuity or even extension of the existing order rather than its dismantling.

Other developments, however, reinforce the notion that a geopolitical realignment is in process, as the international system is reconfigured into what may become 'bounded orders'. The April 2021 G7 foreign ministers' meeting was expanded to include observers from India, Australia, South Korea and South Africa. Its communiqué could serve as a manifesto for the liberal international order,[4] was highly critical of both Russia and China and looked forward to the convening by the US of a Summit for Democracy, a gathering of democracies in the face of rising autocracy and authoritarianism.

There are signs, too, of other bounded orders, either potential or under construction. These are underpinned by the shifting centre of gravity of the global economy. Danny Quah (2011) used an innovative technique of estimating the spatial distribution of economic activity. By his account, in 1980, the spatial distribution of global economic activity or the income-weighted spatial average was located to the west of London, England, towards the middle of the Atlantic Ocean. By 2008, it had drifted east to the same longitude as Izmir and Minsk, and therefore east of Helsinki and Bucharest. This was largely due to the rise of China and the rest of East Asia. By 2050, it was projected to be located between India and China, over 9,300 km away from where it was in 1980. Expressed differently, Tonby et al (2019) report that between 2000 and 2017 Asia's share of global real GDP, in purchasing power parity terms, rose from 32 to 42 per cent; its share of global consumption from 23 to 28 per cent; and its share of the world's middle class from 23 to 40 per cent. By 2040, these shares are expected to increase to 52, 39 and 54 per cent respectively. From 2007 to 2017, global flows continued to shift to Asia. This includes trade flows (27 to 33 per cent), capital flow (13 to 23 per cent), worldwide patents (52 to 65 per cent) and global container shipping traffic (59 to 62 per cent). Intraregional trade has further expanded, including 60 per cent of goods traded by Asian economies, and 59 per cent of foreign direct investment. This integration and interregional flows across Asia have created powerful networks.

China has played a leading role in establishing an Asian Infrastructure Bank (that now has more than 140 members supplying funds to it) which could eventually rival the IMF. Its One Belt, One Road initiative (BRI) (Drache et al, 2019) is a massive programme of investments (at least $10 trillion) and establishes links between China and about 150 countries on every continent except North America. China's participation in the RCEP brings together 15 Asia-Pacific states, comprising a third of the world's population and global GDP. It will be the world's largest trading bloc. In addition to the Association of Southeast Asian Nations (ASEAN) members, the RCEP includes Australia, China, Japan, New Zealand and South Korea. Its terms are less intrusive and more compatible with national sovereignty than most trade agreements of the modern era. Notably, the US is not part of this agreement. Nor, because it withdrew under President Trump, is it part of the CPTPP. Neither is China. But the emergence of these blocs is a sign of intentional modification of the international order. The One Belt, One Road initiative, in particular, has been described as an effort to remake the global economic order. Even after controlling for inflation its scale dwarfs the post-war and much vaunted Marshall Plan.

Russia is a much weaker player than China in economic terms. Yet it is at the centre of a group of currently weak regional organizations (Mearsheimer, 2019, p 48, n 96) that could be invigorated under the right circumstances to create a smaller bounded order. And the country retains sufficient economic strength to render demands for behavioural change attached to multiple rounds of economic sanctions ineffective. Imposed by the US, and its allies including the EU, the sanctions may be inconvenient to Russia but have not so far produced policy changes.[5] Indeed, they may be counterproductive if the US and the EU are concerned by the prospect of closer relations between that country and China, the two main challengers to the international order. Sanctions may hasten the dissolution of the international system to which the EU and the US are committed.

In June 2021, the G7 met in the United Kingdom, and proposed the establishment of the Build Back Better World (B3W) initiative. The B3W initiative aims to provide a values-driven and transparent infrastructure partnership to help narrow the $40 trillion needed by developing nations by 2035. Through B3W, the G7 (alongside other partners) will coordinate in mobilizing private sector capital in four areas: climate, health and health security, digital technology, and gender equity and equality. This initiative is intended to be global in scope and to cover low- to middle-income countries (White House, 2021). The shared G7 agenda for global action promotes strengthening partnerships, including through magnifying support from the IMF for countries most in need (primarily focused in Africa), and promoting collaboration within the multilateral rules-based system (G7 Summit Communiqué, 2021). With the US leading these efforts, it is clear that the B3W means more than helping developing countries, and may represent the larger intention of maintaining US hegemony and the liberal-international order.

The anti-China rhetoric used by the US has generated mixed feelings, as countries such as Canada, Britain and France largely support this position, while Germany, Italy and the EU more generally remain more hesitant (Guarav, 2021). This ultimately may have an impact on international cooperation.

The B3W has also been criticized as hardly rivalling the BRI. The American strategy will require dealing with a patchwork of separate programmes, and the Western insistence towards environmental and human rights practices may become less appealing to developing nations than Beijing's all-in-one package of financing and new technology. Many BRI countries also appreciate China's willingness to build what the host country wants, as opposed to being told what they should do. As a result, China's BRI represents a more coherent, single group of builders, financiers and government officials (Sanger and Landler, 2021).

Apart from intentional redesign, the liberal international system remains under pressure from increased protectionism (Everett, 2019), widespread imposition of economic sanctions,[6] imposition of unilateral tariffs, including on allied countries, and attempts to exclude Chinese actors from high-technology markets such as that for 5G (Huawei).

What is the relative role of the private sector?

Various liberal reform initiatives have been advanced. Most require significant expenditures of public funds, a feature they share with the shorter-term recovery projects stemming from the pandemic. They also require 'buy-in' from a private sector used to operating under neoliberal rules. How reasonable is it to expect capital to deliver?

One approach calls for an operational transition from exclusively furthering 'shareholder' value, a concept that often leads to short-term profit maximization, to a concept of 'stakeholder' value. The latter supposedly takes into account the interests of a broader group of actors. By including customers, suppliers, employees, shareholders and local communities, corporations are impelled to focus on long-term interests of the firm and to balance profits with other deliverables.

Articulated by the World Economic Forum and popularized by leading figures like Karl Schwab (Schwab and Malleret, 2020) and Mark Carney (2021), the new direction finds expression in advocacy for 'responsible capitalism' or 'purposeful capitalism'. Related concepts include ESG (Environmental, Social, Governance) principles as a guide for investment in profitable, but socially beneficial directions. To take Carney's climate change recommendations as an illustration, we find an important role for government, including the use of market mechanisms and carbon taxes that affect the price of carbon, and thus discourage its use, assuming that the costs cannot simply be passed on to consumers. The other side of this equation is to induce or incentivize massive private investment in green energy projects. One way in which governments can help is by legislative or regulatory adjustments that enable a broader range of criteria than the fiduciary duty of tending only to shareholder value.

It remains at best an open question whether this approach can trigger the necessary behavioural changes. In part this is because the metrics for ESG are very hard to measure, and performance under different versions of the indices is not well correlated. One critic argued that the indices are 'as shaky as a fiddler on the roof' (Mintz, 2021). At the very least, this opens the way to 'index shopping' on the part of corporations aiming to project a favourable image based on these criteria.

Liberal reformers agree that large-scale private investments will be needed. They agree that the role of the state and increased state expenditures is to 'lever', 'induce' or 'catalyze' private investment in infrastructure and green technology through greater collaboration between governments and the private sector (Yellen, 2021). Yet, there seems little sign of a new radical paradigm in much of this. Bill Gates (2021) depicts a market-friendly and highly supportive government role. Among other things, governments should invest in research and development, where the private sector will not do so, but the state should move aside in favour of private involvement once it becomes clear that profits can be generated. The state should nudge private investments towards carbon neutrality through pricing mechanisms, supply needed infrastructure, and the like, but its expanded role is merely one of scale and not of methods or instruments.

Nonetheless, between its own investments and its provision of incentives to private industry to invest in new technologies, infrastructure and digital transformation, there is plenty of scope for increased state spending when compared to the neoliberal era. Yet so far, all is not as it appears. Or, at least, all has not yet been revealed.

Existing economic recovery plans in state budgets project a return to pre-pandemic levels of spending (as a percentage of GDP), within a very few years. Much of the additional spending to bring about the Great Reset, and a green and digital economic transformation based on inclusivity has not yet been included in these projections or, in many cases, has not been specified in detail. Assuming that (a) pre-pandemic levels of spending to GDP will be insufficient to get the liberal reform job done; and (b) to get it done will be very expensive, even if the exact amounts are unknown, where is the money to come from?

How is all this to be paid for?

Four broad options can be considered. First, if economic growth is high, then government revenues will be correspondingly high, even without major changes to the tax system. There are two problems. Economic growth rates are projected to be low once an anticipated post-pandemic mini-boom is over. Further, if the growth rates did turn out to be higher, in the absence of transformation to an inclusive and green economy they would exacerbate the major crises of the environment and of inequality and hence, ultimately, of democracy. Resumed growth might be the answer to handling the financial costs of short-term pandemic spending but would need to be managed carefully to avoid contributing to the continuation or worsening of the other crises.

Second, the vast amounts of accumulated private wealth could be deployed to meet the costs of the transition.[7] Liberal reformers believe this could happen voluntarily. This is really what calls for responsible capitalism and ESG criteria governing investment are all about. Critics maintain that, however well intentioned these ideas are, it is unlikely that sufficient investments will transpire as a result of this attempt to reorient capitalist values to favour the long-term and broader social benefits.

Third, the taxation system can be used to raise the necessary revenues. This might include a general increase in the level of taxation and/or more specific taxes designed to increase revenues from affluent individuals and households, including their accumulated private wealth, and corporate earnings and assets.

Fourth, money creation using monetary policy instruments could be pursued more comprehensively. Through so-called quantitative easing (QE), monetary policy has already featured in financing the emergency responses to the pandemic, as it also did, in some jurisdictions, with respect to the GFC. A new and heterodox branch of economic theory, MMT, could provide a rationale, although its precepts are not accepted by more orthodox economists, including those in the post-Keynesian school (Palley, 2020). MMT suggests that government spending and use of budget deficits is much less constrained than mainstream economics concedes. More specifically, governments with sovereignty over their currencies, which have flexible rather than fixed exchange rates, and are not overburdened by foreign-denominated debt, can create money to operate and pay any domestic debts. There are some resource constraints, otherwise inflation might occur, but these are not viewed as major hindrances to expansionary fiscal policies (Mitchell et al, 2019; Kelton, 2020). Of course, eurozone members lack the control of monetary policy that might make this possible. In any case, there is little sign of mainstream buy-in to this theory, which suggests that under conditions of rising inflation, for example, orthodox prescriptions would be reintroduced. That said, the level of debate about options, combined with the demonstration effects of QE, means that the old neoliberal certainties are under greater challenge than for many years.

Independent studies of the global impact of tax cuts in the neoliberal period suggest that there is room to increase taxes on the rich. The claimed beneficial consequences of neoliberal tax cuts for economic performance were non-existent, although they did, of course, produce increased inequality within countries (Hope and Limberg, 2020). Quite apart from this, the amount of revenue lost due to tax evasion and avoidance is astronomical: 'multinational corporations are shifting US$1.38 trillion worth of profit into tax havens each year, causing governments around the world to lose US$245 billion a year in direct tax revenue … [TJN] estimates a further $182bn in direct tax revenue is lost from private offshore tax evasion' (Tax Justice Network et al, 2020).

Corporate tax rates have declined on a global basis, as Table 7.1 indicates. In 1980, the unweighted average worldwide statutory tax rate was 40.11 per cent. By 2020, the average was about 23.85 per cent (Asen, 2020). Harmful tax competition is often referred to as the 'race to the bottom' in which individual countries alter their corporate income tax systems to attract investors, revenue or other resources away from other countries (Faulhaber, 2018). As globalization has allowed corporations to choose where they record profits, the race to the bottom in corporate tax rates allows corporations to evade high-tax jurisdictions in favour of lower-tax jurisdictions to reduce their tax liability (Zucman and Wezerek, 2021).

There would certainly seem to be lots of tax room if national governments were prepared to occupy it. Some efforts at tax reform

Table 7.1: Statutory corporate income tax rates

Country	2001	2011	2021
Canada	28.1	16.5	15
United Kingdom	30.0	26	19
United States	35.0	35	21
EU average	29.1	22.4	20.25
OECD average	28.5	25	21.5

Note: For the EU average, I included the UK in 2001 and 2011

Source: OECD Stat (2021). *Corporate Tax Statistics: Statutory Corporate Income Tax Rates*

feature in the UK 2021 Budget,[8] but their scope and impact are hard to gauge at this point in time.

Internationally, President Biden's proposal for a global minimum 15 per cent corporate tax rate was adopted by the G7 finance ministers' meeting in June 2021. Alex Cobham of the Tax Justice Network hailed the agreement as a historic breakthrough, while also condemning it for being grossly unfair because most of the revenues would flow to the rich G7 countries. Oxfam International's executive director, Gabriela Bucher, also criticized it for having set the rate too low to end the race to the bottom on corporate tax rates, and curtail the use of tax havens (Meyer and Walt, 2021). Here, too, the devil will be in the details, but the initiative does point to the possibilities of taxing capital to pay for the economic and ecological transitions that are necessary.

Summing up: the limits of liberal reform

The aim of liberal reform is to solve the inequality and democracy crises by inclusive growth mechanisms. The problem of inequality, with all its negative consequences, is seen as a by-product rather than a fundamental feature of the neoliberal growth model. Espousing a positive-sum scenario, the OECD asserts that technology and digitalization, for example, can be harnessed to investments in skills, green infrastructure and innovation, and can deliver optimum results. A more active state role, described as a 'whole-of-government' response, is envisaged. Moderating outcomes in this way will offset inequality and discontent. Other measures are proposed to train and reskill workers whose human capital is unfit for purpose in the new economy. Properly retrained they will benefit from the move to a digital and green economy.

If the positive-sum scenario does not take hold, then a more segmented, more unequal labour market with a continuing gap between productivity and wage levels will continue. Nowhere is empowering trade unions on the agenda. Yet their collective actions can perhaps do more to make the positive-sum outcomes a reality.

If arguments are correct that inequality before and since the GFC is 'systemic' (Tooze, 2018, p 459) then liberal reform recommendations simply will not work. The problem, and its spillover into other crises, will persist. Addressing inequality that is the product of concentrated wealth and the returns its owners are able to obtain (Piketty, 2014), or of policies adopted as a result of naked class politics favouring capital (Hacker and Pierson, 2010), requires a different and more radical approach. Notably, the recommendations on macroeconomic policy do not aim at full employment, or deploy demand-side measures that might produce it (TUAC, 2018, p 6) but remain locked into supply-side assumptions that if individuals are equipped with the right human capital and given opportunities then supply will create its own demand.

Liberal reformers are correct in acknowledging the interconnectedness of the various crises. In general, they put more emphasis on establishing international norms or goals with which nation-states and subnational entities should conform but concede that much of the implementation will necessarily occur at the national level. They fail to consider how the international tensions associated with trying to rebuild the liberal international order may impede the realization of other goals.

Often their proposals privilege the private sector as the main contributor of solutions (albeit with extensive public assistance). This combination of methods creates significant obstacles to the successful implementation of the recommended policies. To the extent they are implemented, which is itself uncertain, these reforms may ameliorate but will not overcome the contradictions between the crises that have produced the dystopian threat from which we need to escape.

Importantly, liberal reforms do not acknowledge how much powerful interests may defend their privileged position. In essence they must either be persuaded to give up some of their current advantages and modes of operating or they must be compelled to give them up. However, liberal reformers are hesitant to address the power issue that must be applied if persuasion or the prospect of imminent catastrophe does not provoke a change of course by the elite.

8

Radical Transformation

Several decades of neoliberal globalization has meant catering to the interests of the private sector. It has caused, fuelled or contributed to the multiple crises. Over this period the institutional political architecture has been reshaped to serve a narrow range of purposes and interests. The goals of global capitalism centre on maximization of wealth and its upward distribution to reward owners and managers of capital. This has involved pursuit of unlimited growth policies that imperil the environment, and permitting irresponsible speculative financial practices. Vast sums of public money have been spent to clean up the mess left behind. It has also increased inequality through the suppression of average labour incomes and social assistance measures of various types, and a tax system designed to keep taxes low for the affluent and enable tax evasion or avoidance by wealth holders. Under neoliberalism, capital has enjoyed a form of sovereignty, the results of which we experience on a daily basis.

Given the dead end of 'back-to-normal' approaches, and the limits of liberal reform, what remains? Could different political choices make a difference? The short answer is 'yes'.

Of course, just as Rome was not built in a day, neither was the architecture for neoliberal globalization. Equally, its undoing will prove a lengthy and complex affair. The neoliberal components – flexibilization, deregulation, privatization, the austerity state, international capital mobility – are woven together, so unravelling them will be complicated. Still, it seems unduly pessimistic and passive to conclude that nothing can be done to escape the situation we find ourselves in.

Achieving radical transformation of the system is necessary to overcome the multiple crises. Achieving it depends on the assertion of popular sovereignty over the sovereignty of capital. That will involve imposing controls on capital and rebuilding the public domain and state. The goals of state policy need to shift from satisfying the conditions for profit maximization by private interests, to the construction of a prosperous and socially just economy functioning in a context of environmental sustainability. These connections are illustrated in Figure 8.1.

Described in that way it doesn't sound a particularly radical destination. It may represent an escape from dystopia but is hardly utopia. But getting there means substituting public priorities for private ones, and social needs for individual wants. That means that a radical transformation will be to some form of socialism. There is no blueprint available, so its precise characteristics will be worked out in the course of the political struggles and conflicts that displace the current arrangements by ones that are attuned to the needs of society.

Figure 8.1: Radical transformation

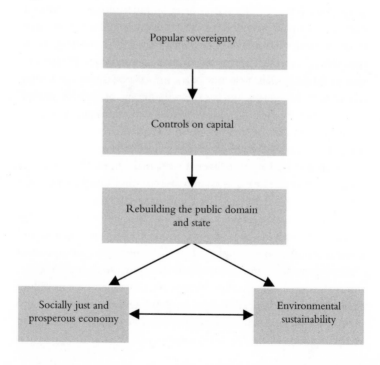

Controlling capital, building the public domain

Imposing controls on capital and building up the state and public domain are the key. Working towards and obtaining a socially just and environmentally sustainable economic and social system will also involve the construction of a new international order based on different principles from the existing one, which must first be modified and then undergo a radical transformation.

Neoliberalism succeeded admirably from the point of view of capital. Considered from a society-wide perspective, its economic record was unimpressive at best and disastrous at worst. Economic growth was slower than in the previous Keynesian era. Enriching the already rich through tax policies did not trickle down to produce general prosperity. Instead, it generated inequalities of wealth and income distribution on an unprecedented scale. This posed challenges for social cohesion and political stability. For large proportions of the population real incomes remained stagnant, social mobility declined, employment became increasingly precarious and social support declined or became available only under disciplinary conditions. Importantly, the system is unstable, with endemic crises that bring misery to millions. Most of these economic crises have been regionally contained but they eventually culminated in a more generalized one, with the 2007–08 GFC. In managing that crisis, the needs of those responsible for it – capital and in particular finance – were addressed. The cost was paid by ordinary people with no responsibility for causing it. The costs were imposed by austerity policies of various kinds and the state assumed both economic and political liability for an economic disaster driven by an unleashed private sector.

As the crisis-prone economic system inflicted great costs, neoliberal political systems failed their citizens. They had enabled finance capital in the first place, then failed to impose prudential regulations, and then responded with austerity measures. And if the COVID-19 pandemic could not be attributed directly to neoliberalism, neither was it blameless. The assault on the public sector in a series of austerity-driven budget cuts and insistence on market methods being applied within public services meant they were ill equipped to respond adequately. Allen (2021) identifies a number of issues that the experience of COVID-19 has brought into focus. These include the continued importance of the public sector even though it had been diminished by decades of austerity and neoliberalism, the vital role of key workers despite the low wages and insecure conditions that had been imposed upon them, the importance of the spending power of the state, and the multiple failures of privatization.

Under neoliberal global capitalism the environmental crisis continued to deepen. Massive environmental damage was caused by an economy built on unlimited growth, fossil-derived energy, extraction of natural resources, and expanded transhipment of supplies along lengthy global supply chains (Di Muzio, 2015b). This was compounded by obscure provisions and interpretations of international economic agreements that led to goods produced with lax environmental regulation and/or inferior labour conditions being treated as the 'same' as goods produced under higher standards. They were thus immune from discriminatory tariffs. In effect, outsourcing certain types of production to havens of deregulation was encouraged. All these caused environmental problems while serving the accumulation needs of capital. Global and national political institutions that were permissive or encouraging of such practices did not limit environmental damage in any effective way.

After the Bretton Woods system broke down, the liberal international order increasingly reflected the interests of internationally oriented financial interests and became much less accommodating to expressions of national autonomy. To achieve radical transformation requires a greater degree of national autonomy or capacity that is rooted in popular sovereignty and democracy.

Similarly, the international order needs to be recast. Proponents of the liberal international order missed an opportunity after the rival socialist system of the Eastern bloc disintegrated after 1990. They could have worked towards a non-hierarchical and peaceful international system. It was a unique historical moment. Instead, the US, amid claims that history had come to an end and that the only imaginable future was continuation of liberalized global capitalism and light-touch liberal democracy, sought to reinforce its hegemony and achieve a unipolar world order under US domination. There was no significant objection from its allies. In socioeconomic terms, the rules in this rules-based international order would benefit capital and, in political terms, the US and a cohort of allies. The brazen assertion of the Western right to engineer regime change and to intervene militarily almost at will led to whole regions, such as the Middle East, becoming zones of endless conflict, instability and human rights disasters. Predictably, the assertion of Western primacy soon led to the (re)assertion of opposition to the international order from countries like China and Russia. The short-life, and still-in-progress unravelling, of this order is a further expression of the failure of neoliberal global capitalism and a key reason why radical transformation of the entire system, rather than piecemeal reform, is necessary.

Proposals for a radical transformation of the existing system vary in scope and details. In common there are a set of goals that involve subordinating the economy to the service of society, rather than the other way around as is characteristic of neoliberal global capitalism. If society trumps the assertion of private and individualist priorities, then we can speak of some form of social-ism.

As outlined in Chapter 1, this would include a prosperous, relatively egalitarian society characterized by full employment, security, decent jobs and well-organized public services to meet social needs – health, education, ageing and housing. Such an economy would be based on carbon neutrality. Internationally, the one-size-fits-all approach of the liberal economic order would be replaced by a more permissive one allowing for re-politicization, and the expression of popular sovereignty at national and local levels. With some redistribution of resources and sufficient economic growth to meet crucial goals, such as elimination of poverty and conversion to a green economy, the resulting international order would be composed of relatively prosperous, harmonious and environmentally sustainable societies coexisting together.

Goals of this type could certainly be added to, outlined in more detail, and would in any case actually be defined in the process of a radical transition. That process, it might be anticipated, would last some years or even decades rather than be an overnight event. More importantly at this stage, what would need to be done to get the process moving with some chance of success?

If global capitalism and the pursuit of private interests over those of society is the problem, then getting capital under better control and asserting the primacy of public interests is a big part of the solution. Controlling capital is actually the key to implementing other measures to escape from the dystopian experience of multiple crises. Controls could be imposed on the mobility of capital, the rewards derived from its deployment, the purposes for which it may be invested, and the rights conferred on it by domestic or international law.

Capital mobility

The architects of the Bretton Woods system, including John Maynard Keynes and Harry Dexter White, among others, saw capital controls as an important feature of a well-functioning global financial system. Bringing international finance under public control was the objective (Helleiner, 1994; Gallagher, 2012; Gallagher et al, 2012). This is because it was recognized that the interests of international finance were by no means the same as those of society. Capital control measures were seen as a means to enhance macroeconomic policy effectiveness, and to control and promote financial and currency stability (Grabel, 2006). The regime governing capital flows has been coined 'cooperative decentralization' by Eric Helleiner and Stefano Pagliari (2011), denoting interstate cooperation across divergent national regulatory approaches. Thus, nations were able to regulate capital flows as they deemed necessary and were able to cooperate with each other to make them effective. As a result, countries around the world – including the United States – deployed capital controls fairly successfully during the Bretton Woods era, including controls on both inflows and outflows of investment (Gallagher, 2015).

By the 1970s, financial power began dominating global economic policies due to the internationalization of capital markets and growing political strength of the financial sectors in the US and Europe. The convergence of power, interests, ideas and institutional structure promoted new international rules to replace cooperative decentralization (Gallagher, 2015). The rules dismantled controls and regulations. They were rationalized as being necessary to promote market-led growth. Financial deregulation and globalization were the objectives of the strategy (Madhyam, 2018). Replacing public control with the 'invisible hand' of the market, and rolling back the regulatory role of the state, were the new priorities (Crotty, 2000). As capital's power was enhanced, that of labour became further subordinated (Epstein, 2005).

Since then, liberalization of capital mobility has produced a series of speculative financial crises. The damage inflicted by these crises makes a compelling case for imposing controls on capital. Yet it remains contested. Sometimes this is on theoretical/ideological grounds because controls are said to distort markets, increase inefficiencies and encourage rent-seeking behaviour (Henry, 2007; Caballero, 2012). Others view them as ineffective, or as creating more problems than they solve (Forbes et al, 2016). Still others point out that they do not necessarily lead to system transformation. Controls may be useful in reducing speculative financial operations and dealing with the threat of short-term capital flows, but they still operate to maintain and/or fortify existing power relations within the countries using them (Soederberg, 2004).

A number of studies have made the case for the technical effectiveness of capital controls (Grabel, 2010). Essentially controls can be imposed on the inflow or outflow of foreign investment, using various techniques. These may be based on price mechanisms, including taxes, quantity-based regulations, or by conditionalities, as with performance requirements before incoming investment is approved. The latter might include technology transfer, establishing research and development facilities, hiring quotas to ensure local managers, and local content provisions for supplies.

The often proposed 'Tobin Tax' is an example of a price-based mechanism. It envisaged a small percentage tax on all foreign exchange transactions, designed to discourage excessive short-term speculation without reducing longer-term capital flows. An example of a complementary measure might be a tax on the sale of any financial asset held for less than a specified length of time. This would discourage capital flight. The taxing of the sale of the asset or taxing the foreign exchange rate transaction should have similar effects.

However, beyond the technical case for or against controls lies their potential for promoting democratic control over economic policy and transformative change (Crotty and Epstein, 1996; Epstein, 2009; 2012). In the radical transformation arsenal, the real purpose of capital controls is political and goes well beyond the technical goals outlined above. It is to reduce the power that capital currently wields over nation-states (through currency speculation, debt ratings and the like), and over labour (through capital flight or the threat of it).

Their transformative purpose means deliberately using capital controls as a method of increasing national democracy and autonomy. The ability of speculators and other external actors to influence domestic decision-making – a key feature of the neoliberal financialized era – can be reduced. Performance requirements can also ensure a variety of host country benefits. As a result, capital controls contribute to and must be accompanied by more profound changes in the political and economic structures of society (Epstein, 2012).

This means that capital controls can only bring about social justice and economic equity if they are designed and applied with that intent and if they are accompanied by restructuring the social relations of economic and political power within a country (Soederberg, 2004). Eric Helleiner (2005) suggested that some of the techniques developed through international cooperation and coordination to address money laundering might be extended to curb tax evasion and capital flight (also referenced in Crotty and Epstein, 1996).

The primary impediment to the successful use and implementation of capital controls is political, not technical. It will require the creation of a new set of domestic political arrangements that will bind labour, capital and the state to egalitarian policies (Crotty and Epstein, 1996).

Rewards and taxes

Corporations today are taxed at lower levels than in the past (see Table 7.1 in the previous chapter). Domestically, most countries have constructed a taxation system that favours the affluent. Billionaire Warren Buffett famously observed that he was paying tax at a lower rate than his secretary. Internationally, the potential for corporations, and rich individuals, to avoid or evade taxes through tax havens has long been acknowledged. Not all these tax havens are remote tropical islands. Countries in the top 20 of the Tax Justice Network's Tax Haven List include the Netherlands, Switzerland, France, the UK, Belgium and Ireland.[1]

Corporations operating multinationally have become adept at making profits in one location and declaring them in the lowest tax rate country available to them. The ability of technology and communication giants like Facebook and Apple to evade taxation has infuriated many, contributing to a public mood that demands governmental action. Apart from the unfairness of highly profitable corporations paying little tax, the effects on government revenues that could be used to fund social or environmental necessities are serious. Many of these public priorities wither because of imposed fiscal limits, while capital continues to accumulate in private hands.

There are some signs of corrective actions being taken on this issue. In June 2021, the G7 agreed to US-sponsored reforms intended to make multinationals pay what it considered to be their 'fair share' of tax in the countries in which they do business, with the principle that they would pay a global minimum rate of at least 15 per cent. The largest and most profitable mutinationals will be required to pay some taxes in countries they operate in (not just where they are headquartered) (White House, 2021).

This agreement has been hailed 'historic', 'seismic' and a 'landmark deal' by the G7 (G7 UK, 2021). The global minimum tax rate would apply to overseas profits. Countries would be able to tax some of the profits made by big companies based on the revenue generated there, rather than tax being paid where the firm is located for tax purposes. However, if corporations still declare the bulk of their profits in a low-tax location, there would be a minimum global corporation tax rate that would top up the tax paid to the 15 per cent level. But, under these proposals, the first right to top-up tax goes to the headquarters' country. For instance, a US multinational using a low-tax country to achieve a near-zero effective rate on profits generated in, say Spain, would see its tax topped up by the US, not by Spain. Alex Cobham, chief executive of the Tax Justice Network, states that this deal would give the lion's share of revenue to the largest OECD members at a time where lower-income countries already lose the greatest share of tax revenue to corporate tax abuse (Cobham, 2021; see also Meredith, 2021).

While hardly the complete solution, these proposals arguably provide an indication of how taxes might be levied on multinational capital, and with more radical provisions in future. A starting point would be to increase the minimum rate and transfer the right to top up the global minimum tax to the countries where the profits were generated.

Socialization of capital investment

Capital can also be directly controlled by state regulation and planning. In this case, investment is conducted directly by the state or directed by it in some way. The use and direction of investment is prioritized by politically defined objectives rather than calculations of profit maximization. This requires a strong interventionist state with sufficient resources itself to directly invest in important areas like education, health, transport, housing and reversal of privatization. To take control of finance, nationalization of banks would be an important instrument. In fact, public ownership, or use of state-owned enterprises, could be the most important way of controlling capital. Private investment would become supplementary to publicly owned initiatives.

Given the democratic crisis and consequent legitimacy deficit of the state, making the case for this type of state intervention will not be easy. Yet there is no other entity remotely capable of controlling capital. So, to coin a phrase, there is no alternative.

If public authority is to be imposed on the private, deregulated and global capital markets it will be through the state – in both its guises. First, as an ensemble of public institutions making up the political system, the state is the only body with the authority and potential legitimacy to achieve this goal. Second, the jurisdictional form of a technically sovereign actor exists at the nation-state level, not at any international level. It is true that states differ in power, and weaker states may be less able to exploit the possibilities until a path has been cleared by the actions of stronger states. However, they still might enjoy more room for manoeuvre than under the existing liberal rules-based order.

To be able to direct investments, states need to control or, at the very least, have much greater influence over the credit system. A first step towards this will be the reversal of central bank independence (CBI) from governments. Monetary policy needs to be brought back into the realm of politics and to be determined by public and democratic processes and not by technical processes that mask private interests.

Under neoliberalism, issuing credit and therefore determining the supply of money has been largely privatized. When private banks make loans, they create deposits in the accounts of borrowers. In effect, money is created. There are a number of problems with leaving this in private hands. Because private bank loans are not backed up by adequate reserves, they are highly susceptible to a psychological variable – 'confidence', in the economy, in the specific markets that have received investment or in the banks themselves. The result is volatility and frequent bubbles and crises. In fact, as Heather Whiteside (2021) notes in a damning portrait of private finance, the problems are multiple and, among others, extend to bankruptcies, publicly financed buyouts, and assumption by the public sector of risks supposedly transferred to the private sector under public–private partnerships.

The issuing of private credit is governed by calculations of profit maximization. This has produced dysfunctional investments such as those in the real estate market which is especially prone to bubble-and-bust cycles. One effect has been that affordable housing has been driven beyond the reach of large parts of the population.

If, as is amply apparent, one cannot rely on the private banking and finance sector to support socially necessary investments, then the solution is to establish a public bank or banking sector. Initially this might exist in parallel to the private banking sector. Ultimately it might displace it in whole or in part. Public banks would be mandated to channel investment to projects meeting criteria of environmental sustainability, job creation, affordable housing and other socially useful initiatives.

The task of reining in global capital may seem a formidable one. However, looked at from another perspective, global capital and global finance already is entirely dependent on the nation-state which enables but could instead substantially condition and control its activities because, 'taxpayer power sustains and finances the public institutions that underpin the private monetary system' (Pettifor, 2021, p 207). Anyone who doubts this should observe the utter dependence of the private financial sector as the state provided assistance during the GFC and the recent pandemic.

Only a democratic state would assert public control over private capital. Institutional redesign and empowerment of the population are essential ingredients for radical transformation. As that process starts and continues it will be necessary to achieve the dominance of public over private authority. This is possible at the national level but not at the global. The modern political left rejects the nationalism it associates with the nation-state but has little to offer as an alternative vehicle for change. If not the nation-state, what? Can it be stripped of undesirable characteristics of nationalism? Perhaps.

Apart from increased public ownership, a key instrument in controlling the direction of investment will be economic planning. The concept of planning a national economy has been derided and largely disappeared from 'respectable' economic discourse in the neoliberal period, and many will find advocacy of its return surprising. In fact, it has never really been away (Jones, 2020, p 6).

Even as China has moved away from its originally centrally planned command economy through decentralizing and deregulating the economy, the state still plays an important role (Bekkevold et al, 2020). State-owned banks continue to favour state-owned enterprises over private enterprises (IMF, 2019), and strategic industries have remained under the control of state-owned enterprises (Naughton and Tsai, 2015).

China's 'Made in China 2021' initiative strives to reduce reliance on foreign technology imports and invest heavily in its own innovations to enhance competitiveness. This is done largely through state financial support (bonds, low-interest loans, and subsidies) and mobilizing state-owned enterprise (McBride and Chatzky, 2021). Similarly, the highly successful developmental state model followed in Japan and some East Asian countries was hardly devoid of state planning or coordination (see Clift, 2014, ch 8).

All successful capitalist enterprises, like Walmart and Amazon, engage in meticulous planning (Phillips and Rozworski, 2019). Developing states like India and China practise state planning of different sorts. Technological developments in algorithms and big data make planning easier and more attractive than in some historical examples (Durand and Keucheyan, 2019).

Pat Devine (1988) makes the case for *democratic* planning of the economy. The superiority of planning lies in the application of collective conscious control over economic processes and outcomes. This, because it is envisaged to be democratic, also implies equal input from various social forces. Both elements are lacking when the economy is left to market forces. More specifically, planned economies have three main advantages, according to Devine. The allocation of resources and the general direction the economy takes can be linked to social priorities, themselves politically (that is, democratically) determined. The uncertainties of leaving matters to decision by atomized individuals is removed. Finally, rather than being adjusted after the act, as may be accomplished by a market system operating through the price mechanism, the interaction of related decisions can be adjusted prior to implementation.

Having to operate within a planned economy context constitutes a major control on capital. Its activities can be aligned with the public purpose.

Redefining rights conferred on capital by domestic or international law

The power of capital is expressed in and reinforced by the provisions and implementation of international trade and investment agreements, regional economic pacts, and in the practices of international organizations like the IMF and the World Bank. Enforcement ultimately is always in the hands of the nation-states that enter such arrangements. For example, under the WTO, in the event that a country does not comply with a ruling, the WTO can authorize retaliatory action. It is up to the state that originally launched the complaint to take the action.

Often operational and discretionary decision-making is devolved to private authority, meaning that the state voluntarily surrenders its sovereignty. A good example is the investor-state dispute settlement provisions of many international agreements. These essentially empower capital by enabling it to bring cases against states before what is basically a private commercial arbitration process. Many of the decisions rendered in these forums have thwarted state efforts at environmental regulation (Sinclair, 2018). Regulatory actions anticipate the trade impact of such measures, as this will be construed by arbitration tribunals. Thus, a new and higher level of (undemocratic) accountability intrudes into the democratic process. Governments contemplating 'measures' face uncertainty, a condition that has been linked to reluctance to regulate, sometimes termed 'regulatory chill'.

For example, an initial effort in Ontario, Canada to construct a green energy sector based on local content and procurement was struck down by the WTO. Sinclair (2019) concluded that trade treaties obstruct the use of public services and government purchasing from playing a pivotal role in a domestic Green New Deal strategy. Relevant provisions are investor-state dispute settlement, procurement provisions which cover purchasing by national and subnational state-owned enterprises, local governments and the broader public sector, and the so-called market access provisions. To these might be added (excessive) protection of intellectual property rights. Modifying or removing such provisions in international agreements would be an important element of radical transformation.

Radical transformation of economic and social policy

Inequality needs to be reduced. Insecurity for people needs to be eliminated. Doing these things would be an immediate priority of radical economic and social policy. Committing to a full employment economy and provision of decent jobs for all capable of and wanting to work is an effective contribution to achieving these goals. It would, of course, need to be accompanied by other measures. Redistribution of income through taxation is one example, taxation of accumulated wealth another.

The welfare state should be reformed to concentrate on meeting actual needs rather than serving as a disciplinary adjunct that conditions labour force attachment. Huge and already identifiable needs in areas like long-term care should be the subject of public investment and increased public sector employment. An industrial policy, including filling infrastructure deficits, should be deployed. On grounds of greater efficiency alone, these will likely be public ventures rather than private or P3 collaborations. Clearly the list could be extended.

Adjustment of fiscal and monetary policy to produce full employment could be supplemented by a public sector job guarantee to make sure everyone wanting work was able to get it. There would no doubt be some room for flexible employment. Some would prefer to work part time, or on temporary contracts.

Pay and benefits would be prorated to hours worked, removing some of the incentive for employers to instigate this type of employment. There would be no room for precarious employment as it is currently understood. A job guarantee is far preferable to a basic universal income (BUI), another proposal often made in the context of recovering from the crisis in an equitable way. BUI would be expensive if provided at adequate levels and wasteful if received by everyone. A job guarantee is only needed for those not otherwise employed: incumbents pay taxes, and the jobs they occupy would be designed to be socially useful. Many could be provided in areas like childcare, education, services for older people, environmental clean-ups, and other areas that would improve the quality of social life. To consolidate the employment package, institutional reforms to empower workers and trade unions, along with recipients of public services, would be useful (Lehndorff, 2021). Measures favourable to trade union organization, high minimum wages and standards, provision of training and adjustment services, and accountability mechanisms – of governments to organizations, and organizations to their members – are important elements. Employment-creating initiatives that lead to greater equality can be financed partly by taxes, including higher corporate taxes and higher taxes on individual wealth and income. Serious prosecution of tax evaders and avoiders would be important. Some existing spending, such as military expenditures, could be reduced and reallocated.

Further resources can be supplied by an expansive implementation of fiscal and monetary policy. The rapid turning-on of the financial taps in response to both the GFC and the pandemic has laid to rest the neoliberal argument that there is not enough money available. How much additional spending can be provided is a political decision, not an economically determined one. Of course, there are limits, but for countries that have control over their own banking and financial sector, a central bank, and their own currencies, these are created by the ability of an economy's productive capacity to sustain spending and money creation, not by some pre-ordained neoliberal theory (Stanford, 2021, pp 265–6).

With these resources in place and a political leadership willing to use them, a new growth model can be constructed (Urban and Kramer, 2021, pp 280–1). This will involve displacing wasteful and luxury consumption by well-designed investments and provision in the areas of social security, health-care, education, culture, mass transit, social housing and many others. Institutional reforms to align with the new priorities and strategy would also be essential.

Radical transformation of climate and environmental policy

In his book *A Good War*, Seth Klein (2020) invoked the mobilization of resources and people to fight fascism in World War II. In applying the lessons to the fight against climate change today, Klein contrasts current climate change policies with those that will be needed if a climate disaster is to be averted. Current policies – and this applies to most liberal reform proposals as well – depend on instruments like incentives, rebates and carbon pricing. What is needed is a combination of 'strong regulatory measures, effective economic planning, and large-scale public investment' (Klein, 2020, p 174). In his vision this would be based on an inventory of what is needed to convert to a green economy. The inventory would feed into the planning process, with public spending being provided as required on infrastructure, training, new enterprises including state-owned ones, and mandatory changes to alter behaviour at the household, industry and community levels. Setting clear targets and using planning mechanisms to make sure they are met is part of the approach. Klein argues that the strategy should seek to combine centralized coordination but empowerment of leadership at more local and sectoral levels.

Within this general approach, specific measures are listed. The list is similar to many renditions of a Green New Deal that aspire to address the global warming problem. At the centre of most of them is the need to phase out fossil fuels and replace them by renewable energy sources, mostly solar and wind. Taken out of context, these measures in isolation are subject to the same objections that Ozzie Zehner (2012) raised about alternative energy and technological fixes to the climate crisis – that solutions lie in shifting the social determinants of energy usage rather than in the adoption of new technologies. To be part of a radical solution, alternative energy proposals must be embedded in a broader context that includes but extends beyond energy policy per se.

Thus sequencing, speed and, perhaps most importantly, whether the process is market-led or public authority-led all matter. For radical transformation, the mass production of necessary equipment and technologies such as turbines and solar panels is a proposal that feeds into the full-employment economic agenda, or could do so if international trade agreements did not obstruct the process. A huge amount of green economic employment could also be generated in areas like retrofitting existing building stocks, expanding mass transit operations, constructing electric charging stations to facilitate elimination of internal combustion vehicles and replace them with electric or hybrid ones. Similarly, climate adaptation measures will undoubtedly be necessary and could include flood control construction projects and expansion of fire-fighting capacity to deal with forest fires, as well as expanded green spaces and recreational areas in cities. Major expansion of the caring services for older and younger people is another area where employment creation would be socially useful and have little negative environmental impact. In addition, the expansion of social supports is an essential condition of keeping the population on-side in what will be an era of undoubted social upheaval.

Rather than rely on price mechanisms to persuade people to convert from carbon use, a device that favours the affluent who may be inclined to buy their way out of some of the worst effects, carbon quotas might be used to equalize changes in lifestyle costs. Essentially a form of rationing, it will produce greater equity than use of the price system. Above all, the radical transformation of climate policy will require the private sector to align with public authority rather than to demand incentives from the public sector. As Klein (2020, p 205) puts it with reference to the private sector's role in Canada during World War II:

> The private-for-profit sector had an important role to play in the war – it produced much of what we needed, and people made money doing so. But critically, the private sector – at both the corporate and household level – didn't get to decide on the allocation of scarce resources in a time of emergency. Rather, our governments directed what needed to happen to rise to the task at hand. That's the kind of thinking we need today.

Proposals to radically transform climate and environmental policy are cognizant of the need to do so in ways that minimize the social and economic dislocation experienced by those formerly dependent on polluting activities. This is not just a matter of fairness. It is important to build support for the transformation project and to minimize resistance on the part of those who must undergo the transition. The concept of making sure it is a 'Just Transition' has been developed to cover this situation. This consists of a package of measures to cover the various eventualities that individuals, businesses and communities may face. Examples might include retraining to ensure employment continuity as jobs are phased out, accompanied by a job guarantee, early retirement allowances for some who may not benefit from further employment, relocation assistance to help individuals move, and housing purchases to offset losses in towns where businesses are closing down due to the transition.

Conclusions

The goal may be modest – construction of a prosperous and socially just economy functioning in a context of environmental sustainability. But in getting there, all the ingredients of the neoliberal package – labour market flexibility and insecurity, the unequal society, austerity, a reduced and constrained state, deregulation, privatization, free trade, and capital mobility – would be challenged. The new paradigm would need to prioritize security over flexibility, greater equality rather than inequality, public and state over private and market, and national obligations to citizens over international ones to capital.

And, of course, it would not be cost-free. Improvements in labour market conditions and restrictions on imports of cheap goods from abroad would be costly. Consumers would have to pay more for goods and services than they do now (although, of course, many of these consumers would benefit from the improved labour market conditions created). Even so, efforts to mobilize them against change can be anticipated.

Public expenditure would also increase and with it, taxation. Closing tax loopholes that benefit the affluent and by creating a fairer tax system would be helpful, but societies get what they pay for, and tax levels would need to increase to meet the objectives of a more equal society and decent living and working standards for all.

9

Obstacles to Progress

Escaping dystopia means progressing along the path to radical transformation. Nothing else will do.

'Returning to normal' means returning to the pre-crisis situation, allowing the multiple crises to continue, and awaiting the next shock to the system. Liberal reform looks forward to a virtuous cycle in which economic recovery measures that are also inclusive, green and digitally oriented produce improved economic, social and environmental results. These measures claim either to solve the issues posed by the multiple crises or to make them much more manageable. Yet this happy outcome is unlikely because the liberal reforms envisaged do not address the causes of the crises, and because they continue to rely on the social forces and mechanisms that are responsible for them. In short, these efforts are insufficient to avert the crises. Rather than escaping dystopia, the ultimate destination will be to reproduce it.

Radical transformation may be essential, but it is by no means obvious how it can be brought about. It is therefore incumbent on anyone advocating the path of radical transformation to indicate what will be necessary to achieve it. Ideas on this are presented in Chapter 10. But first a review of the obstacles will be useful. Most of the obstacles have been identified or alluded to in earlier chapters. Overcoming them will open the path to radical transformation.

The obstacles fall into three broad categories: the balance of class forces that favour maintenance of the status quo, or only moderate reform to it; the ideological capitulation of the former political left to neoliberalism; and the institutional barriers erected to prevent change and the intrusion of democratic procedures into the application of pre-set rules.

The empowerment of capital and finance

Since the mid-1970s the power of capital has expanded and that of labour has been reduced. More specifically, the era of neoliberal globalization has been depicted as one of 'financialization', in which finance capital has achieved a hegemonic position in leading states and, through them, internationally (Harvey, 2003, p 64).

Financialization means that profit-making is increasingly achieved through financial mechanisms rather than through traditional production activities. This is even true of firms operating in production – automobile companies, for example, often derive as much profit from arranging finance to purchase their vehicles as they do from producing them.

The term 'finance capital' has a long history, dating back at least as far as Rudolph Hilferding's 1910 book of that name. At its core the concept suggests a fusion or integration of forms of capital – industrial, bank, commercial – such that it is no longer reasonable to expect differences of interests between them (see Carroll, 2004, pp 6–8). This is characteristic of the modern period of financialization. Control over capital is consolidated and centralized. The interests of capital are unified because large corporations become involved in both financial and productive activities (Carroll, 2004, p 67), cross-cutting ownership and interlocking directorships are prevalent, and a financial–industrial elite can be identified that sits atop the capitalist class and is affiliated with both 'corporations and financial institutions' (Carroll, 2004, p 8).

Firms operating in the banking, finance, insurance and investment services sectors of the economy have vastly increased their importance in recent decades. There are many definitions of financialization and, consequently, many indicators are advanced, not all necessarily comparable to each other (Karwowski et al, 2020). Global statistics suggest that financial assets were about equal to GDP in 1980 but 4.4 times larger in 2007; between 1980 and 2007 global GDP grew at an average rate of 3.3 per cent, but financial assets at a rate of 8 per cent; the value of the derivatives

market increased from US$92 trillion to US$670 trillion in 2007...
and so on (see Mitchell and Fazi, 2017, p 129). The trend was
more marked in the US, where the total value of financial assets
was five times greater than GDP in 1980, and ten times larger in
2007 (Mukunda, 2014).

Supplying credit has demonstrated the role of finance and
underpinned the neoliberal growth model. The role of private debt
to sustain aggregate demand in the economy has been described
as a system of privatized Keynesianism (Crouch, 2009). Heavily
dependent on increased value of assets in areas like real estate or
equities to sustain debt levels, the system is inherently vulnerable
to periodic crises as 'corrections' occur, and bubbles burst.

Privatization in its various forms (such as sale of assets, outsourcing
of public functions to private providers, and use of P3s) also has
been a key instrument. Asset sales typically make investments
available at an attractive price (read: undervalued sale price), and
P3s guarantee high, state-backed returns on investment with risk
ultimately retained by the state, notwithstanding justifications of
risk transfer built into the P3 concept (Whiteside, 2015).

Concepts like 'shareholder value' have prioritized short-term
economic returns to shareholders, and linking executive salaries to
stock options and performance has meant a managerial cadre fully
integrated into the interests of capital and focused on immediate
financial return rather than longer-term enterprise-building, added
value or increasing market share (Krippner, 2012; Serfati, 2013;
Clark, 2016). This mode of executive compensation, together
with a tax regime that privileges the very affluent, has fuelled the
inequality that plagues the entire economic and political system.
The assets commanded by the elite convey structural power.
Governments find it difficult to ignore the reaction of these
interests to policy decisions and, consequently, seek to shape their
decisions to fit finance's expectations.

Looking at the roots of financialization, Germain (1997, p 106)
argued that the process was linked to the demise of the Keynesian
era and the Bretton Woods international monetary system (see
Helleiner, 1994). Crucially, Bretton Woods had included controls
on capital movements and rejected the laissez-faire ideology and
doctrines of 'sound finance' traditionally associated with banking
and financial interests (Helleiner, 1994, ch 2). It tolerated significant

degrees of national policy autonomy (Harvey, 2003, p 57). Once the Bretton Woods system was abolished in the early 1970s, international finance regained influence that governments had sought to constrain (Helleiner, 1994). However, and importantly, the origins of financialization depended on state sponsorship (Helleiner, 1994, ch 4). That is, far from being an immutable force of nature, it is a political construction. The implication is that however difficult it might be in practice, what has been constructed politically can be renovated or demolished by the same means.

Once financialization was in progress, the increasing fusion of different types of capital created a demand for flexibility in its deployment. The neoliberal policy package, both domestically and internationally, conformed to this requirement on the part of finance capital. Modern 'trade' agreements like the WTO and NAFTA extend far beyond their traditional coverage of trade in goods. Capital mobility is a fundamental element. Investments (very broadly defined), services (supplied in any of a variety of ways), non-tariff barriers, and protection of intellectual property rights loom large in the new agreements. Simply put, they serve to protect almost all forms of economic activity and capital investments from undesired state intervention.

Domestically, the implications of the fusion of control over capital are far-reaching. These can briefly be summarized as: developing new organizational forms for pressing capital's demands on the state at all levels; redefining and articulating business interests to express the general goals of fused, flexible and mobile capital rather than the specific interests of nationally rooted sectoral or fixed capital; increasing structural power of finance capital; implicating states in realizing business's policy goals; and ensuring a major flow of benefits to finance capital. Rather than relying exclusively on its structural power, this elite is active politically to ensure the desired results. Streeck (2011) has argued that states are increasingly accountable to two sets of constituents: citizens, with whom an accountability deficit clearly operates; and 'markets', to which they are in practice much more beholden.

Lobbying activities are intense and, particularly in the US, the system operates a 'revolving door' whereby appointments between the private sector and corresponding state agencies represent a normal career path (Mukunda, 2014; Faroohar, 2016). Starting in the 1970s, coterminously with the shift to neoliberalism, new organizations were devised to integrate, and then represent, business interests.

Founded in 1972, the US Business Roundtable was composed of chief executives of 200 leading corporations. It pioneered the typical format of centralized peak-level associations of business executives from different economic sectors. In Canada the corresponding body was the Business Council on National Issues (Langille, 1987), since renamed the Business Council of Canada.

In Europe, the European Roundtable of Industrialists (ERT) brought together 45 business leaders from Europe's leading international companies (Balanya et al, 2000, Part 1). At the EU level there are some 30,000 registered lobbyists, 63 per cent of them representing business corporations. Recent studies by the Corporate Europe Observatory (for example Cann, 2021) document the degree to which business outscores all other interests in influential EU working committees, sometimes by ratios as high as 13:1 in terms of meetings attended or presentations made. Another report from the Observatory (Corporate Europe Observatory, 2021) records the campaign of big banks, leading law firms and big business lobby groups to establish a parallel European court exclusively to shield business from the financial effects of labour, consumer or environmental regulations. Governments facing financial penalties for enacting regulations would be less inclined to regulate or legislate in the public interest.

National systems for transmitting policy ideas from representatives of the upper reaches of capital to the state have their international equivalents in organizations and forums like the Trilateral Commission, the Bilderberg Group and the WEF. To these can be added older groups, like the International Chamber of Commerce (ICC) which is an important intermediary between business and international organizations like the WTO. The ICC has over 60 national committees and through them exerts pressure on national governments, as well as through international organizations (Balanya et al, 2000, pp 137–8). In addition, the ICC spearheaded business's growing relationship with the United Nations, a 'proactive move to ensure that any regulation of the global economy will be tailored to the interests of international business' (Balanya et al, 2000, p 144).

Side by side with interest representation is funding of sympathetic political parties and leaders. More broadly, elite influence extends well beyond the business world and is partially expressed by membership on corporate boards of 'organic intellectuals ... lawyers, accountants, academics and retired politicians who provide crucial technical experience.... Such advisors make up an important stratum of the corporate elite, one that exercises not only economic power, but also the second characteristic form of corporate power: hegemony' (Carroll, 2004, p 9). Moreover, corporate influence extends well into civil society, as exemplified by membership of boards of universities (see Carroll, 2004, ch 9), health authorities, charities, and other associations, not to mention corporate ownership of most mass media.

Taken together, the structural power of capital and the existence of a powerful political bloc dedicated to its defence represents a formidable obstacle to change. These interests are the architects of the system we currently live under, and they have, most assuredly, been its main beneficiaries. They can be expected to defend those interests robustly. Their task is made all the easier by the decline of labour and the ideological disarmament of the social democratic left, and the fragmentation of the potential alternatives bloc.

The disempowerment of labour

As capital's power has increased, that of labour has diminished. A number of indicators show by just how much. Table 9.1 shows 'union density' (the proportion of the workforce which belongs to trade unions) for the OECD and several states. This captures one aspect of the decline of labour.

In a few cases, union density has been maintained or even increased. However, in the vast majority of cases the trend is downwards, and the OECD average figure tells the general story – a decline from 38.7 per cent in 1975 to 16.5 per cent in 2015. National legislation on union rights and collective bargaining varies so the percentage of the labour force covered by collective agreements can be very close to union density (as in Canada, for example), or very different (as in France and Spain). However, the general picture is one of declining coverage from 37.4 per cent coverage in the OECD area in 2000, to 32.7 per cent in 2015.

Table 9.1: Trade union dataset

Frequency	Annual									
Measure	Percentage of employees									
Time	1975	1980	1985	1990	1995	2000	2005	2010	2015	2020
Country										
Canada	34.8	34.0	35.3	33.6	..	28.2	27.7	27.2	26.5	27.2
France	22.6	18.6	13.8	10.7	..	10.8	10.5	10.8	..	..
Germany	34.6	34.9	34.7	31.2	29.2	24.6	21.5	18.9	17.6	..
Spain	..	13.3	12.7	14.1	18.6	17.5	15.5	18.2	14.4	..
United Kingdom	43.8	52.2	45.3	39.6	33.9	29.8	28.6	26.6	24.7	..
United States	25.3	22.1	17.4	15.5	14.3	12.9	12.0	11.4	10.6	10.3
OECD – total (E)	38.7	36.5	32.1	28.8	24.2	20.9	19.0	17.8	16.5	..

Note: E = estimated value

Source: OECD, 2022

These trends are reflected in outcomes. Between 1990 and 2009 labour's share of national income declined in 26 out of 30 advanced countries. The median decline was from 66.1 to 61.7 per cent. Over the longer term, and using a different averaging measure, the decline between 1975 and 2011 was from 65 to 56 per cent (ILO/OECD, 2015). Various explanations were advanced, but the declining power of workers was clearly a major one. Consequences include: greater inequality; a disconnect between increases in productivity and wages, with investment lagging due to lack of demand; and use of profits to pay dividends and reward shareholders who have invested in financial assets. In turn, wages that are inadequate to sustain demand have led to increased reliance on personal and household debt, and to export-led growth strategies.

Another consequence has been the construction and extension of sizeable low-wage sectors in most economies (McBride and Muirhead, 2016). The increase in 'active' rather than passive income support measures has been enabled by union weakness. At one time, 'active' referred to the policies themselves. Now it is applied to individuals who are unemployed or in receipt of other income supports. These individuals must be 'activated' by means that make receipt of benefits conditional on compliant actions on their part. The implication is that it is the individuals who are responsible for their plight, and they need to be assisted or coerced into becoming part of the labour force and hence more model citizens (McBride, 2019).

Recent decades have seen a surge in the relative share of wealth holders and high-income earners in a number of industrial countries (Piketty, 2014). At the other end of the spectrum is the stagnation or fall in the real incomes of the lower and middle strata of the population. This move towards greater inequality has coincided with the transformation of work and employment relations, involving increased precarity among large sections of the labour force whose economic prospects have dimmed considerably (Standing, 1997). More generally, low-wage sectors defined by low wages and precarious work appear to be endemic and show no signs of abatement. In the United States, for example, the Bureau of Labor Statistics reported in 2017 that eight of the ten fastest-growing job categories were low-wage services, such as personal care and home health aides (cited in McBride, Mitrea and Ferdosi, 2021).

Less quantifiable but equally indicative of reduced labour influence is its political track record. Even among its notional social democratic allies, organized labour has had less political influence than formerly. These parties, dominated by party professionals, became neoliberalized in recent decades and often act in ways as hostile to labour as their liberal and conservative counterparts. Essentially, labour now has no reliable political allies. Similarly, unions' role in neo-corporatist institutions of social dialogue or social partnership has also declined. As much a device for incorporating and moderating labour (Panitch, 1980), in some countries these institutions did provide voice and a degree of influence on a wide range of issues. However, as labour strength declined, and particularly in the post-GFC period, its influence was eroded as the institutions were ignored, had their mandates narrowed or, in some cases, were abolished (Bryan Evans et al, 2021).

Labour is not just weaker. It has been deliberately weakened as a result of state and international strategy. As far as unions are concerned, Steffen Lehndorff (2021, p 64) argues that the state has changed from an enabling to a disabling state. Labour reform measures have aimed at cutting labour costs and the power of unions to negotiate wages (Lehndorff, 2021, pp 77–8). Insecure, precarious work has been promoted and tolerated; outcomes imposed on bargaining through legislated wage cuts, freezes, or back-to-work orders; collective bargaining systems have been hollowed out; and social supports have been reduced, targeted and made more conditional. All this adds up to class struggle from above, with the state acting as the conduit for the demands of capital for greater flexibility in how it treats its employees (Whiteside et al, 2021, ch 5).

The rationale for the offensive against labour was provided in the OECD Jobs Strategy developed in the 1990s (McBride and Williams, 2001) and since periodically updated (McBride and Watson, 2019). Its central point was to flexibilize employment relations to the benefit of employers. Many of the purported benefits of flexible labour markets did not materialize. However, the goal of keeping labour quiescent was achieved. Implementation of the policies was primarily at the state level, although there was considerable variety in compliance with OECD recommendations.

The EU, too, played a key role in implementation (McBride and Mitrea, 2017). The thrust, justified in the name of competitiveness, was to control the price of labour, expressed as 'unit labour costs'. Often this was dubbed 'internal devaluation' to signify that the suppression of working-class living standards was the only alternative to other means of achieving competitiveness (such as 'external devaluation' or currency devaluation, which remained possible for countries outside the eurozone, but was not possible for those within).

Ideological capitulation of the former left

Traditionally, working-class movements have had two arms or wings. One is based on unions operating in the economic sphere; the other is political. Typically, working-class organizations have allied or aligned with left-wing political parties, usually communist or social democratic depending on time period and place. Obviously, the distinction between the two spheres is one of convenience. In reality, economy and politics are linked intimately. Labour's ability to influence its fate has been handicapped by the collapse of its major political options. Communist parties that were very powerful in some countries in the twentieth century have for the most part disappeared or become marginal players. And social democracy, the ideology of the reformist alternative to communism, became thoroughly neoliberalized, with the result that it is incapable of playing a role that expresses labour's interests.

If one reaches far enough back into the history of social democratic parties, evidence can be found of an intention to transform capitalism into an alternative political economy – socialism (Evans, 2014). For many years, however, it has been apparent that while social democratic parties may advocate some reforms, they accept the fundamentals of capitalism and consider it a permanent system. As social democracy's goals became more moderate, so too did its inattention to the interests of its working-class base. Many social democratic parties were linked in some way to trade unions and other working-class organizations and saw their mission as improving conditions for working people. To an extent this is still reflected in the rhetoric and values expressed by these parties but rarely in their performance while in office.

In seeking to escape the dystopia caused by multiple crises it is logical to look for alternatives at those organizations that traditionally focused on reform and change. Perhaps the severity of the crises has prompted a re-evaluation of past adaption to capitalism and made the organizations available for a progressive bloc engaged in the politics of transformation? Or, perhaps the current rendition of social democracy renders them an obstacle to the realization of such a project rather than a partner in it?

Colin Hay (1999) identified some of the components of social democratic strategy in the Keynesian era. These included social dialogue initiatives which could be considered a form of economic democracy and thus reduce the democratic deficit. Redistribution through social policies designed to protect all citizens in areas like health and education was an integral part of social democratic politics in that era. These policies would reduce inequality. In the period of the Keynesian welfare state such policies and programmes were relatively easy to deliver. In the economy there were high levels of productivity growth that enabled high wages and some redistribution of income through taxes and social policies (Schmidt, 2012). The international situation also played a significant role. During the Cold War, Western capitalism faced an ideological adversary and an actually existing alternative economic system. In this context, capital was cautious in its approach to potential social discontent and relatively supportive of the welfare state, at least in comparison to its attitudes before and after the Keynesian interlude.

However, social democracy had already lost its analytical focus on capitalism and class. The post-war Keynesian consensus was viewed as a triumph of technocratic and rational ideas about how best to manage the economy. Labour and capital were thought to have more in common than what divided them. Consequently, ideas about class struggle belonged in the past. They were certainly not a basis on which to conduct modern social democratic politics.

Class analysis and efforts to mobilize workers to demand radical change were abandoned. Instead, expert, technocratic manipulation of the big levers of economic policy was the ethos of Keynesian social democracy. Fundamental reform no longer featured and eventually even catering to the interests of its working–class base fell by the wayside. This led these formerly reformist parties to be characterized as practising 'reformism without reforms' (Liebman, 1986).

One could argue that this approach worked well enough as long as capital retained its commitment to Keynesianism. Social democrats were possibly the only true believers in the 'end of ideology thesis' that became popular in the 1960s (Bell, 1962). That school of thought argued that the changing social structure of post-war capitalism (if, indeed, that word was still an appropriate description of the system) had induced an ideological consensus in these societies. In order to survive in such changed circumstances, the traditional socialist working-class parties were forced to dilute, even liquidate their socialist doctrines to explicitly accept the continuation of the capitalist system. Certainly, their commitment to Keynesian technocratic management was wholehearted, whereas that of conservative and liberal formations was contingent and easily dropped when conditions changed. Having abandoned any trace of analysis suggesting that capitalism needs drastic reform if not replacement, and having long since abandoned methods for bringing that about, including planning and nationalization of significant parts of the economy, the social democrats had nowhere to go – except to trail neoliberalism. An alternative view would have rooted capital's temporary acquiescence to the balance of forces between labour and capital in the post-war world, an acquiescence that could be withdrawn as circumstances changed (McBride, 2005).

Once capital shifted its allegiance to neoliberalism in the 1970s the vacuity of social democracy was exposed. After a brief interregnum, social democratic parties mostly adapted to the new form of capitalism that predominated and sought to present themselves as a moderate option within that camp through doctrines such as the 'Third Way' popularized in Britain by Tony Blair, and in Germany by Gerhard Schröder. Berman and Snegovaya (2019) note that Bill Clinton's 'New Democrats', Tony Blair's 'New Labour', and Gerhard Schröder's SPD in Germany accepted neoliberal policies and the idea that the government's ability to shape economic and social development was restricted. Instead of presenting as a party that would protect society from capitalism's downsides, social democrats presented their mission in technocratic, 'efficiency' terms. As well, this was seen with a shift in the centre-left's leadership towards highly educated elites whose preferences on many issues differed from those of traditional left-wing voters.

Berman and Snegovaya (2019) argue that from the nineteenth to the late twentieth century, the main feature of the social-democratic left was its belief that it was possible to use the democratic state to mitigate or eliminate capitalism's most destructive effects. The social-democratic left's economic course shifted during the late twentieth century and entailed a significant watering-down of what made it appealing and distinctive. Berman and Snegovaya note that once the negative economic and social effects of neoliberalism became obvious, voters decided there was little reason to vote for the left. These parties endorse neoliberal policies, notwithstanding significant challenges within those parties such as those of Jeremy Corbyn in the UK Labour Party and of Bernie Sanders in the US Democratic Party.

Taken together, the 2017 and 2019 Labour Party Manifestos in the UK moved away from the dominant neoliberal framing characterizing the market as the key site of wealth creation, instead emphasizing the role of working people and state agencies in fostering growth (Byrne, 2019). They presented a critique of austerity capitalism, and opened up an image that alternatives were possible (Maiguashca and Dean, 2019; Batrouni, 2020). In this sense, Labour sought to re-embed non-market forces (including workers and public values – especially green ones) in the reproduction of social life (Basset, 2019). Through a group called Momentum, the leftist cause proved capable of rejuvenating the party's membership, literally since many new members were youth, and figuratively by overcoming years of membership decline. Momentum therefore offered a means for ordinary people to influence and change the party and the country (Cop and Erturk, 2021).

Although there has been much debate about how 'left' these developments were (Gjerso, 2017; Basset, 2019; *Financial Times*, 2019; Batrouni, 2020; Loucaides, 2020), the media's hostility to Momentum and the Corbynism movement was overt and predictable. Similarly, any doubts that the mainstream of the Labour Party might be open to radical change were dispelled by the degree of hostility towards Corbyn throughout his tenure as party leader (Helm and Hacillo, 2017; Maiguashca and Dean, 2019). A widely shared assumption that Labour could never improve upon its prior election results by moving politically to the left and the election of radical leadership was undermined by the 2017 election results. Labour achieved its best results for years, and Prime Minister May was forced into a minority government (Gilbert, 2021). Despite this, the implacable opposition continued by the social democratic apparatus firmly ensconced within the Parliamentary Labour Party and the staff employees tells all (Gilbert, 2021). Social democratic organizations are an obstacle, not potential participants in radical transformation.

Bernie Sanders' campaigns to shift the Democratic Party to the left emphasized economic, racial, social and environmental justice (Sanders, 2020). In his *2020 Campaign Platform* Sanders advanced proposals for a Green New Deal (GND) that would: transform the energy system to 100 per cent renewable energy; ensure a just transition for all workers; provide $200 billion to a Green Climate Fund; and rejoin the Paris Agreement. The GND also proposed infrastructure grants and technical assistance for municipalities and/ or states to build publicly owned and democratically controlled co-op or open access broadband networks. Other ideas involved establishing a medicare system for all with a single-payer, national health insurance programme, expanded to include dental care, hearing and vision, home- and community-based long-term care, mental health and prescription drugs.

Bernie Sanders' mobilization efforts sought to reignite class politics within the United States. He consistently employed the slogan of wanting to create a country that works for all (read: all working people), not just the 1 per cent of billionaires. Both Sanders and ally Alexandria Ocasio-Cortez sought to address rallies in 'red states', comprising remnants of the old working class. In this way, they were attempting to establish class unity between the old and new working classes (de Miranda, 2020). Sanders was able to capture much of the youth vote through articulating the relationship between the political system and substantive, programmatic and intelligible reforms (free college, cancelling student debt, among other allegedly 'radical' changes). If achieved, these would make a genuine impact on life chances of the younger generations.

The established leaders of the party that Sanders sought to lead in presidential elections were hardly receptive to the programme he advanced. Inside the organization Biden won the 'electability' argument, because the establishment and their media relations declared it, and the party's voters listened, demonstrating the legitimacy the Democratic establishment holds during elections (Arbour, 2020; Heideman and Thier, 2020). Establishment politics, paired with the looming threat of Trump, stood in the way of a progressive agenda offered by Sanders. This has led to an inconclusive discussion of the rival strategies of working within the Democratic Party or creating a new one, a People's Party that could break the mould of having two capitalist parties bankrolled and controlled by big business (Selfa and Smith, 2016; Trudell, 2016).

Sanders dropped out of the presidential campaign in 2020 and endorsed Joe Biden. He became the chair of the Senate Budget Committee and established a joint task force covering issues including health-care, criminal justice, education and climate change (Unity Task Force, 2020). While the task force document included a collection of widely acceptable liberal proposals, many of which Biden had already embraced during his bid for party unity, the recommendations on economics include broader and costlier plans. Biden's own spending proposals have involved major initiatives, though falling short of what Sanders had advocated in his campaign (Americans for Tax Fairness, 2020). Similarly, Sanders' Medicare For All idea was watered down into an approach resembling Biden's approach on the Affordable Care Act, and simply ignores tuition-free public college and cancelling student debt (Ember and Kaplan, 2020). Sanders is still calling for a 'course correction' that focuses on fighting for the American working class and standing up to powerful corporate interests but appears to be making little headway.[1] The administration's climate agenda was both less ambitious than that put forward in the Green New Deal (zero emissions by 2050 rather than 2030) and contained many ambiguities such as continued subsidization of technologies like carbon capture that in practice enable fossil fuel companies to continue to release climate warming gases (Brown, 2021). Moreover, fracking has not been banned (Snaith, 2021). Biden's clean electricity standard (CES) was hailed the most aggressive initiative to shut down polluting power plants in American history. Yet, even before being dropped, it was criticized as a 'half-measure', promoting false climate solutions such as natural gas, nuclear and biomass power plants. Critics feared that Biden's CES would be a complex technical scheme designed to avoid radical transitions, dubbed 'Obamacare for electricity' (Grunwald, 2021). Advocates of the Green New Deal conceded that it was a step in the right direction, but the size and scale was lacking (Kurtzleben, 2021).

Similarly, much of the social spending, while welcome and helpful to recipients, consists 'one-off or temporary payments that leave the systemic reproduction of inequality unchanged' (Watkins, 2021, p 14).

Overall, there has been some movement towards a progressive agenda, perhaps more than many would have predicted. But the grounds for optimism about the capacity of the Democratic Party to shift to a permanently progressive focus remain highly qualified at this point in time. So far, the internally divided Democratic Party has not done enough to move beyond its track record as a bastion of neoliberal globalization under Clinton, Obama and, in his earlier roles, Joe Biden.

For these reasons, many of those left behind by neoliberalism and globalization no longer look to the traditional left-of-centre parties to address their needs. This has resulted in some voters turning to anti-system parties and protests. Furthermore, the political space opened up by the left's economic transformation helps to explain the rise of populist parties. Far right-wing parties with libertarian or conservative economic profiles transformed themselves into defenders of interventionist states and social safety nets, thus taking advantage of the backlash against austerity and globalization to increase their appeal.

Global insulation and institutional and democratic deficits: the problem of scale

Assuming political forces developed that mobilized for radical transformation of the system, they would find existing institutions unfit for purpose. Democracy itself is in crisis and the nature of its defects creates an obstacle that would have to be overcome. The nation-state is the jurisdictional level that houses the most developed democratic institutions. Compared to it, supranational institutions are far less democratic, less representative, less accountable and more likely to be dominated by appointees whose connection with any part of the democratic process is remote.

Yet national-level political systems are plagued by the same issues, even if to lesser degree. Such deficits in democracy are partly fuelled by neoliberal distrust of democratic procedures that reflects the self-interest of the wealthy and is backed by neoliberal theoretical arguments. These perspectives try to confine the democratic element of our political systems to a choice between leaders and leadership teams that, apart from their personal characteristics, are largely indistinguishable. What these leaders should do when in office is regarded as better handled by experts.

Many functions of government are in fact 'depoliticized' to facilitate this. This can involve creation of 'arm's length' agencies to administer public programmes and farming out of state functions to the private sector. Central bank independence (from government and hence democratic accountability) is a prime example of this since the policy area it affects – monetary policy – is of central importance to the operation of neoliberalism. But many other examples can be found in the health, education, transport, and other sectors. Representation in and accountability of arm's-length agencies is minimal.

Political parties are in decline as they transition from being vehicles in which members might have a voice to supply-side organizations, staffed and run by professional experts (in communications, fundraising, and so on), and offering their wares in the electoral marketplace. There is increased distance now between party leaders and members and, more broadly, between leaders, or elites, and citizens. The ideological convergence of the parties offers little choice about 'what is to be done', only 'who is to do it'. And the outcomes or results of several decades of this are unacceptable to those left behind. The effect is damaging for democracy. The left behind either fail to participate in politics at all, or engage fully in occasional referenda that offer protest opportunities, or they join or vote for anti-system parties that appear to offer a choice or, at least, appear to be listening to concerns that established elites ignore or condemn.

In addition, large areas of policy have been removed from the nation–state level of politics, in whole or in part. Often referred to as constitutionalization, because of its binding characteristics, this process has empowered capital and protected its interests from democratic challenge. Constitutionalization embeds neoliberal rules in national constitutions and in various international agreements, and in polities like the European Union. Authority has been relocated to remote and unaccountable places and venues. The nation-state, which offers the best available prospects for democratic input, however imperfect they may be, has been disempowered.

Conclusions

I have argued in this book that a radical transformation of the existing economic and political system is a logical necessity if the multiple crises are to be confronted and an escape from an approaching dystopia is to be possible. The argument is based on the fact that 'back-to-normal' efforts, even if they were to prevail in the short term, will do nothing to solve the crises or the impact they are having. Conditions will continue to deteriorate, and another situation will arise putting all options back on the table, but with valuable time having been lost in the intervening period. Liberal reform proposals take matters more seriously and offer solutions that, to the extent they were implemented, could mitigate some of the effects of the crises. They are judged too limited in scope to have a major impact. More importantly they are too dependent on the very actors responsible for our present situation. Given the good intentions of many liberal reformers, it may be too harsh to evaluate their proposals as a slower route back to renewed crises. However, in failing to address the roots of the problems that does seem the most reasonable conclusion. Since radical transformation will be a lengthy process, it may be that some liberal reforms might be integrated into the process, something that could also help with constructing a new alliance of interests and ideas.

The purpose of this chapter has been to review the obstacles to the implementation of radical transformation, something that is logically necessary but will certainly be politically difficult to achieve. Broadly, the obstacles are found in the current constellation of interests, ideas and institutions. The interests of capital, especially of finance, prevail. The state has been reconfigured to serve these interests and they are not challenged by politicians or political parties of any stripe. Left-of-centre parties have been looked to as sources of alternative ideas. They have none. They have long been ideologically adapted to the context in which they operate – neoliberal capitalism today – and have failed to offer real alternatives. Existing institutions at both international and national levels have been partially repurposed to obstruct radical change to the existing economic order.

Overcoming this constellation of obstacles is a daunting political challenge. Ways in which it might be done can be readily identified. Some of these are outlined in the next chapter. The argument focuses on what is logically needed.

10

How Is It to Be Done?
Democratic Process and
Building the Public Domain

Radical transformation is necessary.

How can we imagine it taking place? What would the process look like? Since the transformation will not be according to any blueprint but largely an iterative and probably conflictual process, it is impossible to say with any certainty. One envisages a great deal of trial and error and experimentation to see what works and how it can be implemented and institutionalized, though with the main goals and objectives remaining in focus.

Clearly, radical transformation will not happen in one fell swoop but rather in disjointed stages. One anticipated sequence of events would be when nation-states of some significance begin to establish more democratic institutions to rebuild their own public domain and state capacity and, probably simultaneously, begin to disentangle themselves from the existing international order. Imagining and beginning the process of building an alternative international order through cooperation between newly invigorated nation-states would be part of that process.

Focusing on the national level first, because that is the only location where radical change can begin, examples from the past can be instructive. Steffen Lehndorff (2020) conducted such an exercise to determine what the adoption of the New Deal in 1930s' America might have to tell us about the battle for a Green New Deal elsewhere and now.

He identified a series of factors from that period that will likely be present in any radical transformation. Many of these may not seem to be on the horizon in today's political universe. However, if we look back on the twentieth and early twenty-first centuries we see that change, often unexpected, has been a constant.

Once some powerful event or social force has set change in motion, Lehndorff notes the following characteristics of the New Deal which may have broad applicability. First, is a willingness to experiment and look for non-orthodox solutions. Second, strong democratic and charismatic leadership was available then in the form of Franklin D. Roosevelt. The emergence of such leaders cannot be presumed. Still, the reform of democratic institutions by restoring substance and the possibility of alternatives to the existing political process might encourage such a development. Third, institutions and policies that are supportive of change, and particularly of those who will find it difficult to adjust, need to be in place. Fourth, for this to happen, the public domain and the use of the state needs to be expanded. The mantra of 'private is better than public' is demonstrably false and needs to be reversed. Unless there is overwhelming evidence to the contrary public solutions should be assumed to be superior to private ones. This will require, fifth, a 'mutually reinforcing interplay of government policy and social pressure for change' (Lehndorff, 2020, p 83). The state must empower social forces working for radical transformation. Those social forces and movements must rid themselves of 'state hesitancy' and instead commit to use its power to the full in order to constrain the exercise of private interests and the structural power of capital. Finally, Lehndorff notes, conflict with capital during the transformation of the neoliberal order is inevitable and should be assumed and preparations made.

Most of these factors involve an expanded public domain in which the state, other public institutions, and social forces working for change interact in new and democratic ways. The repudiation of the existing orthodoxy by alternative ideas needs to proceed in tandem with the construction of new institutions to embed the new approach, otherwise it and the new ideas will wither on the vine. Although conflict with capital is inevitable as its current privileges are challenged, conceivably efforts at radical transformation, like Keynesianism and the 1930s New Deal, might end up saving capitalism from itself. More likely, radical transformation would confine and contain it within a narrow sphere of activity. Either way there is no getting away from the fact that escaping dystopia will involve some degree of social conflict.

To bring about the types of policies necessary for radical transformation will require a realignment and mobilization of social forces. In addition, however, institutional redesign, a neglected item in radical thinking, will be important. This is because existing institutions are not fit for (radical) purposes. On the contrary, they constitute obstacles to radical change. They are also unpopular and distrusted by significant sections of the population. Proposals to change them and make them servants of popular demands could attract many to the cause of radical transformation.

Popular sovereignty

The remoteness and poor performance of representative and accountability functions by existing institutions serves capital's agenda for the most part. Their redesign needs to ensure that popular sovereignty, the authority of the people to determine priorities, prevails over that of special interests such as capital.

Institutional redesign and reform in the cause of radical transformation involves some basic features. First, there needs to be more public domain, more state and more democracy. Second, there needs to be more nation-state, and with it more autonomy. Third, there needs to be a new international order that is based on fewer rules but more cooperation between nation-states, and a sustained effort to overcome structural inequalities. This should be based on the recognition that the focus on inequalities is as much internal to nation-states as between them.

To construct a new social order that is more equal and fair, and is based on environmental prudence and sustainability, involves rolling back neoliberal institutional innovations and constructing new ones. Serious reforms in old institutions that transfer power into the hands of society and make politicians more susceptible and accountable to democratic pressures are also essential.

Making society more democratic in a popular sovereignty and 'majority rules' sense is not a panacea and does carry some risks. There is no guarantee that the outcome of democratic deliberations will be a more egalitarian and sustainable society. But enabling societal interests to hold governments accountable and exert greater influence on policy through new or reformed institutions makes these goals matters of political contestation in which there is a world to win. The record of existing institutions is clear. New institutions that are capable of making progressive solutions possible, rather than inhibiting them, are needed.

Neoliberalism has been a class-based project involving weakening the working class and other subordinate sectors and fostering the power of capital. To counter these trends, the numerically significant but organizationally weak opponents of the neoliberal order need to include an agenda that calls for fundamental change to how politics is done. In other words, the clarion call should go out that old and dysfunctional institutions need to be replaced by ones that are fit for purpose. Discontent with *how* politics currently operates could be an important mobilizing tool for those advocating changes in *what* is done. It could enable the conversion of some right populists to more progressive policies by respecting their discontent with established elites and institutions.

Revamped notions of popular sovereignty will be based in broader concepts of representation than the notional territorial representation we have at present. Institutional mechanisms can be designed to produce better representation and greater accountability to the society in which states are rooted. The concept of popular sovereignty, grounded in the active participation of the population, strongly challenges the neoliberal democratic paradigm. Popular sovereignty expresses the power of the people to determine what is to be done, and how it is to be done. It asserts the primacy of politics over markets and economics.

More public domain, more state and more democracy

Asserting the primacy of politics requires reversing the depoliticization that was a feature of neoliberalism. Important issues belong in the political domain, even if there are no guarantees about what decisions will emerge. Repoliticization is the antidote to depoliticization. Rolling back the transfers of authority to remote and unaccountable locations will represent a start. At the national level, arm's-length agencies enjoying de facto independence from political control need to be brought back and made instruments of public policy and accountable to the public. Governments should use the opportunity to redefine the mandates under which these agencies operate to ensure their activities reflect public purposes.

An important example is central banks, which for years have operated under the principle of central bank independence (CBI). In practice this has meant a focus on inflation control to the exclusion of other economic goals except, as we have noted, under conditions of extreme crisis (the GFC and the pandemic) when their ability to make a different kind of contribution has been revealed. Meeting the other goals, such as a full-employment, socially equitable and green economy, should now be hard-wired into their mandates and an appropriate accountability system constructed such that the monetary policy technicians inside central banks are held to those purposes. Similarly, the personnel of such agencies and their boards and new accountability councils must be more representative of society than is currently the case.

New concepts of representation and accountability are required to supplement the dominant principle of representation and accountability that is based on territory (see McBride and Schnittker, 2021 for a fuller account). Under this principle, individuals in districts elect representatives who are accountable to them (in the sense of being removable at subsequent elections). Few of these districts are natural communities. They tend to be lines on maps within which appropriate numbers of individuals reside. Given executive dominance of the political systems and party dominance of the individual behaviour of elected representatives (Mair, 2013), plus multiple interests within constituencies, effective representation and accountability is impossible.

How representation and greater accountability to society is to be achieved requires intensive debate from which entirely new perspectives might emerge. In the meantime, functional representation and experiential representation offer possibilities that are worth exploring. This presupposes the creation of effective organizations based on these criteria: role or function performed in society; and lived experience of the outputs of the political system. Within new institutions, such organizations can exert influence and power. While being recognized in their representative capacity by the state, the organizations would need to be substantially self-constituted and internally democratic. By politicizing and empowering them, the (re)politicization of the broader society would be promoted. This would require considerable organization at all levels of society, from the grassroots up. Neoliberal society has seen a decline in collective activities. Rebuilding these links is central to the expression of group interests. The antidote to neoliberal individualism is social solidarity and organization.

Functional representation needs to be distanced from its historical associations in the 'corporate states' of fascist regimes. There is no necessary connection. The strength of functional representation is that it can bypass the theatre of legislative politics and reconnect decision-making to organized and informal engagements between the state and grounded organizations (Brenner, 1969, p 123). Most functional interests are engaged in productive activities such as labour, agriculture and industry. They could be subdivided and/or be extended to under-recognized groups based on, for example, social reproduction. The assumption and reality is that common interests are based on activities performed in the economy and society, and that these are in need of direct representation in the political process (Hsiao, 1927, p 66; Devine, 1988, p 148). This type of representation taps into class-based interests. Many currently lack the means and opportunities to articulate and aggregate their interests effectively. Functional representation also means that individuals can use their time, effort and talents inside organizations that focus on the issues most immediate to them (Warren, 2002, p 693). The goal of functional representation is therefore to construct representative bodies to hold the state accountable to societal interests. Being formally included in the political process means these organizations would become insiders rather than lobbyists or campaigners. To avoid dangers of co-optation it would be all the more important that they structure themselves democratically.

Functional representation can operate at a variety of levels. Nationally these could be reflected in formal decision-making structures that represent organizations' interests while negotiating public policy with the state. Similar structures could be envisaged at subnational and community levels, and in non-territorial contexts like workplaces. Works councils in countries like Spain and

Germany provide a degree of state-mandated grassroots influence at the workplace.

It is important neither to romanticize nor dismiss these examples. Potentially they provide an alternative to a situation where there is virtually no representation of, or accountability to, those disempowered by the existing institutional arrangements, to approach one where there is some, and where that can be extended over time. Whatever organizations are included in future institutional reform would need to be representative of their constituency and have some degree of internal democracy (Devine, 1988, ch 9). Each individual functional interest has to have the opportunity for self-government, based on some mixture of grassroots initiation and state recognition for representative purposes. The precise details cannot be stipulated in advance and would need to be the product of negotiation in particular places and contexts, and thus gain the ability to foster particular (and place-specific) means of internal accountability and representation. With these conditions in place, functional representation could enhance popular sovereignty by making the state more accountable to a broader spectrum of the society from which it springs, rather than the current situation of privileging the voice of organized capital behind the trappings of liberal democracy.

A second type of representation might be by experience, reflecting the different ways political decisions affect people according to their class, race, immigrant status, and gender (the differential impact of austerity might serve as an example). These major sectors of society are effectively excluded from the policy process yet have outcomes imposed upon them. Most are organized to some extent, but even the most organized lack effective voice. Trade unions, for example, partially represent class interests but mostly in connection to work-related issues. They strive to influence the broader spectrum of issues that affect their members, but lack institutional opportunities for the most part and, in any case, are not fully representative of the working class, most of which, in most countries, remains unorganized.

To be effective, functional and experiential representation requires a more organized society than at present. The state must encourage and embrace new forms of representation and accountability. Unlike the neoliberal state that sought to insulate itself and political decisions from societal pressures other than those of capital, the radical state should welcome and enable the expression of collective interests (based on function and experience). These interests should be embedded in the political process in the cause of greater democracy. The result will be power-sharing and intense collaboration. This would be reflected too in the creation of publicly owned, or publicly dominated hybrid and/or joint ownership models of state services, and in planning processes to ensure the primacy of public goals.

Provisionally such an approach might be based on the principles we have outlined – of embeddedness (in society and in a network of other institutions), representation (of a broader and deeper kind than current notions of electoral representative government imply), and accountability (to an organized and, to the extent possible, mobilized society). How could these principles be transferred into institutional form?

Representation means inclusion in decision-making processes. Accountability means being required to report on and explain actions already taken. Current lines of accountability run from government to legislatures to, theoretically, the electorate. To put it mildly, they are not effective. Governments, aided and abetted by the party system in many countries, find it too easy to evade responsibility.

An alternative would be to devise mechanisms to make governments deal with functional and experiential organizations in the policy-making process and be accountable for policy implementation. A system of national (and subnational/community) councils or chambers could be established. There are many models that could be followed. Here is one. Monetary, fiscal, environmental, social and health policy, labour policy and so on would each have a policy development, monitoring and accountability council to which relevant ministries and agencies must report. The councils would be composed of appointees from various levels of government, plus those chosen by the functional and experiential representation organizations. The mandates spelling out how radical transformation is to be achieved in areas assigned to the relevant ministries would be public documents, and reports to the councils would focus on policies and measures to be taken to advance them and, once implemented, on the evaluation of the measures taken. The reports would also be public documents, which would need to include the projected impact of policies and record (a) how measures taken were effective (or not) in advancing a radical transformation agenda, and (b) how they differentially affected functional sectors and representation groups. That is, any winners and losers resulting from the policies would be noted. Future corrective measures might also be specified; or, these might be devised by the councils themselves and sent back to government either in form of recommendations or, in stronger accountability systems, conditions. Councils would need their own staff, probably on temporary secondment from universities, research sections of represented organizations, or other bodies. This would help to prevent bureaucratization and professionalization. Staff would be recruited on the basis of diversity and theoretical/ideological variety to ensure critical voices would be heard and considered. Being on temporary secondment they would remain connected to their professional and organizational constituencies.

Establishing the powers and representational structures of such councils would be a crucial part of state restructuring. Powers might range from publicity for moral suasion, but that is far too weak to have any impact; to the right to recommend and receive a response and the right to be consulted, which leads to moderate influence but doesn't really meet the criteria of holding governments accountable; to decision-making or veto rights over certain issues, which is stronger and might evolve over time.

There are various ways of embedding institutions. These include legislative or constitutional measures with special procedures for repeal. Institutions can also be placed in structured power-sharing relationships between different levels of government – federal or national, and subnational including municipal. Finally, new institutions need to be socially embedded into ongoing public relationships with organized groups in society. Empowerment of organizational representation provides an incentive to political participation. Properly conceived, such links between the state and an organized society facilitate new forms of representation and voice, based on function and experience. Needless to say, the mandates of such institutions would need to be radically different from those established in the neoliberal period.

Beyond these examples, other instruments of state policy can both achieve public priorities and encourage more democratic political participation. Two of these are public ownership of economic activities including banking, and detailed state planning for the economy and environment.

Public ownership can be used for lofty and radical goals like getting control of the 'commanding heights of the economy'. More commonly it has been used by states for limited rather than radical purposes. Sometimes, public enterprises are simply profit centres that confer revenues on governments (Bernier et al, 2020). Often, they play important roles in research and innovation, overseeing long-term, capital-intensive investments, and financing projects of social benefit (Florio et al, 2018). The 'national interest' can be expressed by publicly owned enterprises providing supply management of primary products (Haririan, 2019). Additional political economy motives include boosting regional development by improving job creation and income distribution. These firms often have what Haririan (2019, p 108) calls 'dual objectives', which seek to meet social goals and commercial objectives. This means that efficient allocation of resources might be secondary to considerations of wider developmental goals that could stimulate industrialization, technological capacity-building, and regional development. Public enterprise has been used to correct market imperfections, to achieve 'economies of scale' and 'externalities' in areas like utilities, communications and transportation and to help overcome economic crises (Brenner, 1984). Public firms can act as regulators maximizing social welfare, whereby their actions can discipline private firms through their decisions regarding price and quantity (albeit less 'efficiently'). Other policy objectives include nation-building, national security, and changes in the distribution of wealth. To these will certainly be added conversion to a green economy.

The need for state rescue missions in both the financial crisis of 2008 and the 2020 COVID-19 pandemic crisis points to an enhanced long-term role for the public sector (Fanelli and Whiteside, 2020; Mazzucato, 2020). One could imagine an extensive list of new publicly owned corporations, or privatized ones that were renationalized to accomplish objectives where the private sector is unable to make the case that its performance would be superior. Examples, which would vary from country to country, might include railways and mass transit, manufacture of electric vehicles, equipment manufacture for generation of solar, wind or tidal energy, environmental remediation projects, public housing, waste disposal, public banks and so on.

To play an important role in radically transforming the economy and environment, publicly owned industries need to shed some of the baggage attached to them in the past. Frequently they operated in bureaucratic fashion and were as impenetrable to public input as any of their private sector equivalents. Democratization of their governance would be a crucial building bloc of the publicly owned sector and, as that sector expands, of society generally. State control and public participation can be creatively combined. To give one example, a study of a Danish case on wind power revealed that the institutional and regulatory mechanisms of the state in support of renewable energy, through taxation, investment subsidies and the use of price controls, were important in dispersing economic power. The sector was able to create a participatory model of public ownership embedded within existing structures of civil society. These were reciprocal in that they were effective in mobilizing the support for state policies and targets at the national level. The success of the sector therefore relied on both the non-state collective forms of organization, and higher-level state coordination and planning mechanisms to achieve progressive policy goals. Cumbers and McMaster (2012) noted that the central government remained important in overseeing and regulating sectors and markets (including rights of workers and consumers to participate in decision-making), but local-level actors got the power to determine forms of organization and ownership. Mention of a single case does not exhaust the range of possibilities! How to combine state or other forms of public ownership with greater participation in decision-making can be imagined as a process of trial and error, and one with considerable variation in forms. As well as the public goods they provide, publicly owned industries can serve as instruments of democratization. The most important things are: first, that a crucial instrument, public ownership, not be rejected because of a previous negative image; second, that a top-down model not be imposed; and third, that decentring the organizational form does not lead to a lack of focus on fulfilling broader public purposes.

In an era of financialization, public banks are a particularly important example of public enterprise. They can function in ways that are mandate driven and equity oriented, and that promote a green economy with a just transition. Whether they do so or instead act like private profit-seeking banks is shaped and reshaped by power relations, context, social forces, institutional structure and governing priorities. There is nothing inherently dynamic about public financial institutions (Marois, 2021).

That said, while public ownership does not determine how the institution functions, it does create very important alternative possibilities. The benefits that public banks can deliver include: (1) de-financialization; (2) decarbonization; and (3) democratization (Karwowski, 2019).

Public banks can contribute to de-financialization by acting counter-cyclically (that is, lending during financial crises, when private banks are contracting) (Brei and Schclarek, 2013); privileging long-term and stable lending; and better coordinating lending to reduce the cost of borrowing, linked to how public banks can benefit from sovereign guarantees, and lower cost of borrowing in financial markets (McDonald et al, 2021; see also Brown, 2013). Additionally, as public banks operate under public legislation, operational rules and guidelines, they can be used to further national priorities and the common good, rather than profit-making and shareholder value.

Second, public banks can be used to finance decarbonization. Existing public banks often play a key role in infrastructure financing that certainly can be scaled up. As they are located within the public sphere, those banks can be instructed to meaningfully engage with and finance decarbonization (Marois, 2021). Public banks in Brazil, China, Germany, Japan and the EU have already become important financial actors in providing 'patient' funding for projects aiming to address climate mitigation and adaptation (Mazzucato and Semieniuk, 2018). Thus, public banks offer a means to overcome the dead end of private finance and break the deadlock in decarbonization and climate change initiatives.

Finally, democratization, or the ability of citizens to collectively bring societal needs to the forefront of economic planning, will be a necessary and an important force behind de-financializing and decarbonizing operations (Marois, 2021). As public ownership alone is not enough, it must be supported by the democratization of bank governance and accountability towards personnel, clients, social organizations and citizens. This includes checks and balances which tie those who are involved in the bank (management, owners, committees, workers) to the public mandate (Vanaerschot, 2019). Public banks should also be responsible to the relevant monitoring and accountability councils that are representative of economic sectors and experiential groups. This can include enforcing compliance with social, political, economic and environmental mandates. One existing case is Sparkassen – a German public bank. The public mandate is written in law, and municipalities are the responsible institutions but cannot access bank profits. A supervisory board, representing different local stakeholders, oversees whether the management of the bank respects the mandate. While it may not be perfect, it does represent a small step towards making banks accountable to the public (Vanaerschot, 2019). And the basic model could be extended and improved in many ways.

The basic principle is that being accountable to organized public constituencies will help to ensure that strategies do not favour a particular privileged group in society at the expense of others (Romero, 2017). Or, if they do, that this is fully transparent and the reasons are articulated and known. Those authorities which control public banks can determine the extent to which they are shielded from profit and competitive imperatives (Marois, 2021). Consequently, public banks offer an opportunity, if used correctly, for public interest to be a catalytic force in financing progressive goals such as the low-carbon transition, and bypass the need to subordinate climate justice to financialized, private and profit-making imperatives (Marois, 2021). Harnessing the potential of public banks towards progressive ends can therefore create substantial change.

Since the onset of the COVID-19 pandemic, some of the advantages of public financial institutions have emerged. Five overarching lessons have been identified – public banks have the potential: to respond rapidly; to fulfil their public purpose mandates; to act boldly (through offering liquidity with generously reduced rates of interest, preferential repayment terms and eased conditions of repayment); to mobilize their existing institutional capacity; and to build solidarity with other public institutions (such as through central bank and public bank cooperation, and between public banks in different countries). While receiving little media attention, these institutions have been on the frontlines of dealing with the economic and health crisis, avoiding financial collapse, supporting communities and channelling resources into public services (Barrowclough et al, 2020).

Economic planning, broadly defined to include construction of a more equal society and a transition to a green one, is an essential instrument of radical transition. It relies on a strong state employing a variety of powerful instruments such as expanded public ownership, including the use of public banks to dislodge the power of finance. Planning on this scale will be complicated. It involves coordination between decisions at the central level that allocate resources with local input, representation and accountability. Decisions will be needed on the amount and type of growth, and its effects on such issues as land-use, greenspace, transport and housing. Policy needs to achieve sufficient economic growth to achieve a sustainable, fair and equitable economy and society. These priorities need to be reconciled and coordinated with subsidiary levels of planning at the sectoral and community levels. How are these decisions to be made and by whom? How do central decisions affect particular sectors to the economy and particular communities within it? In this context, how do planning decisions affect enterprises, public and private, and how much leeway will they have in modifying them?

These are vitally important processes in which democratic participation will be essential. Two principles would seem important. First, state institutions would work in tandem with some sort of National Planning Council (representative functionally and experientially in the same way as other councils). Equivalent arrangements would apply to planning further down the scale. Second, coordination implies negotiation between different interests, including territorial ones, rather than the imposition of top-down targets or priorities. The challenge is to work out how to apply socially determined goals in a way that permits democratic input, and hence the mobilization of support, without suffocating initiative, but yet avoids anarchy and the possibility of participants in the process working at cross purposes (for a discussion of these knotty problems, see Devine, 1988).

Other experimental and participatory institutional initiatives can be expected during radical transition. Several jurisdictions have established citizens' assemblies to produce recommendations on subjects as diverse as electoral reform, climate action and abortion rights. Typically, these involve a random selection of citizens, structured to be sociologically representative of the general population. They are briefed by experts and then deliberate to recommend courses of action. Evaluations of the results of these vary – some seem to have real impact, others not. Regardless of outcomes, however, they do represent a new way of getting politics done that sidesteps the usual procedures that are baked into existing structures. They may serve a useful purpose for governments by obtaining input on contentious issues and generating legitimacy for measures that governments subsequently decide to implement. Given that governments control whether or not to enact advice received, and the fact that citizens' assemblies may be sociologically representative but are not otherwise connected to society, it is unclear to what extent they shift the parameters of democratic decision-making by enhancing broader participation.

However, the establishment of an assembly or convention to devise a new constitution for Chile points to another possibility in bypassing established political structures. It is interesting for two reasons. First, a rather specific protest about increased transport fares escalated into a judgement on almost fifty years of neoliberalism and led to the demand for a new constitution to replace the one imposed under the Pinochet dictatorship. Chile is the poster child for neoliberalism in Latin America, and remains the most unequal country in the OECD. Chileans have the lowest salaries in the OECD bloc, and many have had to accrue debt to cover basic living costs (Bartlett, 2019). In addition, they have experienced high costs of partly privatized education and health systems, rents and utilities, and have ongoing grievances with the privatized pension system (Laing et al, 2019). The waves of civil unrest therefore exposed cracks in Chile's 'economic success' story (Vilches and Pizarro, 2019).

Second, having won a referendum on the issue, 78 per cent of voters favoured a new constitution. Voters also opted for a newly elected constitutional convention, without automatic inclusion of Congress members (Bonnefoy, 2020). The process of constitutional reform therefore partly escaped the control of established elites and political parties.

The resulting constitutional convention is made up of 155 citizens, based on parity between male and female members (78 men, 77 women). It includes 17 reserved seats for indigenous peoples elected in a parallel ballot. The average age of elected members is 45. At least six of them are members of the LGBTQ+ community, and many come from non-elite economic backgrounds, and include environmental and feminist activists (Tobar, 2021). The established parties had to campaign against an array of 'lists' and other independents. Government-backed candidates (from Sebastian Pinera's right-wing government) only secured 37 seats despite outspending all other coalitions. This means that the right fell short of the number which would make it possible for them to veto sweeping changes (Correa, 2021). That said, it is unclear what common view might emerge from the convention, or if identity politics will thwart progress towards unity (Funk, 2021). The constitutional convention opened on 4 July 2021 and is scheduled to have nine months to draft the new constitution (potentially up to 12 months). Then, after 60 days, it will be approved or rejected in a national referendum (for details of the process see Pérez Dattari, 2021).

'More nation state … more autonomy'

Collective actions advancing radical transformation can occur at any level or scale – global, regional, national, local, community, or workplace. However, the examples I have given of institutional redesign are primarily focused on the national level. There are several reasons for this.

Many advocates of radical transformation tend to minimize the nation-state level and instead focus on the international or local arenas for change. The nation-state has become a somewhat distrusted and underestimated entity. Partly this is because its link to nationalism is distasteful to many. Certainly, nationalist expressions in ethnic or racist terms, as with right populism, contributes to that image. There are, of course, many historical examples. Nationalism has been used to mobilize populations for war, and through colonialism and imperialism has served to justify the oppression of one people by another.

Because of these associations I have sometimes used the expression 'nation-state-*ism*' to depict the nation-state as a jurisdictional entity that, quite independently of ethnic or sociological composition, can play a key role in radical transformation.

The nation-state is also home to the state in its other sense – the complex of institutions that exercise power within its territory and engage in relationships with its counterparts internationally. Many mistrust the state in this sense too. Partly this is because of its association with coercion against its own population. Friedrich Engels observed, as part of his theorization of the state, that it consisted of 'armed men ... and prisons and institutions of coercion of all kinds' (Engels, 1969 [1884], p 577). And the German sociologist Max Weber drew attention to its claim on a 'monopoly of the legitimate use of physical force within a given territory' (Weber, 1968, p 56). These are hardly abstract considerations. States have acted and do act coercively in defence of the established order and hierarchy. Many doubt that they can be repurposed to advance progressive aims.

Then, too, the globalization narrative suggested the obsolescence of the nation-state. It was said to have lost power sideways to 'markets', downwards to subnational jurisdictions, and upwards to global institutions. As a result, nation-states had become 'hollowed-out'. Sceptical analyses were quick to challenge this (Hirst and Thompson, 1996). Moreover, it was clear that to the extent that the trends identified in the globalization narrative were occurring, they were doing so at the instigation of states themselves, acting in concert with the interests of finance capital. That is, if there was a hollowing out of the nation-state (and the extent of this was disputed) it was an act of political choice rather than an act of nature or some unstoppable force. Moreover, 'globalization' was a misnomer for the system that had emerged. That word carries connotations of a true and widespread internationalism. But the global order was a hierarchical one in which advantages for the already-powerful states and interests were locked in, to the disadvantage of most countries outside the Global North, and of subordinate classes and groups everywhere. One implication of this counternarrative is that if neoliberal globalization is really the product of the states themselves, then the states could dismantle it, or alter its central features if enough of them chose to do so. The powerless state is indeed a 'myth' (Weiss, 1998). Like all myths, it is convenient for some. In this case it is convenient for those who wish to evade the controls that nation-states *could* place upon them.

Certainly, the quasi-constitutional trade and investment agreements have been designed to constrain nation-states' regulatory and legislative capacities. If the myth of a powerless state was the reality this would hardly be necessary.

Yet the myth seems to have been internalized by many who otherwise support radical transformation. This is unfortunate, to say the least. Both the nation-state considered as a legal entity and the state considered as a complex of political institutions are the only imaginable vehicles in which popular sovereignty (and therefore democracy) could be realized, and which are potentially powerful enough to effect a radical transformation.

The nation-state as a focus for popular sovereignty and democratic political action has several attributes that are lacking at the international level. Nation-states provide a central institutional focus for political action. At the international level, power is dispersed. There is no central institutional focus. As well, any legitimacy attached to international organizations stems from delegation from member states. Once enmeshed in international organizations or treaty obligations, the relations between the international and the national may be complicated. But the root of any international authority, and hence the ultimate power to rescind it, rests at the national level. This is the case even in the EU, which is the most highly integrated of any international organization.

At the nation-state level, it is possible to speak of the '*demos*', or people who comprise it. This is crucial from the perspective of establishing popular sovereignty. Popular sovereignty and democracy are dangerous to established elites because they threaten the pattern of class-based advantage and inequality that characterizes contemporary society. At the international or global level there is no '*demos*', or people. There are peoples, but they are not cohesive enough to aspire to popular sovereignty. Again, the EU is no exception (Lapavitsas, 2018, p 114). Popular sovereignty blends into national contexts. It cannot do the same internationally because there is no 'people' or citizenry to serve as a referent.

Highlighting the nation-state in this way does not imply any form of isolationism. Nor does it overcome power differentials between nation-states, some of which will be more capable than others of taking advantage of new opportunities. However, it does imply a new international order that is voluntarily arrived at, and which is tolerant of a greater degree of national autonomy and therefore different strategies to be adopted by states, than the existing order that is crumbling around us.

Towards a new international order

If the liberal international order is under challenge, what might a positive replacement look like? Recognizing that international orders are not just about relationships between states but also relations between social classes might be a useful starting point. An important study on trade wars concluded that '[t]rade war is often presented as a conflict between countries. It is not: it is a conflict mainly between bankers and owners of financial assets on one side and ordinary households on the other – between the very rich and everyone else' (Klein and Pettis, 2020, p 221). The subtitle of the study is 'How rising inequality distorts the global economy and threatens international peace', and the inequality in question pertains to that within states as much as that between them. A class-based response towards constructing a more egalitarian international order would be a promising avenue. It would necessarily start at the national level and have, as one of its purposes, creating a more permissive international context.

Even with greater autonomy for nation-states they will still want to engage in a wide variety of interactions, including economic ones. If not on the basis of neoliberal rules, on what basis might this occur? Clearly, this will involve a rejection of liberal and neoliberal theoretical constructions based on Ricardo's theory of comparative advantage. Rather, a pragmatic assessment of what is mutually advantageous should replace that theory-driven and highly flawed approach.

Two examples from the past, even though of roads not taken, are instructive. Their precise details will not be appropriate for today. Nevertheless, the approach they represent and their goals, objectives and broad strategies may serve as an inspiration as to how to construct a new internationalism. The examples are the International Trade Organization (ITO), proposed in the immediate aftermath of World War II, and the NIEO movement of the 1970s.

The ITO Charter, proposed but subsequently not ratified by the United States, encouraged economic development and full employment, as well as trade and investment. For Jean-Christophe Graz (2000, p 21) it represented an effort to reconcile, on an international basis, 'the historic antagonisms of capitalism between an open international economy and the socio-economic functions of the state'. Its statutes:

> acknowledged a conception of trade regulation that shielded substantial economic and social functions of the state: heavy agricultural support, quotas on a discriminatory basis for development or balance of payment purposes, a wide range of safeguards to avoid international propagation of recessions, intergovernmental agreements for primary commodities and recognition of the legitimate right of expropriation for capital-importing countries. (Graz, 2000, p 22)

A modern version would need to build in other goals such as transitioning to a green economy. While isolationist fears played some role in its non-ratification, economic liberals and interests such as the International Chamber of Commerce, hostile to the broad goals and state interventionism conveyed by the ITO Charter, were more important (O'Brien et al, 2000, p 69).

Some of the eventual American opposition to the ITO was based on its deviation from the principle that trade is about private gain and profit and should not be subject to other, public, priorities (Drache, n.d., p 19). The ITO was a compromise between liberal and non-liberal views of trade. As such, it did not fully endorse the iron law of comparative advantage. Indeed, it sought to insulate governments from regulations that compromise their ability to pursue broad economic and social goals like full employment (Drache, n.d., p 10). Included in its detailed rules were ones that would hold business to account for restrictive practices. All subsequent trade agreements, starting with the General Agreement on Tariffs and Trade, limited their regulations to the conduct of states and were silent on the conduct of businesses and multinational corporations. One purpose in constructing a new international economic order would be to impose constraints on capital. It is time to reconsider and reconstruct international trade agreements, and some elements of the ITO will be instructive.

The second example is the NIEO. It was the product of national liberation movements that emerged across the 'Third World', with demands emphasizing their opposition to colonialism, increased cooperation between governments, and self-determination, among others (Berger, 2004).

It was dedicated to closing the gap between developing and developed countries. United Nations development targets (including increasing agriculture production and development aid) were only half achieved by the early 1970s, and service charges on debts were beginning to accumulate. There continued to be poor progress in commodity trade, and inadequate access to markets, and tariffs escalated (Gebremariam, 2017). Moreover, Raul Prebisch's (1950) work on development economics began to gain attention. It provided a critique of the subordinate economic position that imperial powers had transferred to their colonies as primary producers. It also held that international trade must be managed to prevent the erosion of terms of trade, and that governments and corporations from the North should provide capital, technology and expertise to allow the South to develop an industrial base. This thesis also produced the rationale for import-substitution industrialization strategies (Gathi, 2009; Gilman, 2015).

The political objective of the NIEO was to create a global democracy of equal sovereign states, thus completing the process of decolonization (Gilman, 2015). The NIEO included: the absolute right of states to control the extraction and marketing of their domestic natural resources; the regulation of transnational corporations; conditionality-free technology transfers from the North to the South; granting preferential trade preferences to countries of the South; and forgiveness of certain debts owed to the North (Gilman, 2015). It also included the right to nationalize and transfer ownership of foreign entities, and turning over the resources to the state or its citizens (Gordon, 2009). Overall, these proposals called for the 'economic sovereignty' of postcolonial states (Gilman, 2015). But they also attempted to establish that assisting developing countries should be an obligation of developed countries, due to the history of colonialism and imperialism that had placed them in an unfavourable position in the first place (Gordon, 2009; Gebremariam, 2017). This represented a radical break from the traditional economic liberalism.

The NIEO attracted the enmity of powerful states, interests and adherents of liberal trade theory. To them it was seen as an antithesis of international economic relations, as it seemed to undermine their underlying assumption that the economic sphere is market driven and self-regulating and should not be subject to regulatory intervention by governments (Gordon, 2009). The NIEO became a casualty of the rise of neoliberalism domestically and internationally.

Yet, as Gilman (2015) notes, for many poor countries the NIEO remains a dominant frame for the question of climate justice. The G77, now composed of 134 member states, remains the South's main organizing agent for collective climate bargaining with the North. It has pursued similar economic reasoning to that outlined in the NIEO. This includes the concept of the North agreeing to bear historic responsibility for producing greenhouse gases, recognition that the South still has a 'right to development', and that any fair climate deal should be 'nonreciprocal', with respect to binding responsibilities such as emission reductions mandates (Gilman, 2015).

Radical ideas based on the NIEO may be more realizable than formerly. The original version faced neoliberal enthusiasm for markets in its messianic phase. The GFC and pandemic have eroded trust in the efficacy of open, deregulated markets and moderated distaste for the role of state intervention in the economy. Even if considered solely from the point of view of self-interest, the urgency of the climate crisis places more pressure on rich countries to do more to help developing countries tackle the crisis, especially through large technology transfers for mitigation and adaptation (Chang, 2020). Revisiting the abandoned road of the NIEO could help denaturalize the existing inegalitarian global political economy (Gilman, 2015) and serve as a model for moving forward on the climate change as well as the economic fronts.

Writing in the mid-2010s, Uddin (2017) argued that the industrialized countries were unwilling to give up their position of advantage and that this is at the core of global environmental politics. Countries in the Global North are not ready yet to take historical responsibility for carbon emissions nor to advance sufficient assistance to countries in the Global South to ensure an international just transition to a green economy to complement the one being talked about internally.

Previous rounds of climate talks have fallen short of the challenge. Kyoto, with its mandatory requirements, fell by the wayside as powerful countries either failed to ratify or else withdrew. The Paris Agreement substituted an approach of voluntary pledges. It, too, is seen as having failed to meet its goals. Pledged targets have often not been met and the world is on a trajectory for higher warming than would have been the case if they had been. The latest round of talks, organized under the United Nations COP26 rubric, took place in Glasgow in November 2021. Prior to the event the main goals were clear: to achieve net-zero emissions by 2050, a target that would require significant reductions by 2030. In general terms, the measures to be taken could include phasing out the use of coal, ending deforestation, substituting electric vehicles for those powered by petrol, and investing in renewable energy generation. As always, the devil was in the details. These measures affect different countries, and within them social classes, differently. Who will benefit and who will pay are issues that are not easy to resolve.

Internationally, poor countries need economic growth, as quickly and as cheaply as possible, to overcome their poverty. More than a hundred countries set out their demands for the COP26 conference. They included funding to adapt to climate change, compensation for the impact it will have, and financial assistance to convert to green economies. Wealthy countries had already promised $100 billion per year by 2020 to advance these goals but the amounts provided came to only $80 billion, and most of that was in the form of repayable loans, obligations that already indebted countries might not want to incur.

The COP26 meeting culminated in the adoption of the 'Glasgow Climate Pact', an effort towards a more ambitious climate response. Like its Paris predecessor, this text 'requests' that countries attempt to revisit and strengthen their climate pledges by the end of 2022, thus maintaining the reliance on voluntary contributions from members. It also calls for a 'phasedown' of the use of coal (instead of a 'phase-out'). Most blame for this dilution fell on India and China, but other countries, such as Japan, Australia and Saudi Arabia, also played down the need to move rapidly away from fossil fuels. The agreement establishes processes to deliver greater adaptation, higher levels of climate finance, and finance for loss and damage (Simon Evans et al, 2021; Sharma Poudel, 2021). The text urges developed countries to double their collective provision of climate finance for adaptation from 2019 levels by 2025, and reaffirms the duty to fulfil the sum of US$100 billion annually. The parties also committed to a process to agree on long-term climate finance beyond 2025 (Sharma Poudel, 2021). Moreover, the agreement suggests that more money needs to be given in the form of grants over loans, although the details on this commitment are limited (Morris, 2021).

The Glasgow meeting did call attention to 'loss and damage' – referring to the unavoidable impacts of climate change that cannot be adapted to. This is often framed as climate reparations, due to the historical responsibility of developed countries for climate change (Simon Evans et al, 2021). Developed countries resist this idea because it may force them to pay compensation for their historical responsibility, and they succeeded in delaying it for now. On the positive side, the agreement is the first to include the phasing down of fossil fuel, and to name coal as the root cause of the problem (McGrath, 2021b), and, overall, it keeps the hope of achieving the 1.5° target faintly alive.

Military blocs

Ideally, a new international order would demand that military spending be reduced and any reductions reallocated to climate, anti-poverty or other socially useful projects. Global spending on the military amounts to about $2 trillion per year. Of this, the US alone accounts for 39 per cent, and seven of the top 15 largest defence budgets come from NATO members (the US, France, the UK, Germany, Italy, Canada and Turkey). Adding in the rest of the 30-country military bloc would boost the share considerably.

Legitimate defence spending would no doubt continue to be a priority for the more autonomous nation-states comprising a new international order. But the shift away from a unipolar order, and non-military developments like Brexit, might be extended to military alliances. NATO, in particular, has undergone repeated mission creep since the dissolution of the Soviet bloc. Whatever its origins, it is clearly not a defensive alliance. The enemy to be defended against has continually to be re-invented. In reality, the alliance serves to project Western power, at the behest of the US, in corners of the world far from the North Atlantic. It is also a somewhat captive market for some of the US's arms exports, though dwarfed by armaments sales to other American allies like Saudi Arabia. The US has a 37 per cent market share of world armaments sales, and another 25 per cent belongs to seven other NATO countries (France, Germany, the UK, Spain, Italy, Netherlands, and Turkey). By comparison, Russia has a 20 per cent market share, and China 5.2 per cent.[1]

Together with the EU's Eastern Partnership project, NATO's expansion to the East has been a destabilizing factor in that region. Its regime change activities in places like Libya, Iraq and elsewhere in the Middle East have produced failed states and stimulated the rise of non-state terrorist groups. Its disastrous war in Afghanistan failed to achieve its long-term objectives, and its ignominious defeat and withdrawal promises an even more unstable future in that country.

Occasionally, one heard world leaders' comments that suggested a rethinking of the alliance – President Trump observed that NATO was 'obsolete', President Macron that it was 'brain dead' – and US unilateralism in various foreign policy contexts, including nuclear weapons treaties, the Iran agreement, and Afghanistan, must have prompted private apprehension within the alliance that the US is a far from reliable partner. However, following the Russian invasion of Ukraine in February 2022, the NATO bloc underwent a rapid consolidation rendering such internal tensions moot. The American-led European security order has been reconstituted. At the same time the idea of a single liberal rules-based international order, let alone a unipolar one, seems broken. It is clear that the war in Ukraine and new security situation, and the subsequent Western economic sanctions and other measures directed against Russia, will have a collateral impact that deepens the crises in the economy, the environment and climate, migration, and democracy in ways that cannot be predicted at this moment in time.

Putting radical transformation in motion

This series of political, policy and institutional changes offers a route away from impending dystopia. It emphasizes certain essential features: more national autonomy and fewer rules from international authorities, and more democracy to embed representation and accountability in ways that express the interests of organized society. Since governments will still be selected using the old criteria of territorial representation (even though, in essence, it is undermined by party discipline), contestation between different modes of representation can be anticipated. The new ones will be the most important because, as outlined in earlier chapters, existing representational and accountability mechanisms are somewhat fictional. Legislatures in the modern period do little to hold governments accountable.

The formula will be a larger and stronger state (with less influence from international organizations and agencies), more democracy (based on new representational and accountability criteria), more influence for workers and other currently under-recognized sectors of society (and less influence for business).

It might be objected that the process will have to begin within existing institutions. Given what has been said about their lack of democracy and the way they have been configured to lock in neoliberalism and obstruct alternatives, how can we imagine this happening? The question is especially pertinent given that no political formation currently on the scene looks remotely capable of pushing for or bringing about a radical transformation.

This can be readily conceded. But it is also true that a number of pre-conditions for radical change are in place even though no political entity has yet set them in motion. In the political sphere that encompasses the crisis of democratic institutions, the preconditions can be observed at the level of ideas and of institutions. Neoliberal ideas served to convert and mobilize large numbers of people in the past. They provided, like any ideology, a set of goals, a guide to actions, and a range of justifications for actions taken or planned. Neoliberalism's period of missionary-like zeal is long gone. Its record is appalling since it must bear the responsibility for the multiple crises. It still has powerful and self-interested backers, but its mantras of private sector superiority, private sector efficiency, austerity as the remedy for economic crisis, and the public sector as the problem not the solution, are discredited. No one rushed to the private sector to save the day in the GFC or the pandemic. Instead, states had to step in to save society from the full impact of private sector financial irresponsibility in the GFC, and scramble a response to the health pandemic, despite their capacity having been undermined by decades of neoliberalism. For those pushing for radical transformation there is, if not an ideational vacuum, at least a major opportunity.

Neoliberalism's institutional basis too is increasingly unpopular and discredited. Globalization is under challenge from a variety of sources, most obviously from those who quite rightly consider they have been 'left behind', but also from many who believe it has become economically and environmentally dysfunctional. Few look to the international sphere or the international capital for solutions. While it is true that shifting authority to the nation-state level and to public institutions has hardly become the new common sense, there is a greater willingness to explore options at these levels, if for no other reason than because the alternative has failed.

The neoliberal economy has been operated in favour of capital. The newspaper headline at the beginning of the book recording that CEOs in the US now earn 351 times as much as workers earn, compared to 15 times as much in 1965, tells the story of the era. The working class has experienced stagnant living standards, increased insecurity and precarity, and declining social mobility opportunities. There is thus a large, currently dormant, pool of working-class discontent on which to draw. The environmental crisis encourages a 'whole of society' potential constituency for radical change. Literally the whole of society stands to lose as the spectre of climate change and global warming deepens. Vested interests in the fossil-producing industries, financial interests that make money out of them, and climate deniers would seem to be in the minority. They would be unable to block radical transformation if the potential majority were properly mobilized.

Within the political system, the economy and the environment, the power of capital seems entrenched and often looks impregnable. But the crises have exposed its vulnerabilities. Capital's insulation from the impact of the crises and its ability to transfer the costs of its own errors onto the backs of others depend entirely on states. Should it lose control of the state its demise as a powerful actor would follow. Yet the political momentum to convert states from the instruments of capital to the instruments of popular sovereignty is nowhere apparent.

At least two of the critical ingredients that Lehndorff (2020) identified in the New Deal developments in 1930s' America are missing. The first is strong and democratic leadership, and the second is organized and sustained social pressure for broad-ranging change. There is lots of pressure aimed at narrower targets that are unlikely to lead to system change, although as mentioned briefly, this can sometimes happen.

My argument has been that these deficiencies will only be overcome at the national level because this is the only imaginable site for the expression of popular sovereignty. Clearly this will have to be achieved in some significant nation-state(s) first of all. There are a number of plausible scenarios about how it might happen.

First, expressions of political discontent over some specific issue could be transformed and achieve a broader focus. Which issue might trigger this is unpredictable. In all the many protests against austerity in the 2010s, most had specific targets and remained that way. A few broadened into movements against austerity policies as a whole. Protests against housing evictions in Spain led to the formation of a new political party, Podemos, and other movements that captured control of many cities. Protests against water rates in Ireland led to the anti-austerity party, Sinn Fein, outdistancing the traditional parties that had dominated the country's politics for a century. Most relevant to the present discussion, protests against a transport fare increase in Chile escalated into successful demands for a constitutional convention to be established with the aim of ridding the country of some of its neoliberal inheritance. In this context, new leadership and links to new social forces can emerge quickly.

Second, the structure of the liberal international order is already under great pressure. The UK's exit from the EU, though hardly a model for radical transformation, suggests that national defections from the order are not impossible. Were some other significant nation-states to withdraw from the EU, or the eurozone for that matter, political opportunities would become far more open. Whether this would lead to radical transformation or a regression to a different form of neoliberal globalism, as has clearly been the case with Brexit, would be the issue to be settled. But once again, what might be called a Great Unravelling of the international order would break the logjam that obstructs change in institutions and politics.

Another possibility would arise if an important nation-state were to disintegrate due to minority nationalist pressures. The entire institutional structure of the now separate units would be open for (re)construction. Countries with some risk of undergoing this process include the UK and Spain. Again, the outcome of devising new constitutional and institutional arrangements for England after Scottish independence and possibly status changes for Northern Ireland and Wales, or for the rest of Spain after a Catalonian departure, cannot be predicted. What is for sure is that such events would demand new political organizations and leadership. Possibly this could come from within established political parties or elites, even though they are deeply implicated in the existing system. Its collapse would certainly open up other possibilities, such as the formation of new parties and organizations, including ones based in the class and other constituencies affected by the multiple crises.

Finally, the urgency of the multiple crises might itself enable radical transformation. Climate is the most obvious candidate. Militarism and the threat of war between major powers is another. Either or both might push politics in significant nation-states to a major rethink about what their national interests really are and what kind of political changes need to be made to address them.

I have argued that, faced with the intractable and dangerous intersection of multiple crises, radical transformation is necessary. The scenarios just outlined suggest ways in which the process could be set in motion. Once in motion the possibilities for progress at the national level and for new forms of international cooperation can develop. There are, of course, no guarantees as to outcomes or that globally oriented capital can be constrained in the public interest. Without breaking the institutional and political roadblocks, however, there is no possibility of this happening. Once the barriers are down, the game is on.

11

Escaping Dystopia

The various crises in the economy, environment, security, international economic order, health and migration areas are serious and in need of urgent political attention. Unfortunately, the world's political systems have been unable to respond adequately.

The fact that the crises are interconnected means that partial responses focused on one or other area will not be sufficient. Rather an approach targeted at the underlying cause of all of them is necessary.

The underlying cause is the neoliberal global variant of capitalism. Its unlimited and unconstrained growth objective has fuelled the environmental crisis, destabilized the economy and wreaked havoc with working life and solidarity within societies. In conjunction with the military and economic international orders, it has led to other crises like that of migration.

Political systems are blocked partly by the institutional constraints placed on governments at the national level, and partly by the limiting effects of neoliberal ideas. These preclude critical analysis of the multiple crises and the links between them, and of the powerful interests that created the system and continue to benefit from it. Many important policy areas have been 'depoliticized' with the result that the scope for the exercise of democratic politics is diminished. The lines of accountability in liberal democratic systems have shifted anyway. Streeck (2014) noted that states were trying to be accountable to two constituencies – the people, or citizenry, and the markets. The desire or perceived need to maintain the second line of accountability, to capital in general and globally active financial interests in particular, rules out any assessment that the crises are caused by global capitalism itself.

The nation-state, considered as a vehicle in which action could be taken, has been hollowed out, and the state, in its other meaning of public institutions, has been deliberately weakened in areas connected to social policy and equity as a result of the long neoliberal hegemony. This is a problem because the nation-state and the state offer the best prospects for confronting the multiple crises.

One consequence of the crisis in liberal democratic institutions has been the rise of anti-system politics. This has been associated with a state of malaise and disaffection in many liberal democracies. Mainstream critics (like Zakaria, 1997) have identified a danger of illiberal democracy as liberal values get sacrificed in the name of nationalism. In reality, the problem could be restated as one of undemocratic economic liberalism. Some see a crisis of legitimacy and point to the growth of right-wing populism. Other challenges, of a different sort, are represented by the growth of minority nationalist movements that challenge the legitimacy of some existing nation-states.

There are many detailed proposals about how to resume economic growth after the pandemic, what to do about global warming, how to stabilize the international system and so on. They have been grouped here into three broad categories. Which will prevail, or what mix of approaches will emerge as a result of experimentation or sequencing, will be determined by the battle of ideas and interests. These rarely contend directly but find expression in the context of existing institutions.

In the battle of ideas, neoliberalism has lost ground. Ideas are partly judged on their visions of the future. Neoliberalism has little to offer but more of the same. Ideas are partly judged on their record. Neoliberalism's record is dismal. Its intellectual foundations are discredited. Powerful interests continue to support it but the concepts it was built on, such as the efficiency and superiority of the private sector when compared to the public sector, that markets know best, and that austerity is sound public policy, are unconvincing. Its ability to serve as an allegedly scientific guide to action and source of justification for policies favouring private interests is stretched, perhaps to breaking point. Neoliberal institutions are also increasingly unpopular and discredited. Globalization is under challenge from a variety of sources. Perhaps as importantly, the vulnerabilities in the apparently entrenched power of capital have been exposed as a result of the economic crises in particular. Its survival in the face of crisis and its ability to transfer blame and costs to others depends entirely on nation-states.

Returning to the broad options, the first is the 'back-to-normal' school of thought that emphasizes the need to restore fiscal sustainability, if not now, then as soon as possible. The connection between crises is hardly acknowledged, and none of the main ingredients of neoliberalism – reliance on private sector and 'for profit' solutions, unlimited growth, the need for low taxes, balanced budgets and limits on public indebtedness – are challenged. Voices for change and reform are certainly predominant in current discussions. But neoliberal spokespersons and organizations are far from silent in highlighting the need to wind down stimulus packages. They draw on austerity discourses used for decades. Their preferred way to deal with the long-term effects of the pandemic is the same as before, with minor tweaks to adjust to new circumstances. It is not impossible that this approach will prevail in the short-term. If it does, the simmering crises will continue until attention becomes focused on options and alternatives again. This would be the result of the eruption of one or other of these crises to a level requiring emergency action.

Second, liberal reformers do take matters more seriously and see the connections between the crises, or some of them. Therefore, they have outlined proposals to restore economic growth, for example, in ways that promote transition to a green economy, and simultaneously address the plight of those excluded from economic opportunities. These initiatives are described as green growth and inclusive growth, and are seen as compatible with the objectives of greater environmental sustainability and social equity. The solutions, to the extent they were implemented, could mitigate some of the effects of the crises. These ideas, or a different version of them, could feature under radical transformation too. Indeed, one could see some untidy mix of the two approaches coexisting for some time, depending on the balance of political forces.

The problems with liberal reform are that its goals are too limited in scope to have a major impact on the underlying cause of the multiple crises. Furthermore, they are too dependent on the very actors responsible for them. Liberal reformers tend to see inequality as a by-product rather than a necessary characteristic of the neoliberal growth model. There is a great reliance on new technologies and digitalization to overcome problems. Linked to investments in skills, green infrastructure and innovation, it is believed that results of inclusive growth can reduce inequality and discontent in the labour market and thus alleviate the eroding trust in liberal democratic institutions. However, there are reasons to think that this happy outcome may not occur. The adverse labour situation is built into the neoliberal growth model itself. This means that a more segmented, more unequal labour market with a continuing gap between productivity and wage levels would persist, and with it the associated problems of disaffection and alienation from the existing system.

Similarly, advocates of liberal reform fail to consider how the tensions associated with trying to rebuild the liberal international order may be counterproductive to achieving other goals. They continue to see the private sector as the main source of solutions (albeit with expanded public assistance through spending and creating 'incentives' to induce private sector investments in new technologies). By failing to recognize that the powerful interests they seek to mobilize in favour of green and inclusive growth may be part of the problem, they evade the issue of power which may have to be applied if persuasion, incentives or the prospect of imminent catastrophe does not provoke a change of course.

Radical transformation involves challenging all the components of neoliberalism – labour market flexibility and insecurity, the unequal society, austerity, a reduced and constrained state, deregulation, privatization, free trade and capital mobility. A new approach involves prioritizing security over flexibility, greater equality over inequality, public and state concerns over those of private and market actors, and national obligations to citizens over international ones to capital. More to the point, it attacks the social base of neoliberal global capitalism by focusing on bringing capital under public control. A variety of means can be contemplated, encompassing capital control measures, expanded state ownership including in the financial sector, and democratically organized economic planning.

Radical transformation emphasizes more national autonomy and fewer rules from international authorities, and more democracy to embed representation and accountability in ways that express the interests of organized society. It places a lot of trust in the power of the (admittedly imperfect) people. It assumes that on a more even political terrain provided by new institutions of representation and accountability, people collectively can control their own destinies. Under these conditions it assumes they will do so in an informed and rational way. Faced with the impact and known consequences of the multiple crises, they will gravitate to the logical conclusion that radical transformation is needed.

That transformation includes a larger and stronger state which is not as subject to the rules of international organizations and agencies, is more democratic by being based on new representational and accountability criteria that apply in new institutions, including planning bodies, and provides more influence for workers and other currently under-recognized sectors of society. The corollary is that business and capital will have less influence.

One important difficulty is that no political formation currently looks remotely capable of pushing for or bringing about a radical transformation. However, a number of pre-conditions for radical change are in place, even though no political entity has yet mobilized them effectively. The ideational and interest-based foundations of neoliberal global capitalism are damaged goods.

Specific protests abound, but large constituencies among the population await mobilization for more comprehensive purposes. The neoliberal economy is a creature of capital. The working class has a very different composition from that of 50 years ago when neoliberalism began to develop. It has experienced stagnant and sometimes declining living standards, insecurity because of employment that is precarious, and diminished social services and supports. There is a reservoir of working-class discontent on which to draw. Environmentalists are justly enraged by environmental degradation and political inaction. Racialized communities, women, youth, migrants and others experience the failures of the neoliberal strategy more harshly.

Preconditions exist that might trigger radical change, and a number of scenarios have been outlined that might set the process in motion. They include specific protests expanded into ones that represent a systemic challenge, further nation-state defections from international institutions, reconstruction of nation-states after separatist movements prevail, and an intensification of one or other of the multiple crises such that action becomes radical action and the assertion of popular sovereignty unavoidable. Others are certainly conceivable. However it happens, once the dam obstructing action to address the multiple crises bursts, a new politics is possible. With it, the path opens to escaping dystopia.

Notes

Chapter 2

1 https://www.imf.org/en/Publications/WEO/Issues/2020/09/30/world-economic-outlook-october-2020
2 https://data.undp.org/vaccine-equity/
3 For accounts using the accumulation/legitimation schema, see O'Connor (1973); Panitch (1977); and McBride (1992).
4 Subprime markets are those which are involved with making the most risky consumer loans. Borrowers tend to have the lowest credit rating scores, the least amount of credit history, excessive debt and/or a history of missing payments, defaulting on loans or declaring bankruptcy. Subprime lending markets typically involve a variety of credit types, such as mortgages, auto loans and credit cards.
5 https://www.statista.com/statistics/812053/youth-unemployment-rate-in-greece/
6 https://www.imf.org/en/Publications/WEO/Issues/2021/03/23/world-economic-outlook-april-2021
7 https://www.theguardian.com/environment/2007/nov/29/climatechange.carbonemissions
8 Most of the examples in the following paragraph are drawn from Harvey's account.
9 https://bush41library.tamu.edu/archives/public-papers/3886
10 https://1997-2001.state.gov/statements/1998/980219a.html

Chapter 3

1 An elite-level forum founded by David Rockefeller in July 1973 to foster closer cooperation between Japan, Western Europe and North America. See Sklar (1980).
2 It is important not to idealize the past in these discussions. As long ago as 1911, Robert Michels, in his classic book *Political Parties*, coined the expression the 'iron law of oligarchy' to describe trends in the social democratic parties and trade unions of his day.

[3] The exceptions are the UK and the Czech Republic.

[4] The 'European Semester' is designed to give the EU more oversight and surveillance capacity over member states' budgets through a yearly cycle of surveillance, reporting, evaluation, and recommendations aimed at policy convergence (Degryse, 2012, p 28; De La Porte and Pochet, 2014; Cacciatore et al, 2015).

[5] https://www.ecb.europa.eu/pub/pdf/infobr/ecbbren.pdf

[6] The distinction between member and nation-states is one made by Bickerton (2012) and utilized by Anderson in his own work.

Chapter 4

[1] Although Corbyn became party leader he was never accepted by the majority of Labour MPs and thus the 'dissident' label seems fair.

[2] Renamed National Rally in 2018.

[3] https://lordashcroftpolls.com/2016/06/how-the-united-kingdom-voted-and-why/

Chapter 5

[1] In general, 'golden age' imagery is questionable. The post-war settlement was always a gendered and racialized one, and the so-called Cold War period included major wars, such as that in Vietnam, and many other armed conflicts. The designation of the post-war period as 'golden' therefore must be on the basis of comparisons with what came before, and after.

[2] For an application of the impact of these multiple crises on the developing world see Rivarola Puntigliano (2020).

Chapter 6

[1] https://blog-pfm.imf.org/pfmblog/2020/04/-do-whatever-it-takes-but-keep-the-receiptsthe-public-financial-management-challenges-.html

[2] https://www.bankofengland.co.uk/independent-evaluation-office/ieo-report-january-2021/ieo-evaluation-of-the-bank-of-englands-approach-to-quantitative-easing

[3] https://www.crfb.org/blogs/updated-budget-projections-show-record-debt-2031#:~:text=New%20estimates%20from%20the%20Committee,Office's%20(CBO)%20July%20baseline

[4] The Parliamentarian is the official who advises on and interprets its rules and procedures for the United States Senate.

[5] https://www.courthousenews.com/house-approves-1-85-trillion-spending-bill-to-expand-social-programs/

Chapter 7

[1] The discussion is based on: the OECD, as a key player in ideational development (Woodward, 2008); the EU; the World Bank; and some of the bigger nation-states.

[2] Assessments of how valid this self-portrayal is can be found in McBride and Watson (2019) and Janssen (2019).

[3] In *National Post*, 2 October 2018, p A2.

[4] http://www.g7.utoronto.ca/foreign/210505-foreign-and-development-communique.html

[5] Whether this will also be true of the more draconian sanctions imposed because of the war in Ukraine remains to be seen.

[6] https://news.bloomberglaw.com/tech-and-telecom-law/banks-urge-treasury-to-ease-burden-of-complying-with-sanctions?context=article-related

[7] For estimates of private wealth see Credit Suisse (2020).

[8] https://taxfoundation.org/2021-uk-budget-tax-proposals/

Chapter 8

[1] https://cthi.taxjustice.net/en/

Chapter 9

[1] https://www.theguardian.com/us-news/2022/jan/10/bernie-sanders-democrats-failing-working-class-interview

Chapter 10

[1] https://www.statista.com/statistics/267131/market-share-of-the-leadings-exporters-of-conventional-weapons/

References

Achcar, Gilbert. 2020. 'The Great Lockdown hits the Third World hard', *Le Monde Diplomatique*, November, pp 4–6.

Ackerman, Seth. 2021. 'Biden's COVID Relief Bill is the biggest anti-poverty program in … months', *Jacobin*, 19 March. https://www.jacobinmag.com/2021/03/joe-biden-relief-bill-child-benefit-anti-poverty

ActionAid. 2020. 'The pandemic and the public sector'. https://actionaid.org/sites/default/files/publications/The%20Pandemic%20and%20the%20Public%20Sector.pdf

Adamczyk, Alicia. 2021. 'The Senate just passed the American Rescue Plan – Here's how it differs from the House version', *CNBC*, 6 March. https://www.cnbc.com/2021/03/06/how-the-senates-american-rescue-plan-differs-from-the-house.html

Aguado, Jesus and Emma Pinedo. 2020. 'Spain heads for its worst recession on record, Central Bank says', *Reuters*, 8 June. https://www.reuters.com/article/us-spain-economy-outlook-cenbank/spain-heads-for-its-worst-recession-on-record-central-bank-says-idUSKBN23F1CJ

Aiello, Rachel. 2020. '"The challenge of our lifetime": Federal deficit to hit $343 billion this year', *CTV News*, 8 July. https://www.ctvnews.ca/politics/the-challenge-of-our-lifetime-federal-deficit-to-hit-343-billion-this-year-1.5015467

Ali, Tariq. 2015. *The Extreme Centre: A Warning*, London: Verso.

Allen, Patrick. 2021. 'Introduction', in: P. Allen, S. Konzelmann and J. Toporowsky (eds), *The Return of the State: Restructuring Britain for the Common Good*, Newcastle-upon-Tyne: Agenda Publishing, pp 1–18.

Altman, Roger C. 2009. 'The Great Crash, 2008', *Foreign Affairs*, January/February. http://www.foreignaffairs.com/articles/63714/roger-c-altman/the-great-crash-2008

Americans for Tax Fairness. 2020. 'Analysis of Biden-Sanders Unity Tax Force Policy Plan Recommendations', ATF. https://americansfortaxfairness.org/issue/analysis-biden-sanders-unity-task-force-tax-policy-recommendations/

Anderson, Perry. 2021. 'Ever closer Union?', *London Review of Books*, 7 January, pp 25–34.

Arbour, Brian. 2020. 'Tiny donations, big impact: How small-dollar donations are eroding the power of party insiders', *Society*, 57: 496–506.

Arias, Maria A. and Yi Wen. 2015. 'Recovery from the Great Recession has varied around the world', Report by the Federal Reserve Bank of St Louis. https://www.stlouisfed.org/publications/regional-economist/october-2015/recovery-from-the-great-recession-has-varied-around-the-world

Arntz, Melanie, Terry Gregory and Ulrich Zierahn. 2016. 'The risk of automation for jobs in OECD countries: A comparative analysis', *OECD Social, Employment and Migration Working Papers No. 189*, OECD Publishing.

Asen, Elke. 2020. *Corporate Tax Rates Around the World, 2020.* Tax Foundation Fiscal Fact, No. 735. https://taxfoundation.org/publications/corporate-tax-rates-around-the-world/

Atkinson, Andrew. 2020a. 'UK faces biggest budget deficit in peacetime history', *Bloomberg* [online], 14 July. https://www.bloomberg.com/news/articles/2020-07-14/u-k-faces-biggest-budget-deficit-in-peacetime-history-obr-says

Atkinson, Andrew. 2020b. 'George Osborne, architect of U.K. austerity, says new cuts needed post-crisis', *Bloomberg* [online], 20 April. https://www.bloomberg.com/news/articles/2020-04-20/architect-of-u-k-austerity-says-retrenchment-needed-post-crisis

August, Martine and Alan Walks. 2018. 'Gentrification, suburban decline, and the financialization of multi-family rental housing: The case of Toronto', *Geoforum*, 89: 124–36.

Ayres, Jeffrey M. 2004. 'Framing collective action against neoliberalism: The case of the "anti-globalization" movement', *Journal of World-Systems Research*, 10(1): 11–24.

Bachman, Daniel. 2021. 'United States Economic Forecast, First Quarter 2021', Deloitte. https://www2.deloitte.com/us/en/insights/economy/us-economic-forecast/united-states-outlook-analysis.html

Balanya, Belen, Ann Doherty, Olivier Hoedemann, Adam Ma'anit and Erik Wesselius. 2000. *Europe Inc: Regional and Global Restructuring and the Rise of Corporate Power*, London: Pluto Press.

Bank, Andre, Christiane Frohlich and Andrea Schneiker. 2017. 'The political dynamics of human mobility: Migration out of, as and into violence', *Global Policy*, 8(Supplement 1, February): 12–18.

Bank of Canada. 2020. 'Our COVID-19 response: Large-scale asset purchases'. https://www.bankofcanada.ca/2020/08/our-COVID-19-response-large-scale-asset-purchases/

Bank of England. 2021. *Monetary Policy Report, May*. https://www.bankofengland.co.uk/-/media/boe/files/monetary-policy-report/2021/may/monetary-policy-report-may-2021.pdf

Barkin, Noah. 2016. 'EU globalization fears most acute in Austria and France: Study', *Reuters*, 30 November. https://www.reuters.com/article/us-europe-globalisation-survey-idUSKBN13P0C0

Barlow, Maude. 2015. 'Fighting TTIP, CETA and ISDS: Lessons from Canada', The Council of Canadians. https://www.globaljustice.org.uk/sites/default/files/files/resources/fighting-ttip-ceta-isds-lessons-from-canada-maude-barlow.pdf

Barrowclough, Diana, Thomas Marois and David A. McDonald. 2020. *Public Banks and COVID-19: Combatting the Pandemic with Public Finance*, Kingston, ON: Municipal Services Project, UNCTAD and Eurodad.

Bartlett, John. 2019. 'Chile students' mass fare-dodging expands into city-wide protest', *The Guardian*, 18 October. https://www.theguardian.com/world/2019/oct/18/chile-students-mass-fare-dodging-expands-into-city-wide-protest

Basset, Lewis. 2019. 'Corbynism: Social democracy in a new left garb', *The Political Quarterly*, 90(4): 777–84.

Batrouni, Dimitri. 2020. 'Corbynism: The Left's resurgence', in: Dimitri Batrouni (ed), *The Battle of Ideas in the Labour Party: From Attlee to Corbyn and Brexit*, Bristol: Bristol University Press, pp 119–50.

BBC. 2019. 'Violent clashes erupt as Spanish court jails Catalonia leaders', *BBC News*, 14 October. https://www.bbc.com/news/world-europe-49974289

BBC. 2021. 'In numbers: How has life changed in Afghanistan in 20 years?', BBC News, 26 November. https://www.bbc.com/news/world-asia-57767067

Beider, Harris and Kusminder Chahal. 2020. *The Other America: White Working Class Perspectives on Race, Identity and Change*, Bristol: Bristol University Press.

Bekkevold, Jo Inge, Arve Hansen, and Kristen Nordhaug. 2020. 'Introducing the Socialist Market Economy', in: Arve Hansen, Jo Inge Bekkevold and Kristen Nordhaug (eds), *The Socialist Market Economy in Asia Development in China, Vietnam and Laos*, Singapore: Palgrave Macmillan, pp 3–26.

Bell, Daniel. 1962. *The End of Ideology: On the Exhaustion of Political Ideas in the Fifties* (2nd edn), New York: Free Press.

Benn, Tony. 1989. *Against the Tide: Diaries, 1973–1976*, London: Hutchinson.

Berger, Mark T. 2004. 'After the Third World? History, destiny and the fate of Third Worldism', *Third World Quarterly*, 25(1): 9–39.

Berger, Thor and Benedikt Frey. 2016. 'Structural transformation in the OECD: Digitalization, deindustrialization and the future of work', *OECD Social, Employment and Migration Working Papers No. 193*, OECD Publishing.

Bergvall-Kareborn, Birgitta and Debra Howcroft. 2014. 'Amazon Mechanical Turk and the commodification of labour', *New Technology, Work and Employment*, 29(3): 213–23.

Berman, Sheri. 2019. 'Populism is a symptom rather than a cause: Democratic disconnect, the decline of the center-left, and the rise of populism in Western Europe', *Polity*, 51(4): 654–67.

Berman, Sheri and Maria Snegovaya. 2019. 'Populism and the decline of social democracy', *Journal of Democracy*. https://www.journalofdemocracy.org/articles/populism-and-the-decline-of-social-democracy/

Bernier, Luc, Massimo Florio and Philippe Bance (eds). 2020. *The Routledge Handbook of State-Owned Enterprises*, New York: Routledge, pp 12–68.

Bickerton, Christopher. 2012. *European Integration: From Nation-States to Member States*, Oxford: Oxford University Press.

Bieling, Hans-Jurgen. 2021. 'Austerity-induced populism: The rise and transformation of the New Right', in: Stephen McBride, Bryan M. Evans and Dieter Plehwe (eds), *The Changing Politics and Policy of Austerity*, Bristol: Policy Press, pp 213–29.

Birch, Anthony H. 2007. *The Concepts and Theories of Modern Democracy* (3rd edn), London and New York: Routledge.

Blinken, Anthony J. 2021. *A Foreign Policy for the American People*, US Department of State. https://www.state.gov/a-foreign-policy-for-the-american-people/

Blyth, M. 2013. *Austerity: The History of a Dangerous Idea*, Oxford: Oxford University Press.

Bofinger, Peter. 2021. 'The ECB Strategy Review is a missed opportunity'. https://braveneweurope.com/peter-bofinger-the-ecb-strategy-review-is-a-missed-opportunity

Bolton, Joshua. 2020. Phase 4 Letter. *Business Round Table*. https://s3.amazonaws.com/brt.org/BusinessRoundtable_Phase_IV_Letter_2020.07.21.pdf

Bonino, Stefano and Lambros G. Kaoullas. 2015. 'Preventing political violence in Britain: An evaluation of over 40 years of undercover policing of political groups involved in protest', *Studies in Conflict and Terrorism*, 38: 814–40.

Bonnefoy, Pascale. 2020. 'An end to the chapter of dictatorship: Chileans vote to draft a new constitution', *The New York Times*, 25 October. https://www.nytimes.com/2020/10/25/world/americas/chile-constitution-plebiscite.html

Boone, Laurence. 2020. 'Turning hope into reality'. The OECD. https://oecdecoscope.blog/2020/12/01/turning-hope-into-reality/

Bracking, Sarah. 2015. 'The anti-politics of climate finance: The creation and performativity of the Green Climate Fund', *Antipode*, 47(2): 281–302.

Brandt, Maricke. 2017. *Tribes and Politics in the Yemen: A History of the Houthi Conflict*, Oxford: Oxford University Press.

Brei, Michael and Alfredo Schclarek. 2013. 'Public bank lending in times of crisis', *Journal of Financial Stability*, 9(4): 820–30.

Brenner, Michael. 1969. 'Functional representation and interest group theory: Some notes on British practice', *Comparative Politics*, 2(1): 111–34.

Brenner, Reuven. 1984. 'State-owned enterprises: Practices and viewpoints', in: R. Hirschorn (ed), *Government Enterprise: Roles and Rationale*, Ottawa: Economic Council of Canada, pp 12–68.

Brexit Party. 2019. *Contract with the People*. The Brexit Party. https://www.thebrexitparty.org/wp-content/uploads/2019/11/Contract-With-The-People.pdf

Brown, Alleen. 2021. 'Bipartisan Infrastructure Bill includes $25 billion in potential new subsidies for fossil fuels', *The Intercept*, 3 August. https://theintercept.com/2021/08/03/bipartisan-infrastructure-bill-climate-subsidies-fossil-fuel/

Brown, Ellen. 2013. *The Public Bank Solution: From Austerity to Prosperity*, Baton Rouge: Third Millennium Press.

Bruff, Ian. 2014. 'The rise of authoritarian neoliberalism', *Rethinking Marxism*, 26(1): 113–29.

Burgen, Stephen. 2021. 'EU Parliament strips Carles Puigdemont and two other Catalans of immunity', *The Guardian*, 9 March. https://www.theguardian.com/world/2021/mar/09/eu-parliament-strips-carles-puigdemont-and-two-other-catalans-of-immunity

Burnham, Peter. 1999. 'The politics of economic management in the 1990s', *New Political Economy*, 4(1): 37–54.

Burtenshaw, Ronan. 2020. 'There is finally an alternative in Ireland', *Jacobin*, 14 February. www.jacobinmag.com/2020/02/irish-election-sinn-fein-fianna-fail-fine-gael

Business Roundtable. 2020. 'CEO Economic Outlook Index', Business Roundtable. https://www.businessroundtable.org/media/ceo-economic-outlook-index

Butcher, Jim. 2019. 'Brexit: Working class revolt or middle class outlook?'. https://archive.discoversociety.org/2019/07/03/brexit-working-class-revolt-or-middle-class-outlook/

Byrne, Liam. 2019. 'How Jeremy Corbyn brought Labour back to the future: Visions of the future and concrete utopia in Labour's 2017 electoral campaign', *British Politics*, 14: 250–68.

Caballero, Ricardo. 2012. 'Notes on capital-account management', in: Oliver Blanchard, David Romer, Michael Spence and Joseph Stiglitz (eds), *In the Wake of the Crisis: Leading Economists Reassess Economic Policy*, Cambridge, MA: MIT Press, pp 129–32.

Cacciatore, Federica, Alessandro Natalini and Claudius Wagemann. 2015. 'Clustered Europeanization and national reform programmes: a qualitative comparative analysis', *Journal of European Public Policy*, 22(8): 1186–211.

Cann, Vicky. 2021. 'Business lobbies offered privileged access to secretive EU Council group', *Social Europe*, 15 July.

Care International. 2021. 'Developed nations hugely exaggerate climate adaptation finance for Global South'. https://www. care-international.org/news/press-releases/developed-nations-hugely-exaggerate-climate-adaptation-finance-for-global-south

Carney, Mark. 2021. *Values: Building a Better World for All*, Toronto: Signal.

Carroll, William. 2004. *Corporate Power in a Globalizing World*, Toronto: Oxford University Press.

Carter, Angela V. 2020. 'Canadian ecological political economy', in: Heather Whiteside (ed), *Canadian Political Economy*, Toronto: University of Toronto Press, pp 103–20.

Casciani, Dominic. 2018. 'Metropolitan Police admits role in blacklisting construction workers', BBC, 23 March. https://www. bbc.com/news/uk-43507728

Castanho Silva, Bruno, Federico Vegetti and Levente Littvay. 2017. 'The elite is up to something: Exploring the relation between populism and belief in conspiracy theories', *Swiss Political Science Review*, 23(4): 423–43.

Castells, Manuel. 2019. *Rupture: The Crisis of Liberal Democracy*, Cambridge: Polity Press.

Chan, Szu Ping. 2020. 'Coronavirus: UK faces "explosive" debt levels', BBC News [online], 14 July. https://www.bbc.com/news/business-53402176

Chang, Ha-Joon. 2020. 'Building pro-development multilateralism: towards a "New" New International Economic Order', *CEPAL Review*, 132. https://repositorio.cepal.org/bitstream/handle/11362/46928/1/RVI132_Chang.pdf

Chomsky, Noam. 1999. *Profit over People: Neoliberalism and Global Order*, New York: Seven Stories Press.

Chrisafis, Angelique. 2017. 'Marine Le Pen rails against rampant globalisation after election success', *The Guardian*. https://www. theguardian.com/world/2017/apr/24/marine-le-pen-rails-against-rampant-globalisation-after-election-success

Christophers, Brett. 2021. 'Mind the rent gap: Blackstone, housing investment and the reordering of urban rent surfaces', *Urban Studies*: 004209802110264.

Clark, Dave. 2016. *The Global Financial Crisis and Austerity*, Bristol: Policy Press.

Clark, John D. and Nuno S. Thermudo. 2006. 'Linking the web and the street: Internet-based "dotcauses" and the "anti-globalization" movement', *World Development*, 34(1): 50–74.

Clarkson, Stephen. 1993. 'Constitutionalizing the Canadian–American relationship', in: D. Cameron and M. Watkins (eds), *Canada under Free Trade*, Toronto: Lorimer, pp 3–20.

Clémençon, Raymond. 2016. 'The two sides of the Paris Climate Agreement: Dismal failure or historic breakthrough?', *Journal of Environment and Development*, 25(1): 3–24.

Clift, Ben. 2014. *Comparative Political Economy: States, Markets and Global Capitalism*, London: Palgrave Macmillan.

Cobham, Alex. 2021. 'Is today a turning point against corporate tax abuse?', *Tax Justice Network*, 4 June. https://taxjustice.net/2021/06/04/is-today-a-turning-point-against-corporate-tax-abuse/

Cockburn, Andrew. 2021. *The Spoils of War: Power, Profit and the American War Machine*, London: Verso.

Committee for a Responsible Federal Budget. 2021. *President Biden's Full FY 2022 Budget*, 28 May. https://www.crfb.org/papers/president-bidens-full-fy-2022-budget

Committee on Migration, Refugees and Displaced Persons. 2016. *Violence against Migrants*, Council of Europe, Parliamentary Assembly. https://www.refworld.org/pdfid/5836fc7c4.pdf

Conway, Janet M. 2016. 'Anti-globalization movements', in: Nancy A. Naples (ed), *The Wiley Blackwell Encyclopedia of Gender and Sexuality Studies*, Chichester: John Wiley and Sons Ltd.

Cop, Burak and Ahmet Erturk. 2021. 'The rise and fall of Corbynism', *Journal of Social Sciences*, 2(2): 287–307.

Corporate Europe Observatory. 2021. *Conquering EU Courts? Big Business Lobbies in Secret for New Legal Privileges in the EU*. https://corporateeurope.org/sites/default/files/2021-06/Conquering%20EU%20courts.pdf

Correa, Daniel. 2021. 'Chile's Constitutional Convention: The ascent of the anti-establishment left and the death of the moderate centre', *The Dialogue*, 3 June. https://www.thedialogue.org/blogs/2021/06/chiles-constitutional-convention-the-ascent-of-the-anti-establishment-left-and-the-death-of-the-moderate-center/

Council on Foreign Relations. 2021. 'The state of US infrastructure', Council on Foreign Relations, https://www.cfr.org/backgrounder/state-us-infrastructure

Coyne, Andrew. 2020. 'There's less to this snapshot than meets the eye', *The Globe and Mail* [online], 9 July. https://www.theglobeandmail.com/opinion/article-theres-less-to-this-snapshot-than-meets-the-eye/

Credit Suisse. 2020. *Global Wealth Report 2020*, Credit Suisse Research Institute.

Cross, Philip. 2020. 'A modest proposal on public service pay to help tackle the ballooning deficit', *Financial Post* [online], 9 April. https://financialpost.com/opinion/philip-cross-a-modest-proposal-on-public-service-pay-to-help-tackle-the-ballooning-deficit

Crotty, James. 2000. 'The case for capital controls', *Political Economy Research Institute*. https://peri.umass.edu/fileadmin/pdf/published_study/PS8.pdf

Crotty, James and Gerald Epstein. 1996. 'In defence of capital controls', *The Socialist Register*, 32: pp 118–49.

Crouch, Colin. 2009. 'Privatised Keynesianism: An unacknowledged policy regime', *British Journal of Politics & International Relations*, 11(3): 382–99.

Crouch, Colin. 2020. *Post-Democracy After the Crisis*, Cambridge: Polity Press.

Crozier, Michel, Samuel Huntington and Joji Watanuki. 1975. *The Crisis of Democracy: Report on the Governability of Democracies to the Trilateral Commission*, New York: New York University Press.

Cumbers, Andrew and Robert McMaster. 2012. 'Revisiting public ownership: Knowledge, democracy and participation in economic decision making', *Review of Radical Political Economies*, 44(3): 358–73.

Daly, Herman. 1996. *Beyond Growth: The Economics of Sustainable Development*, Boston: Beacon Press.

Davis, Mike. 2020. *The Monster Enters: COVID 19, Avian Flu, and the Plagues of Capitalism*, New York and London: OR Books.

Degryse, Christophe. 2012. 'The new European economic governance', ETUI Working Paper 2012.14. https://ssrn.com/abstract=2202702 or http://dx.doi.org/10.2139/ssrn.2202702

De La Porte, Caroline and Philippe Pochet. 2014. 'Boundaries of welfare between the EU and Member States during the "Great Recession"', *Perspectives on European Politics and Society*, 15(3): 281–92.

De Miranda, Alvaro. 2020. 'Class and nation in the age of populism: The forward march of labour restarted?', *Soundings: A Journal of Politics and Culture*, 75: 124–43.

Devine, Pat. J. 1988. *Democracy and Economic Planning: The Political Economy of a Self-Governing Society*, Cambridge: Polity Press.

Dewan, Angela. 2017. 'Catalonia independence referendum: What just happened?', CNN. https://www.cnn.com/2017/10/02/europe/catalonia-independence-referendum-explainer

Dewilde, Caroline. 2018. 'Explaining the Declined affordability of housing for low-income private renters across Western Europe', *Urban Studies*, 55(12): 2618–39.

Di Muzio, Tim. 2015a. 'The plutonomy of the 1%: dominant ownership and conspicuous consumption in the New Gilded Age', *Millennium: Journal of International Studies*, 43(2): 492–510.

Di Muzio, Tim. 2015b. *Carbon Capitalism: Energy, Social Reproduction and World Order*, London: Rowman & Littlefield.

Di Muzio, Tim and Richard H. Robbins. 2016. *Debt as Power*, New York: Bloomsbury.

Dincer, Nergiz and Barry Eichengreen. 2014. 'Central bank transparency and independence: updates and new measures', *International Journal of Central Banking*, 34, March: 189–253.

Dodge, David and Michael Horgan. 2021. 'With a budget pending do fiscal anchors still matter?', *Globe and Mail*, 25 February, p B.6.

Doern, Bruce and Brian Tomlin. 1991. *Faith and Fear: The Free Trade Story*, Toronto: Stoddart.

Dolan, Michael. 2020. 'Ireland: regression or revolution?', *Cherwell*, 16 February. https://cherwell.org/2020/02/16/ireland-regression-or-revolution/

Doling, John and Richard Ronald. 2010. 'Home ownership and asset-based welfare', *Journal of Housing and the Built Environment*, 25(2): 165–73.

Drache, Daniel. n.d. 'The short but amazingly significant life of the International Trade Organization (ITO) free trade and full employment: Friends or foes forever?', Toronto: Robarts Centre for Canadian Studies, York University.

Drache, Daniel, A.T. Kingsmith and Duan Qi. 2019. *One Road, Many Dreams*, London: Bloomsbury Press.

Durand, Cédric and Razmig Keucheyan. 2019. 'Economic planning is back'. https://www.opendemocracy.net/en/oureconomy/economic-planning-back/

Dyke, James, Robert Watson and Wolfgang Knorr. 2021. 'Climate scientists: concept of net zero is a dangerous trap', *The Conversation*, 22 April.

Economist Intelligence Unit. 2021. *How the Pandemic Changed the Global Economy: What Next for Economics and Politics in a World of High Debt and Low Growth*, The Economist Intelligence Unit. https://www.eiu.com/n/campaigns/how-the-pandemic-changed-the-global-economy/

Editorial. 2020. 'The Guardian view on austerity: a grotesque failure that must not be revived', *The Guardian*, 22 July. https://www.theguardian.com/commentisfree/2020/jul/22/the-guardian-view-on-austerity-a-grotesque-failure-that-must-not-be-revived

Editorial Board. 2020. 'The death of austerity should not be mourned', *Financial Times*, 16 October. https://www.ft.com/content/2f4ef5ab-e07b-4666-8367-e8750817a97e

Eidlin, Barry. 2021. 'To pass the PRO Act, we need to examine past labour law reform failures', *Jacobin*, 24 June. https://www.jacobinmag.com/2021/06/pro-act-collective-bargaining-labor-law-legislation

Elliot, Larry. 2020. 'Spend what you can to fight COVID-19, IMF tells member states', *The Guardian*. https://www.theguardian.com/business/2020/apr/15/spend-what-you-can-to-fight-covid-19-imf-tells-member-states

Ember, Sydney and Thomas Kaplan. 2020. 'Joe Biden and Bernie Sanders deepen their cooperation', *The New York Times*, 8 July. https://www.nytimes.com/2020/07/08/us/politics/biden-bernie-sanders.html

Engelhardt, Tom. 2014. *Shadow Government: Surveillance, Secret Wars, and a Global Security State in a Single-Superpower World*, Chicago, IL: Haymarket Books.

Engels, Friedrich. 1969 [1884]. 'Origins of the family, private property and the state', in: *Marx Engels Selected Works, First Edition*, London: Lawrence and Wishart, pp 461–583. https://www.marxists.org/archive/marx/works/sw/progress-publishers/sw.pdf

Epstein, Gerald. 2005. *Capital Flight and Capital Controls in Developing Countries*, Northampton, MA: Edward Elgar.

Epstein, Gerald. 2009. 'The Case of Capital Controls Revisited', in: Jonathan P. Goldstein and Michael G. Hillard (eds), *Heterodox Macroeconomics: Keynes, Marx and Globalization*, New York: Routledge Advances in Heterodox Economics.

Epstein, Gerald. 2012. 'Capital outflow regulation: Economic management, development and transformation', in: *Regulating Global Capital Flows for Long-Run Development*, Pardee Centre Task Force Report, Boston, MA: Boston University.

ESRI (Economic and Social Research Institute). 2020. 'Irish economy faces largest recession in history as lockdown takes it toll', 28 May. https://www.esri.ie/news/irish-economy-faces-largest-recession-in-history-as-lockdown-takes-its-toll

European Commission. 2016a. 'EU Economic Governance. European Commission'. http://ec.europa.eu/economy_finance/economic_governance/index_en.htm

European Commission. 2019. *A European Green Deal*. https://ec.europa.eu/info/strategy/priorities-2019-2024/european-green-deal_en

European Commission. 2020a. *Questions and Answers: Commission Proposes Activating Fiscal Framework's General Escape Clause to Respond to Coronavirus Pandemic*, European Commission. https://ec.europa.eu/commission/presscorner/detail/en/qanda_20_500

European Commission. 2020b. *Questions and Answers on EU Budget for Recovery: Recovery and Resilience Facility*, European Commission. https://ec.europa.eu/commission/presscorner/detail/en/QANDA_20_949

Evans, Bryan. 2014. 'Social democracy in the new age of austerity', in: Donna Baines and Stephen McBride (eds), *Orchestrating Austerity: Impacts and Resistance*, Halifax: Fernwood Publishing, pp 79–90.

Evans, Bryan, Stephen McBride and James Watson. 2021. 'Negotiating Austerity? A Comparative Survey of Social Concertation in Canada, Denmark, Ireland and Spain', in: Stephen McBride, Bryan Evans and Dieter Plehwe (eds), *The Politics and Policy of Austerity*, Bristol: Bristol University Press, pp 176–94.

Evans, Rob. 2018. 'Police spies infiltrated UK leftwing groups for decades', *The Guardian*, 15 October. https://www.theguardian.com/uk-news/2018/oct/15/undercover-police-spies-infiltrated-uk-leftwing-groups-for-decades

Evans, Simon et al. 2021. 'COP26: Key Outcomes Agreed at the UN Climate Talks in Glasgow', *Carbon Brief*, 17 November. https://www.carbonbrief.org/cop26-key-outcomes-agreed-at-the-un-climate-talks-in-glasgow

Everett, Simon J. 2019. 'Protectionism, state discrimination, and international business since the onset of the Global Financial Crisis', *Journal of International Business Policy*, 2(1): 9–36.

Ewall-Wice, Sarah. 2021a. 'Biden's American Jobs Plan and American Families Plan: What's in them and where the funding will come from', *CBC News*, 1 May. https://www.cbsnews.com/news/biden-american-jobs-families-plans/

Ewall-Wice, Sarah. 2021b. 'How taxes for the wealthy and big corporations would change under the new social spending plan', *CBC News*, 29 October. https://www.cbsnews.com/news/build-back-better-tax-changes-wealthy-big-corporations/

Fabbrini, Federico. 2013. 'The Fiscal Compact, The Golden Rule and the paradox of European federalism', *Boston College International and Comparative Law Review*, 36(1): 1–38.

Fanelli, Carlo and Heather Whiteside. 2020. 'COVID-19, Capitalism and Contagion', *Alternate Routes: A Journal of Critical Social Research*, 30(1): 6–27.

Farnsworth, Kevin and Zoe Irving. 2015. 'Austerity: More than the sum of its parts', in: Kevin Farnsworth and Zoe Irving (eds), *Social Policy in Times of Austerity: Global Economic Crisis and the New Politics of Welfare*, Bristol: Policy Press, pp 9–42.

Faroohar, Rana. 2016. *Makers and Takers: The Rise of Finance and the Fall of American Business*, New York: Crown.

Faulhaber, Lilian V. 2018. 'The trouble with tax competition: From practice to theory', *Tax Law Review*, 71(2): 311–66.

Featherstone, David and Lazoros Karaliotas. 2016. 'Scotland and alternatives to neoliberalism: roundtable discussion with Neil Davidson, Satnam Virdee, Jenny Morrison and Gerry Mooney', *Soundings: A Journal of Politics and Culture*, 63: 55–72.

Financial Times. 2019. 'Labour needs to break the grip of the hard left'. https://www.ft.com/content/168f5814-1dc6-11ea-9186-7348c2f183af

Finn, Daniel. 2020. 'Ireland's left turn', *Jacobin*, 13 February. www.jacobinmag.com/2020/02/ireland-election-results-sinn-fein

Florio, Massimo, Matteo Ferraris and Daniela Vandome. 2018. 'Motives of mergers and acquisitions by state-owned enterprises: A taxonomy and international evidence', *International Journal of Public Sector Management*, 31(2): 142–66.

Foley, James and Pete Ramand. 2018. 'In fear of populism: Referendums and neoliberal democracy', *Socialist Register*, 54: 74–98.

Forbes, Kristin, Marcel Fratzscher, Thomas Kostka and Roland Straub. 2016. 'Bubble thy neighbour: Portfolio effects and externalities from capital controls', *Journal of International Economics*, 99(C): 85–104.

Fraser, Nancy. 2017. 'From progressive neoliberalism to Trump – and beyond', *American Affairs*, 1(4): 46–64.

Fukuyama, Francis. 1992. *The End of History and the Last Man*, Toronto: Free Press.

Fung, Crystal, Sahil Parikh and Piotr Zulauf. n.d. 'The Crisis of Affordable Rental Housing in Toronto': 22.

Funk, Robert. 2021. 'The Chilean Constituent Assembly: The identity experiment', *Global Americans*, 21 July. https://theglobalamericans.org/2021/07/the-chilean-constituent-assembly-the-identity-experiment/

G7 UK. 2021. G7 *Finance Ministers Agree Historic Global Tax Agreement*, Summit Communiqué. 5 June. https://www.g7uk.org/g7-finance-ministers-agree-historic-global-tax-agreement/

Galgoczi, Béla. 2021. 'Is Europe fit for the "Fit for 55" package?', *Social Europe*, 19 July.

Gallagher, Kevin P. 2012. 'Regaining control? Capital controls and the GFC', in: Wyn Grant and Graham K. Wilson (eds), *The Consequences of the Global Financial Crisis: The Rhetoric of Reform and Regulation*, Oxford: Oxford University Press, pp 109–38.

Gallagher, Kevin P. 2015. *Ruling Capital: Emerging Markets and the Reregulation of Cross-Border Finance*, London: Cornell University Press.

Gallagher, Kevin P., Stephany Griffith-Jones and Jose A. Ocampo. 2012. 'Capital account regulations for stability and development: A new approach', in: *Regulating Global Capital Flows for Long-Run Development*, Pardee Centre Task Force Report, Boston, MA: Boston University.

Garside, Juliette and Rupert Neate. 2020. 'UK government "using pandemic to transfer NHS duties to private sector"', *The Guardian* [online], 4 May. https://www.theguardian.com/business/2020/may/04/uk-government-using-crisis-to-transfer-nhs-duties-to-private-sector

Gates, Bill. 2021. *How to Avoid a Climate Disaster: The Solutions We Have and the Breakthroughs We Need*, Toronto: Knopf Canada.

Gathi, James Thuo. 2009. 'War's legacy in international investment law', *International Community Law Review*, 11: 353–86.

Gebremariam, Fesseha Mulu. 2017. 'NIEO: Origin, elements and criticisms', *International Journal of Multicultural and Multi-religious Understanding*, 4(3): 22–8.

Georgieva, Kristalina. 2020. 'The Long Ascent: Overcoming the crisis and building a more resilient economy', The IMF. https://www.imf.org/en/News/Articles/2020/10/06/sp100620-the-long-ascent-overcoming-the-crisis-and-building-a-more-resilient-economy

Germain, Randall. 1997. *The International Organization of Credit*, Cambridge: Cambridge University Press.

Germain, Randall. 2019. 'E.H. Carr and IPE: An essay in retrieval', *International Studies Quarterly*, 63: 952–62.

Gilbert, Jeremy. 2021. 'Why wouldn't they be reconciled? Corbyn's leadership and the recalcitrance of the Parliamentary Labour Party', *The Political Quarterly*, 92(2): 172–5.

Gilens, Martin and Benjamin Page. 2014. 'Testing theories of American politics: Elites, interest groups, and average citizens', *Perspectives on Politics*, 12: 564–81.

Giles, Chris. 2021. 'OECD warns governments to rethink constraints on public spending', *The Financial Times*. https://www.ft.com/content/7c721361-37a4-4a44-9117-6043afee0f6b

Gill, Stephen and A. Claire Cutler (eds). 2014. *New Constitutionalism and World Order*, Cambridge: Cambridge University Press, pp 1–23.

Gillingham, John R. 2016. *The EU: An Obituary*, UK: Verso Books.

Gilman, Nils. 2015. 'The New International Economic Order: A reintroduction', *Humanity*, 6(1): 1–16.

Gjerso, Jonas Fossili. 2017. 'Jeremy Corbyn – a mainstream [Scandinavian] Social Democrat', *Open Democracy*. https://www.opendemocracy.net/en/can-europe-make-it/jeremy-corbyn-mainstream-scandinavian-social-democrat/

Globe and Mail. 2020. 'Austerity wasn't the right path before the pandemic, and it can't be the road chosen after it', *Globe and Mail*, 24 July. https://www.theglobeandmail.com/opinion/editorials/article-austerity-wasnt-the-right-path-before-the-pandemic-and-it-cant-be/

Goodwin, Matthew. 2014. 'Explaining the rise of the UK Independence Party', Heinrich Böll Stiftung, European Union. https://eu.boell.org/sites/default/files/uploads/2014/06/ukip_eu.pdf

Gordon, Ruth. 2009. 'The dawn of a New International Economic Order?', *Law and Contemporary Problems*, 72: 131–62.

Gough, Ian. 2011. 'From Financial Crisis to Fiscal Crisis', in: Kevin Farnsworth and Zoe Irving (eds), *Social Policy in Challenging Times: Economic Crisis*, Bristol: Policy Press, pp 49–64.

Gourevitch, Peter. 1986. *Politics in Hard Times: Comparative Responses to International Economic Crises*, Ithaca, NY: Cornell University Press.

Grabel, Ilene. 2006. 'A post-Keynesian analysis of financial crisis in the developing world and directions for reform', in: Philip Arestis and Malcolm Sawyer (eds), *A Handbook of Alternative Monetary Economics*, Cheltenham: Edward Elgar, pp 403–19.

Grabel, Ilene. 2010. *Not Your Grandfather's IMF: Global Crisis, Productive Incoherence, and Developmental Policy Space*, Political Economy Research Institute Working Paper 214.

Graz, Jean-Christoph. 2000. 'The future of Seattle and back', *Studies in Political Economy*, 62(1): 17–24.

Greven, T. (2016) 'The rise of right-wing populism in Europe and the United States: A comparative perspective', *Friedrich Ebert Stiftung*. Available at: https://library.fes.de/pdf-files/id/12892.pdf

Gruber, Lloyd. 2000. *Ruling the World: Power Politics and the Rise of Supranational Institutions*, Princeton: Princeton University Press.

Grunwald, Michael. 2021. 'The green schism threatening Biden's climate plan', *Politico*, 13 April. https://www.politico.com/news/2021/05/13/green-schism-biden-climate-plan-488037

Guarav, Kunal. 2021. 'Internet shut off during G7 Session as leaders debate over China', *Hindustan Times*, 12 June. https://www.hindustantimes.com/world-news/internet-shut-off-during-g7-session-as-leaders-debate-over-china-report-101623515886002.html

Guardian. 2020. 'The Guardian view on COVID-19 economics: The austerity con of deficit hysteria', *The Guardian* [online], 14 July. https://www.theguardian.com/commentisfree/2020/jul/14/the-guardian-view-on-covid-19-economics-the-austerity-con-of-deficit-hysteria

Guy, Jack. 2019. 'Spain's far-right is back – with a difference', CNN. https://www.cnn.com/2019/04/26/europe/vox-far-right-spain-intl

Hacker, Jacob S. and Paul Pierson. 2010. *Winner-Take-All Politics: How Washington Made the Rich Richer – And Turned its Back on the Middle Class*, Toronto: Simon & Schuster.

Hafez, Farid, Reinhard Heinisch and Eric Milkin. 2019. 'The new right: Austria's Freedom Party and changing perceptions of Islam', Brookings. https://www.brookings.edu/research/the-new-right-austrias-freedom-party-and-changing-perceptions-of-islam/

Hajer, Jesse and Lynne Fernandez. 2020. 'Austerity and COVID-19: Manitoba Government creating, not solving, problems', *CBC News* [online], 21 April. https://www.cbc.ca/news/canada/manitoba/manitoba-government-economy-COVID-19-1.5539666

Hall, Peter A. 1993. 'Policy paradigms, social learning, and the state: The case of economic policymaking in Britain', *Comparative Politics*, 25(3): 275–96.

Haririan, Mehdi. 2019. *State-owned Enterprises in a Mixed Economy: Micro versus Macro Economic Objectives*, New York: Routledge.

Harper, Stephen. 2020. 'After coronavirus, government will have to shrink', *Wall Street Journal* [online], 12 May. https://www.wsj.com/articles/after-coronavirus-government-will-have-to-shrink-11589302337

Harrabin, Roger. 2021. 'John Kerry: US climate envoy criticised for optimism on clean tech'. https://www.bbc.com/news/science-environment-57135506

Harvey, David. 2001. *Spaces of Capital: Toward a Critical Geography*, New York: Routledge.

Harvey, David. 2003. *The New Imperialism*, New York: Oxford University Press.

Harvey, David. 2014. *Seventeen Contradictions and the End of Capitalism*, Oxford: Oxford University Press.

Harvey, Fionna and Jennifer Rankin. 2020. 'What is the European Green Deal and will it really cost €1tn?'. https://www.theguardian.com/world/2020/mar/09/what-is-the-european-green-deal-and-will-it-really-cost-1tn

Hawes, Emily and Sean Grisdale. 2020. 'Housing crisis in a Canadian global city: Financialisation, buy-to-let investors and short-term rentals in Toronto's rental market', in: Susannah Bunce et al (eds), *Critical Dialogues of Urban Governance, Development and Activism*, London and Toronto: UCL Press, pp 158–74.

Hay, Colin. 1999. *The Political Economy of New Labour*, Manchester: Manchester University Press.

Hay, Colin. 2007. *Why We Hate Politics*, Cambridge: Polity.

Hedgecoe, Guy. 2019. 'Spanish elections: How the far-right Vox party found its footing', BBC. https://www.bbc.com/news/world-europe-46422036

Heideman, Paul and Hadas Thier. 2020. 'Bernie's campaign strategy wasn't the problem', *Jacobin*, 20 April. https://jacobinmag.com/2020/04/bernie-sanders-campaign-strategy-democratic-party-biden-trump

Helleiner, Eric. 1994. *States and the Re-emergence of Global Finance*, Ithaca, NY: Cornell University Press.

Helleiner, Eric. 2005. 'Regulating capital flight', in: Gerald Epstein (ed), *Capital Flight and Capital Controls in Developing Countries*, Northampton, MA: Edward Elgar.

Helleiner, Eric and Stefano Pagliari. 2011. 'The end of an era in international financial regulation? A post-crisis research agenda', *International Organization*, 65(1): 169–200.

Helm, Toby and Alex Hacillo. 2017. 'Secret tape reveals Momentum plot to seize control of Labour', *The Guardian*. https://www.theguardian.com/politics/2017/mar/18/secret-tape-reveals-momentum-plot-to-link-with-unite-seize-control-of-labour

Henry, Peter B. 2007. 'Capital account liberalization: Theory, evidence, and speculation', *Journal of Economic Literature*, 45: 887–935.

Hermann, Cristoph and Birgit Mahnkopf. 2010. 'Still a future for the European Social Model?', *Global Labor Journal*, 1(3): 314–30.

Heyes, Jason and Paul Lewis. 2014. 'Employment protection under fire: Labour market deregulation and employment in the European Union', *Economic and Industrial Democracy*, 35(4): 587–607.

Hilferding, Rudolf. 1910. *Finance Capital: A Study of the Latest Phase of Capitalist Development*, (ed) Tom Bottomore, London: Routledge & Kegan Paul.

Hirst, Paul Q. and Grahame Thompson. 1996. *Globalization in Question: The International Economy and the Possibilities of Governance*, Cambridge: Polity Press.

HM Treasury. 2021. *Budget 2021: Protecting the Jobs and Livelihoods of the British People*, HM Treasury. https://www.gov.uk/government/publications/budget-2021-documents

Hobsbawm, Eric. 1995. *Age of Extremes: The Short Twentieth Century, 1914–1991*, London: Abacus.

Hope, David and Julian Limberg. 2020. *The Economic Consequences of Major Tax Cuts for the Rich*, Working Paper 55: London School of Economics, International Inequalities Institute. https://eprints.lse.ac.uk/107919/1/Hope_economic_consequences_of_major_tax_cuts_published.pdf

Hopkin, Jonathan. 2020. *Anti-System Politics: The Crisis of Market Liberalism in Rich Democracies*, Oxford: Oxford University Press.

Horner, Rory, Daniel Haberly, Seth Schindler and Yuko Aoyama. 2018. 'How anti-globalization switched from a left to a right-wing issue – and where it will go next', *The Conversation*, 25 January. https://theconversation.com/how-anti-globalisation-switched-from-a-left-to-a-right-wing-issue-and-where-it-will-go-next-90587

Horsley, Thomas. 2018. *The Court of Justice of the European Union as an Institutional Actor: Judicial Lawmaking and Its Limits*, Cambridge: Cambridge University Press.

Hou, Yilin and Douglas Smith. 2009. 'Informal norms as a bridge between formal rules and outcomes of government financial operations: Evidence from state balanced budget requirements', *Journal Public Administration Research and Theory*, 20(3): 655–78.

Hsiao, Kung Chuan 1927. *Political Pluralism: A Study of Contemporary Political Theory*, London: Routledge.

IER. 2020. 'The Bill that gives M15 carte blanche to spy on trade unions', Institute of Employment Rights. https://www.ier.org. uk/comments/the-bill-that-will-give-mi5-carte-blanche-to-spy-on-trade-unions/

Ikenberry, John. 2011. *Liberal Leviathan: The Origins, Crisis, and Transformation of the American World Order*, Princeton, NJ: Princeton University Press.

ILO. 2021. *ILO Monitor: COVID-19 and the World of Work. 8th edition*, International Labour Organization. https://www. ilo.org/wcmsp5/groups/public/---dgreports/---dcomm/ documents/briefingnote/wcms_824092.pdf

ILO/OECD. 2015. *The Labour Share in G20 Economies*. Report prepared for the G20 Employment Working Group Antalya, Turkey, 26–27 February 2015.

IMF. 2019. 'People's Republic of China: 2019 Article IV Consultation-Press Release; Staff Report; Staff Statement and Statement by the Executive Director for China', 25 November. https://www.imf.org/en/Publications/CR/Issues/2019/08/08/ Peoples-Republic-of-China-2019-Article-IV-Consultation-Press-Release-Staff-Report-Staff-48576

IMF. 2020a. 'The Great Lockdown: Worst economic downturn since the Great Depression', IMF. https://www.imf.org/en/ News/Articles/2020/03/23/pr2098-imf-managing-director-statement-following-a-g20-ministerial-call-on-the-coronavirus-emergency

IMF. 2020b. 'Post-COVID-19 recovery and resilience', IMF. https:// meetings.imf.org/en/2020/Annual/Schedule/2020/10/13/imf-seminar-post-COVID-19-recovery-and-reslience

IOM (International Organization for Migration). 2020. *World Migration Report 2020*, Geneva: IOM. https://publications.iom. int/system/files/pdf/wmr_2020.pdf

IOM. 2021. 'Internal Displacement'. International Organization for Migration. https://www.iom.int/internaldisplacement

IPCC (Intergovernmental Panel on Climate Change). 2018. 'Global warming of 1.5°C', The Intergovernmental Panel on Climate Change. https://www.ipcc.ch/sr15/

IPCC. 2021. 'Climate change widespread, rapid, and intensifying', The Intergovernmental Panel on Climate Change, 18 November. https://www.ipcc.ch/2021/08/09/ar6-wg1-20210809-pr/

IPSOS. 2019. *Populist and Nativist Sentiment in 2019: A 27-Country Survey.* www.ipsos.com

Irani, Lilly. 2015. 'Difference and dependence among digital workers: the case of Amazon Mechanical Turk', *South Atlantic Quarterly*, 114(1): 225–34.

Jackson, Tim. 2009. *Prosperity without Growth: Economics for a Finite Planet*, London: Earthscan.

Jackson, Tim and Peter A. Victor. 2011. 'Productivity and work in the "green economy": Some theoretical reflections and empirical tests', *Environmental Innovations and Social Transitions*, 1(1): 101–8.

Janssen, Ronald. 2019. 'The revised OECD Jobs Strategy and labour market flexibility: a double handed narrative', *Transfer: European Review of Labour and Research*, 25(2): 221–7.

Jones, Campbell. 2020. 'Introduction: The return of economic planning', *South Atlantic Quarterly*, 119(1), January.

Jones, Sam. 2017. 'Spain crisis: "stop this radicalism and disobedience", PM tells Catalan leaders', *The Guardian*. https://www.theguardian.com/world/2017/sep/20/spain-guardia-civil-raid-catalan-government-hq-referendum-row

Justice for Immigrants. 2017. 'Root causes of migration'. https://justiceforimmigrants.org/what-we-are-working-on/immigration/root-causes-of-migration/

Kahler, Miles and David A. Lake. 2013. *Politics in the New Hard Times: The Great Recession in Comparative Perspective*, Ithaca and London: Cornell University Press.

Karwowski, Ewa. 2019. 'Towards (de)financialization: The role of the State', *Cambridge Journal of Economics*, 43(4): 1001–27.

Karwowski, Ewa, Mimoza Shabani and Engelbert Stockhammer. 2020. 'Dimensions and determinants of financialisation: Comparing OECD countries since 1997', *New Political Economy*, 25(6): 957–77.

Kelton, Stephanie. 2020. *The Deficit Myth: Modern Monetary Theory and the Birth of the People's Economy*, New York: Public Affairs.

Kempf, Hervé. 2007. *How the Rich are Destroying the Earth*, Vermont: Chelsea Green Publishing Company.

Kenner, Dario. 2019. *Carbon Inequality: The Role of the Richest in Climate Change*, London: Routledge.

Klein, Matthew C. and Michael Pettis. 2020. *Trade Wars are Class Wars: How Rising Inequality Distorts the Global Economy and Threatens International Peace*, New Haven, CT: Yale University Press.

Klein, Seth. 2020. *A Good War: Mobilizing Canada for the Climate Emergency*, Toronto: ECW Press.

Koch, Max. 2011. *Capitalism and Climate Change: Theoretical Discussion, Historical Development and Policy Responses*, London: Palgrave Macmillan.

Kohler, Pierre and Servaas Storm. 2016. 'CETA without blinders: How cutting "trade costs and more" will cause unemployment, inequality, and welfare losses', *International Journal of Political Economy*, 45: 257–93.

Kose, M. Ayhan, Franziska Ohnsorge and Naotaka Sugawara. 2021. *A Mountain of Debt: Navigating the Legacy of the Pandemic*. Policy Research Working Paper No 9800. Washington, DC: World Bank.

Krekó, Péter, Bulcsú Hunyadi and Patrik Szicherle. 2019. 'Anti-Muslim populism in Hungary: From the margins to the mainstream', Brookings. https://www.brookings.edu/research/anti-muslim-populism-in-hungary-from-the-margins-to-the-mainstream/

Krippner, Gretta R. 2012. *Capitalizing on Crisis*, Cambridge, MA: Harvard University Press.

Kundnani, Hans. 2017. 'What is the Liberal International Order?'. https://www.gmfus.org/news/what-liberal-international-order

Kurtzleben, Danielle. 2021. 'Green New Deal leaders see Biden climate plans as victory, kind of', *PBS*, 4 April. https://www.gpb.org/news/2021/04/04/green-new-deal-leaders-see-biden-climate-plans-victory-kind-of

Kurzer, Paulette. 1988. 'The politics of central banks: Austerity and unemployment in Europe', *Journal of Public Policy*, 8(1): 21–48.

Laing, Aislinn, Dave Sherwood and Fabian Cambero. 2019. 'Explainer: Chile's inequality challenge: what went wrong and can it be fixed?', *Reuters*, 23 October. https://www.reuters.com/article/us-chile-protests-explainer/explainer-chiles-inequality-challenge-what-went-wrong-and-can-it-be-fixed-idUSKBN1X22RK

Lakner, Christoph, et al. 2021. 'Updated estimates of the impact of COVID-19 on global poverty: Looking back at 2020 and the outlook for 2021', *World Bank Blogs*. https://blogs.worldbank.org/opendata/updated-estimates-impact-covid-19-global-poverty-looking-back-2020-and-outlook-2021 [accessed 19 November 2021].

Lancaster, Thomas D. 2017. 'The Spanish General Election of 2015 and 2016: A new stage in democratic politics?', *Western European Politics*, 40(4): 919–37.

Langille, David. 1987. 'The Business Council on National Issues and the Canadian State', *Studies in Political Economy*, 24 (Autumn).

Lapavitsas, Costas. 2011. 'Theorizing financialization', *Work, Employment and Society*, 25(4): 611–26.

Lapavitsas, Costas. 2018. *The Left Case Against the EU*, Cambridge: Polity Press.

Lehndorff, Steffen. 2020. *'New Deal' Means Being Prepared for Conflict: What We Can Learn from the New Deal of the 1930s*, Hamburg, VSA: Verlag Hamburg in Cooperation with transform! Europe.

Lehndorff, Steffen. 2021. 'A fragile triangle: Collective bargaining systems, trade unions and the state in the EU', in: Stephen McBride, Bryan Evans and Dieter Plehwe (eds), *The Changing Politics and Policy of Austerity*, Bristol: Bristol University Press, pp 63–81.

Lemann, Nicholas. 2021. 'The stimulus Bill is the most economically liberal legislation in decades', *The New Yorker*, 13 March. https://www.newyorker.com/magazine/2021/03/22/the-stimulus-bill-is-the-most-economically-liberal-legislation-in-decades

Liebman, Marcel. 1986. 'Reformism yesterday and social democracy today', *Socialist Register*, 22: 1–22.

Lobosco, Katie, and Tami Luhby. 2021. 'Here's what's in the bipartisan infrastructure package', *CNN*, 16 November. https://www.cnn.com/2021/07/28/politics/infrastructure-bill-explained/index.html

Losurdo, Domenico and Gregory Elliott. 2011 [2005]. *Liberalism: A Counter-History*, New York: Verso.

Loucaides, Darren. 2020. 'Democratic socialists lost, but their ideas have won', *Foreign Policy*. https://foreignpolicy.com/2020/10/30/democratic-socialists-corbyn-sanders-momentum-lost-ideas-won/

Lovergine, Saverio and Alberto Pellero. 2018. 'This time it might be different: Analysis of the impact of digitalization on the labour market', *European Scientific Journal*, 14(36): 68–81.

Lubbers, Eveline. 2015. 'Undercover research: Corporate and Police Spying on Activists', *Surveillance and Society*, 13(3/4): 338–53.

Lynch, Kevin and Paul Deegan. 2021. 'Five steps to sustainable fiscal management for Canada', *Globe and Mail*, 29 January, p B4.

Lynch, Peter. 2009. 'From social democracy back to no ideology? The Scottish National Party and ideological change in a multi-level electoral setting', *Regional and Federal Studies*, 19(4–5): 619–37.

MacEachen, Ellen, Jessica Polzer and Judy Clarke. 2008. 'You are free to set your own hours: Governing worker productivity and health through flexibility and resilience', *Social Science and Medicine*, 66: 1019–33.

Macpherson, C.B. 1965. *The Real World of Democracy*, Toronto: CBC Publications.

Madhyam. 2018. *Capital Controls: The Policy Pendulum Just Keeps Swinging*, Madhyam Policy Brief #3. https://www.somo.nl/wp-content/uploads/2018/12/Paper-3.pdf

Maiguashca, Bice and Jonathan Dean. 2019. 'Corbynism, populism and the re-shaping of left politics in contemporary Britain', in: Giorgos Katsambekis and Alexandros Kioupkiolis (eds), *The Populist Radical Left in Europe*, London: Routledge, pp 145–67.

Mair, Peter. 1992. 'The Question of Electoral Reform', *New Left Review*, I/194 (July/Aug).

Mair, Peter. 2013. *Ruling the Void: The Hollowing of Western Democracy*, London: Verso.

Manzanaro, Sophia Sanchez and Marta Rodriguez. 2019. 'Vox: Who are Spain's far-right party and what do they stand for?', *Euronews*. https://www.euronews.com/2019/11/10/vox-who-are-spain-s-far-right-party-and-what-do-they-stand-for

Marois, Thomas. 2021. *Public Banks: Decarbonisation, Definancialization and Democratization*, Cambridge: Cambridge University Press.

Massetti, Emanuele. 2009. 'Explaining regionalist party positioning in a multi-dimensional ideological space: A framework for analysis', *Regional and Federal Studies*, 19(4/5): 501–31.

Massetti, Emanuele. 2018. 'Left-wing regionalist populism in the "Celtic" peripheries: Plaid Cymru and the Scottish National Party's anti-austerity challenge against the British elites', *Comparative European Politics*, 16(6): 937–53.

Mazzucato, M. 2020. 'Capitalism's triple crisis', Project Syndicate, 30 March. https://www.project-syndicate.org/commentary/covid19-crises-of-capitalism-new-state-role-by-mariana-mazzucato-2020-03

Mazzucato, Mariana and Gregor Semieniuk. 2018. 'Financing renewable energy: Who is financing what and why it matters', *Technological Forecasting and Social Change*, 127(C): 8–22.

McBride, James and Andrew Chatzky. 2021. 'Is "Made in China 2025" a Threat to Global Trade?', 25 November. *Council on Foreign Relations*. https://www.cfr.org/backgrounder/made-china-2025-threat-global-trade

McBride, Stephen. 1992. *Not Working: State, Unemployment and Neo-Conservatism in Canada*, Toronto: University of Toronto Press.

McBride, Stephen. 2003. 'Quiet constitutionalism in Canada: The international political economy of domestic institutional change', *Canadian Journal of Political Science*, 36(2): 251–73.

McBride, Stephen. 2005. '"If you don't know where you're going you'll end up somewhere else": Ideological and policy failure in the Ontario NDP', in: William K. Carroll and R.S. Ratner (eds), *Challenges and Perils: Social Democracy in Neoliberal Times*, Halifax: Fernwood, pp 25–45.

McBride, Stephen. 2006. 'Reconfiguring sovereignty: NAFTA Chapter 11 Dispute Settlement procedures and the issue of public-private authority', *Canadian Journal of Political Science*, 39(4): 755–75.

McBride, Stephen. 2010. 'The new constitutionalism: International and private rule in the New Global Order', in: Gary Teeple and Stephen McBride (eds), *Relations of Global Power: Neoliberal Order and Disorder*, Toronto: University of Toronto Press, pp 19–40.

McBride, Stephen. 2019. 'Two worlds of austerity: Mythologies of activation and incentives', in: Dieter Plehwe, Moritz Neujeffski, Stephen McBride and Bryan Evans (eds), *Austerity: 12 Myths Exposed*, Social Europe, pp 75–80.

McBride, Stephen. 2020. 'Canada's continental political economy', in: Heather Whiteside (ed), *Canadian Political Economy*, Toronto: University of Toronto Press, pp 69–85.

McBride, Stephen and Bryan M. Evans. 2017. 'The austerity state: An introduction', in: Stephen McBride and Bryan M. Evans (eds), *The Austerity State*, Toronto: University of Toronto Press, pp 3–24.

McBride, Stephen and Sorin Mitrea. 2017. 'Austerity and constitutionalizing structural reform of labour in the EU', *Studies in Political Economy*, 98(1): 1–23.

McBride, Stephen and Jacob Muirhead. 2016. 'Challenging the low wage economy: Living and other wages', *Alternate Routes: A Journal of Critical Social Research*, 27(1): 55–86.

McBride, Stephen and Joy Schnittker. 2021. 'Taking institutions seriously: Alternatives for a new public purpose', *Alternate Routes: A Journal of Critical Social Research*, 32(1).

McBride, Stephen and John Shields. 2013. 'International trade agreements and the Ontario Green Energy Act: Opportunities and obstacles', in: Carla Lipsig-Mummé (ed), *Climate@Work*, Halifax: Fernwood, pp 41–56.

McBride, Stephen and James Watson. 2019. 'Reviewing the 2018 OECD Jobs Strategy – Anything new under the sun?', *Transfer: European Review of Labour and Research*, 25(2): 149–63.

McBride, Stephen and Heather Whiteside. 2011. *Private Affluence, Public Austerity: Economic Crisis and Democratic Malaise in Canada*, Winnipeg and Halifax: Fernwood Publishing.

McBride, Stephen and Russell A. Williams. 2001. 'Globalization, the restructuring of labour markets and policy convergence: The OECD "Jobs Strategy"', *Global Social Policy*, 1(3): 281–309.

McBride, Stephen, Sorin Mitrea and Mohammad Ferdosi. 2021. 'The comparative political economy of low wages', in: Bryan Evans, Carlo Fanelli and Tom McDowell (eds), *Rising Up: The Fight for Living Wage Work in Canada*, Vancouver: UBC Press, pp 29–49.

McDonald, David, Thomas Marois and Susan Spronk. 2021. 'Public banks + public water = SDG 6?', *Water Alternatives*, 14(1): 117–34.

McGrath, Matt. 2021a. 'Climate change: IPCC report is "code red for humanity"', BBC News, 9 August. https://www.bbc.co.uk/news/science-environment-58130705

McGrath, Matt. 2021b. 'COP26: Evasive words and coal compromise, but deal shows progress', *BBC News*. https://www.bbc.com/news/science-environment-59277977 [accessed 17 November 2021].

McKenzie, Lisa. 2015. *Getting By: Estates, Class and Culture in Austerity Britain*, Bristol: Policy Press.

McKinsey Global Institute. 2021. *Testing the Resilience of Europe's Inclusive Growth Model*. Discussion Paper: McKinsey and Company. https://www.mckinsey.com/~/media/mckinsey/featured%20insights/europe/testing%20the%20resilience%20of%20europes%20inclusive%20growth%20model/testing-the-resilience-of-europes-inclusive-growth-model.pdf

Mearsheimer, John J. 2019. 'Bound to fail: The rise and fall of the liberal international order', *International Security*, 43(4): 7–50.

Mendoza, Kerry-Anne. 2015. *Austerity: The Demolition of the Welfare State and the Rise of the Zombie Economy*, London: New Internationalist.

Mercer, Greg. 2021. 'Report urges Newfoundland to hike taxes, curb public spending', *Globe and Mail*, 7 May.

Meredith, Sam. 2021. 'G-20's global crackdown could create a new kind of tax haven', *CNBC*, 16 July. https://www.cnbc.com/2021/07/16/oecd-tax-reform-g-20s-crackdown-may-create-a-new-kind-of-tax-haven.html

Mertes, Tom. 2015. 'Anti-globalization movements: From critiques to alternatives', in: Bryan Turner and Robert Holton (eds), *The Routledge International Handbook of Globalization Studies* (2nd edn), London: Routledge, pp 92–110.

Meyer, David and Vivienne Walt. 2021. '"Far too low": Tax justice campaigners push back against the G7's 15% minimum tax-rate pact'. https://fortune.com/2021/06/07/global-minimum-corporate-tax-rate-g7-15-percent-pact/

Miley, Thomas Jeffrey. 2017. 'Austerity politics and constitutional crisis in Spain', *European Politics and Society*, 18(2): 263–83.

Mintz, Jack M. 2021. 'ESG rankings are a mug's game', *Financial Post*, 8 July. https://financialpost.com/opinion/jack-m-mintz-esg-rankings-are-a-mugs-game

Mitchell, William, L. Randall Wray and Martin Watts. 2019. *Macroeconomics*, London: Macmillan.

Mitchell, William and Thomas Fazi. 2017. *Reclaiming the State: A Progressive Vision of Sovereignty for a Post-Neoliberal World*, London: Pluto Press.

Morris, Chris. 2021. 'COP 26: How much are poor countries getting to fight climate change?', *BBC News*, 17 November. https://www.bbc.com/news/57975275

Moylan, Tom. 2000. *Scraps of the Untainted Sky: Science Fiction, Utopia, Dystopia*, Boulder, CO: Westview Press.

Mudde, Cas and Cristóbal Rovira Kaltwasser. 2017. *Populism: A Very Short Introduction*, Oxford: Oxford University Press.

Mukunda, Gautam. 2014. 'The price of Wall Street's power', *Harvard Business Review*, June.

Munck, Ronaldo. 2006. 'The anti-globalization movement: From Seattle (1999) to the future', in: *Globalization and Contestation: The New Great Counter Movement*. New York: Routledge, pp 57–74.

Munevar, Daniel. 2020. 'Arrested development: International Monetary Fund lending and austerity post COVID-19', Eurodad. https://www.eurodad.org/arrested_development

Myant, Martin, Sotiria Theodoropoulos and Agnieszka Piasna (eds). 2016. *Unemployment, Internal Devaluation and Labour Market Deregulation in Europe*, Report. ETUI: Brussels, pp 229–54.

Myers, John. 2020. 'California forces sharp cuts to schools, healthcare in California, Newsom Says', *Los Angeles Times* [online], 14 May. https://www.latimes.com/california/story/2020-05-14/coronavirus-california-shutdown-deficit-may-revise-state-budget

Naughton, Barry and Kellee S. Tsai. 2015. *State Capitalism, Institutional Adaptation, and the Chinese Miracle*, New York: Cambridge University Press.

NCSL (National Conference of State Legislatures). 2010. *NCSL Fiscal Brief: State Balanced Budget Provisions*. https://www.ncsl. org/documents/fiscal/StateBalancedBudgetProvisions2010.pdf

O'Brien, Robert, Anne Marie Goetz, Jan Aart Scholte and Marc Williams. 2000. *Contesting Global Governance: Multilateral Economic Institutions and Global Social Movements*, Cambridge: Cambridge University Press.

O'Connor, James. 1973. *The Fiscal Crisis of the State*, New York: St Martin's Press.

Oberndorfer, Lukas. 2012. 'The Fiscal Compact Bypasses Democracy and the Rule of Law', *Democratizing Europe*, 8 March. Transnational Institute. https://www.tni.org/en/article/the-fiscal-compact-bypasses-democracy-and-the-rule-of-law

Oberndorfer, Lukas. 2014. 'New economic governance through secondary legislation? Analysis and constitutional assessment: From new constitutionalism, via authoritarian constitutionalism to progressive constitutionalism', in: N. Bruun, K. Lorcher and I. Schomann (eds), *The Economic and Financial Crisis and Collective Law in Europe*, London: Bloomsbury Publishing, pp 25–54.

OECD. 2018. *Strategic Orientations of the Director General*, Paris: OECD. https://www.oecd.org/mcm/documents/C-MIN-2018-1-EN.pdf

OECD. 2020a. *Digital Transformation in the Age of COVID-19*, Paris: OECD. https://www.oecd.org/digital/digital-economy-outlook-covid.pdf

OECD. 2020b. 'Building back better: A sustainable, resilient recovery after COVID-19', *The OECD*. https://www.oecd.org/coronavirus/policy-responses/building-back-better-a-sustainable-resilient-recovery-after-covid-19-52b869f5/

OECD. 2020c. 'Turning hope into reality – The Economic Outlook', *The OECD*. https://www.oecd-ilibrary.org/sites/39a88ab1-en/index.html?itemId=/content/publication/39a88ab1-en

OECD. 2020d. *The Territoral Impact of COVID-19: Managing the Crisis across Levels of Government*. OECD Policy Responses to the Coronavirus. www.oecd.org/coronavirus/policy-responses/the-territorial-impact-of-COVID-19-managing-the-crisis-across-levels-of-government-d3e314e1/

OECD. 2021a. *Green Growth Papers*. https://www.oecd-ilibrary.org/environment/oecd-green-growth-papers_22260935

OECD. 2021b. 'The OECD Green Recovery Database: Examining the environmental implications of COVID-19 recovery policies'. https://www.oecd.org/coronavirus/policy-responses/the-oecd-green-recovery-database-47ae0f0d/

OECD. 2022. Labour – Trade Unions and Collective Bargaining – Trade Union Dataset (indicator), OECD Statistics, https://stats.oecd.org/#

Offe, Claus. 2013. 'Participatory inequality in the austerity state: A supply-side approach', in: Armin Schäfer and Wolfgang Streeck (eds), *Politics in the Age of Austerity*, Cambridge: Polity Press, pp 196–218.

Oliver, Eric and Wendy Rahn. 2016. 'Rise of *Trumpenvolk*: Populism in the 2016 election', *Annals of the American Academy of Political and Social Science*, 667(1): 189–206.

ONA (Ontario Nurses' Association). 2020. 'It's a dark day for Ontario nurses and health care professionals as Ford Government passes Bills 195, 197', *Cision* [online], 21 July. https://www.newswire.ca/news-releases/it-s-a-dark-day-for-ontario-nurses-and-health-care-professionals-as-ford-government-passes-bills-195-197855873041.html

Oxfam. 2020a. 'IMF paves way for new era of austerity post-COVID-19', Oxfam. https://www.oxfam.org/en/press-releases/imf-paves-way-new-era-austerity-post-COVID-19

Oxfam. 2020b. *Climate Finance Shadow Report 2020*, Oxford: Oxfam International. https://www.oxfam.org/en/research/climate-finance-shadow-report-2020

Oxfam. 2021. 'Oxfam GB: Poorer nations expected to face up to £55 billion shortfall in climate finance'. Press release, 24 October. https://www.oxfam.org.uk/mc/d5j6zc/

Palombarini, Stefano. 2021. 'Italy returns to the old austerity politics', *Le Monde diplomatique*, 5 April. https://mondediplo.com/2021/04/05italy

Panitch, Leo. 1977. *The Canadian State*, Toronto: University of Toronto Press.

Panitch, Leo. 1980. 'Recent theorizations of corporatism: Reflections on a growth industry', *The British Journal of Sociology*, 31(2): 159–74. doi:10.2307/589686.

Partington, Richard. 2020. 'Rishi Sunak warns public sector workers of new pay squeeze', *The Guardian* [online], 21 July. https://www.theguardian.com/business/2020/jul/21/uk-borrowing-record-coronavirus-pandemic-economy

Paterson, Bill. 2014. *Scotland and International Trade Organisations: A Discussion of Common Weal Approaches to International Organisations and Trade Agreements*, Jimmy Reid Foundation. http://reidfoundation.org/wp-content/uploads/2014/02/ITOs-and-Independence.pdf

Paterson, Bill. 2015. 'Questioning the common sense: Was Scottish Independence really an alternative to UK neoliberalisation?', *Capital & Class*, 39(3): 493–514.

Pauly, Louis. 1996. *The League of Nations and the Foreshadowing of the International Monetary Fund*, Essays in International Finance, no. 201. Princeton, NJ: Princeton University, Department of Economics.

PBO (Parliamentary Budget Office). 2021. *Pre-Budget Outlook March 31*, Ottawa PBO. https://www.pbo-dpb.gc.ca/en/blog/news/RP-2021-046-S--pre-budget-outlook--perspectives-prebudgetaires

Pérez Dattari, Carolina. 2021. 'Chile: the battle for a transformative new constitution', Amsterdam: Transnational Institute, 14 December. https://www.tni.org/en/article/chile-the-battle-for-a-transformative-new-constitution

Pettifor, Ann. 2020. *The Case for the Green New Deal*, London: Verso.

Pettifor, Ann. 2021. 'To restructure the British state the international financial system must be reformed', in: Patrick Allen, Suzanne Konzelmann and Jan Toporowsky (eds), *The Return of the State: Restructuring Britain for the Common Good*, Newcastle-upon-Tyne: Agenda Publishing, pp 201–9.

Pew. 2019. https://www.pewresearch.org/global/2019/04/29/many-across-the-globe-are-dissatisfied-with-how-democracy-is-working/

Phillips, Leigh and Michal Rozworski. 2019. *People's Republic of Walmart: How the World's Biggest Corporations are Laying the Foundations for Socialism*, London: Verso.

Picciotto, Sol. 2003. 'Private rights vs. public standards in the WTO', *Review of International Political Economy*, 10(3): 377–405.

Pickering, Jonathan et al. 2015. 'Acting on climate finance pledges: Inter-agency dynamics and relationships with aid in contributor states', *World Development*, 68: 149–62.

Piketty, Thomas. 2014. *Capital in the Twenty-First Century*, Cambridge, MA: Belknap Press.

Pilon, Dennis. 2007. *The Politics of Voting: Reforming Canada's Electoral System*, Toronto: Emond Montgomery Publications.

Pilon, Dennis. 2013. *Wrestling with Democracy: Voting Systems as Politics in the Twentieth-Century West*, Toronto: University of Toronto Press.

Pittis, Don. 2021. 'Jump in U.S. inflation may signal that history is repeating itself', CBC, 13 May. https://www.cbc.ca/news/business/inflation-history-column-don-pittis-1.6022412

Plehwe, Dieter, Quinn Slobodian and Philip Mirowski (eds). 2020. *Nine Lives of Neoliberalism*, London: Verso Books.

Polanyi, Karl. 1944. *The Great Transformation: The Political and Economic Origins of Our Time*, Boston: Beacon.

Polillo, Simone and Mauro F. Guillen. 2005. 'Globalization pressures and the state: The global spread of Central Bank Independence', *American Journal of Sociology*, 110(6): 1764–802.

Porzio, Steven, Joshua Fox and Elizabeth Dailey. 2021. 'While Democrats whittle down pro-labor provisions of social spending bill, civil penalties remain', *The National Law Review*, 16 November. https://www.natlawreview.com/article/while-democrats-whittle-down-pro-labor-provisions-social-spending-bill-civil

Prebisch, Raul. 1950. *The Economic Development of Latin America and its Principal Problems*, New York: United Nations Department of Economic Affairs.

Press, Jordan. 2020. 'Canadian economy posted steepest decline on record as coronavirus struck: StatCan', *CTV News*. https://www.ctvnews.ca/business/canadian-economy-posted-steepest-decline-on-record-as-coronavirus-struck-statcan-1.5082814

Pylas, Pan. 2020. 'UK economy could see worst slump since 1706 due to COVID-19', *Global News*. 7 May. https://globalnews.ca/news/6915074/coronavirus-britain-economy/

Quah, Danny. 2011. 'The global economy's shifting centre of gravity', *Global Policy*, 2(1): 3–9.

Qureshi, Zia. 2020. 'Tackling the inequality pandemic: Is there a cure?', *Brookings*. https://www.brookings.edu/research/tackling-the-inequality-pandemic-is-there-a-cure/

Ray, Siladitya. 2021. '"Fit For 55": Here's what to expect as the EU unveils its ambitious new climate legislation', *Forbes*, 14 July.

Ripple, William J. et al. 2017. 'World scientists' warning to humanity: a second notice', *BioScience*, 67(12): 1026–8.

Ritt, Madeleine. 2020. 'The crisis of privatized care in Ontario'. https://healthydebate.ca/2020/12/topic/crisis-privatized-care-in-ontario/

Rivarola Puntigliano, Andrés. 2020. 'Pandemics and multiple crises in Latin America', *Latin American Policy*, 11(2): 313–19.

Roberts, J. Timmons et al. 2021. 'Rebooting a failed promise of climate finance', *Nature Climate Change*, 11(3): 180–2.

Romano, Antonio, Giuseppe Scandurra, Alfonso Carfora and Monica Ronghi. 2018. 'Climate finance', in: Antonio Romano, Giuseppe Scandurra, Alfonso Carfora and Monica Ronghi (eds), *Climate Finance as an Instrument to Promote the Green Growth in Developing Countries*, New York: Springer, pp 23–47.

Romero, Mario Jose. 2017. 'Public development banks: Towards a better model', Eurodad. https://www.eurodad.org/public_development_banks_towards_a_better_model

Sánchez-Cuenca, Ignacio. 2020. 'Neoliberal technocracy: The challenge to democratic self-government', in: Eri Bertsou and Daniele Carmani (eds), *The Technocratic Challenge to Democracy*, Abingdon: Routledge, pp 44–60.

Sanders, Bernie. 2020. 'Bernie Sanders on the issues', Bernie Sanders. https://berniesanders.com/issues/

Sandford, Alasdair. 2017. 'What are Marine Le Pen's policies?', Euronews. https://www.euronews.com/2017/02/09/what-do-we-know-about-marine-le-pen-s-policies

Sanger, David E. and Mark Landler. 2021. 'Biden tries to rally G7 nations to counter China's influence', *The New York Times*, 12 June. https://www.nytimes.com/2021/06/12/world/europe/biden-china-g7.html

Sanger-Katz, Margot. 2021. 'Health care renovation', *The New York Times*, 18 November. https://www.nytimes.com/2021/11/18/briefing/biden-health-care-spending-bill.html

Savage, Luke. 2021. 'Joe Biden is not a radical', *Jacobin*, 7 May. https://www.jacobinmag.com/2021/05/joe-biden-radical-policy-liberalism-first-100-days

Sawyer, Malcolm. 2017. 'The Processes of Financialisation and Economic Performance', *Economic and Political Studies*, 5(1): 5–20.

Schäfer, Armin and Wolfgang Streeck (eds). 2013. *Politics in an Age of Austerity*, Cambridge: Polity.

Schmidt, Ingo. 2012. '"It's the economy stupid!" Theoretical reflections on third way social democracy', in: Bryan Evans and Ingo Schmidt (eds), *Social Democracy After the Cold War*, Edmonton: Athabasca University Press, pp 13–44.

Schmidt, Ingo. 2021. 'Market populism, its right-wing off-spring, and left alternatives', in: Stephen McBride, Bryan M. Evans and Dieter Plehwe (eds), *The Changing Politics and Policy of Austerity*, Bristol: Policy Press, pp 195–212.

Schwab, Klaus and Thierry Malleret. 2020. *COVID-19: The Great Reset*, Geneva: Forum.

Selfa, Lance and Ashley Smith. 2016. 'The Sanders campaign and the Left', *New Politics*, 15(4): 13–20.

Seligman, Lara. 2021. 'Biden heads to NATO amid friction over Afghanistan withdrawal', 26 November. https://www.politico.com/news/2021/06/13/biden-nato-afghanistan-withdrawal-493580

Serfati, Claude. 2013. 'The new configuration of the capitalist class', in: Leo Panitch, Gregory Albo and Vivek Chibber (eds), *Socialist Register 2014: Registering Class*, London: Merlin, pp 138–61.

Sevastopulo, Demetri. 2020. 'White House says jobless benefits "disincentive" for work', *Financial Times*, 14 June. https://www.ft.com/content/eab4eef4-a8d3-466f-b9d1-35cde6b22b38

Sharma Poudel, Santosh. 2021. 'COP26 finds its scapegoats – India and China', 17 November. https://thediplomat.com/2021/11/cop26-finds-its-scapegoats-india-and-china/

Shenoy, Rupa. 2020. 'IMF reassures COVID-19 support after hundreds of groups push back against belt-tightening measures', *The World*. https://theworld.org/stories/2020-10-22/imf-reassures-COVID-19-support-after-hundreds-groups-push-back-against-belt

Sinclair, Scott. 2018. *Canada's Track Record Under NAFTA Chapter 11 North American Investor-State Disputes to January 2018*, Ottawa: CCPA.

Sinclair, Scott. 2019. 'Public services, free trade and the Green New Deal', *The Monitor*, 19 November.

Sklar, Holly. 1980. *Trilateralism: The Trilateral Commission and Elite Planning for World Management*, Boston, MA: South End Press.

Slobodian, Quinn. 2019. '20 years after Seattle, the clash of globalizations rages on', *The Nation*, 29 November. https://www.thenation.com/article/activism/seattle-trade-globalization/

Snaith, Emma. 2021. 'What is the Green New Deal and how does Biden's climate plan compare?', *Independent*, 20 January. https://www.independent.co.uk/climate-change/news/green-new-deal-what-is-biden-summary-aoc-b1790197.html

Snell, Kelsey and Brian Naylor. 2021. 'Biden unveils a smaller spending framework. But not all Democrats are onboard', *NPR*, 16 November. https://www.npr.org/2021/10/28/1049973400/biden-unveils-spending-framework-now-he-has-to-sell-it-to-house-democrats

Soederberg, Susanne. 2004. 'Unravelling Washington's judgement calls: The cases of the Malaysian and Chilean capital controls', *Antipode*, 36(1): 45–65.

Sola, Jorge and César Rendueles. 2018. 'Podemos, the upheaval of Spanish politics and the challenges of populism', *Journal of Contemporary European Issues*, 26(1): 99–116.

Sorgner, Alina. 2017. 'The automation of jobs: A threat for employment or a source of new entrepreneurial opportunities?', *Foresight and STI Governance*, 11(3): 37–48.

Sprunt, Barbara. 2021. 'Here's what's in the American Rescue Plan', *NPR*, 11 March. https://www.npr.org/sections/coronavirus-live-updates/2021/03/09/974841565/heres-whats-in-the-american-rescue-plan-as-it-heads-toward-final-passage

Standing, G. 1997. 'Globalization, labour flexibility and insecurity: The era of market regulation', *European Journal of Industrial Relations*, 3(1): 7–37.

Stanford, Jim. 2021. 'The crisis next time: The GFC and the continuing fragility of capitalism', in: Stephen McBride, Bryan Evans and Dieter Plehwe (eds), *The Changing Politics and Policy of Austerity*, Bristol: Bristol University Press, pp 248–71.

Stern, Nicholas. 2015. *Why are We Waiting? The Logic, Urgency, and Promise of Tackling Climate Change*, Cambridge, MA: MIT Press.

Streck, Charlotte and Thiago Chagas. 2011. 'Developments in climate finance from Rio to Cancun', *World Bank Legal Review*, 3: 345–62.

Streeck, Wolfgang. 2011. 'The crises of democratic capitalism', *New Left Review*, 71, Sept–Oct.

Streeck, Wolfgang. 2014. *Buying Time: The Delayed Crisis of Democratic Capitalism*, London: Verso.

Szelenyi, Zsuzsanna. 2019. 'The generation that betrayed Hungarian democracy', *Reporting Democracy*. https://balkaninsight.com/2019/06/20/the-generation-that-betrayed-hungarian-democracy/

Szymborska, Hanna. 2020. 'Coronavirus recovery – the new economic thinking we need', *The Conversation* [online], 8 July. https://theconversation.com/coronavirus-recovery-the-new-economic-thinking-we-need-141339

Tankersley, Jim. 2021. 'Biden signs infrastructure bill, promoting benefits for Americans', *The New York Times*, 16 November. https://www.nytimes.com/2021/11/15/us/politics/biden-signs-infrastructure-bill.html

Tankersley, Jim and Alan Rappeport. 2021. 'Biden finds raising corporate tax rates easier abroad than at home', *The New York Times*, 16 November. https://www.nytimes.com/2021/10/30/world/europe/g20-biden-corporate-tax-agreement.html

Tanuro, Daniel. 2013. *Green Capitalism: Why it Can't Work*, London: Merlin.

Tax Justice Network et al. 2020. *The State of Tax Justice: Tax Justice in the time of COVID-19*, Tax Justice Network. https://taxjustice.net/wp-content/uploads/2020/11/The_State_of_Tax_Justice_2020_ENGLISH.pdf

Teeple, Gary. 2017. 'Austerity policies: From the Keynesian to the corporate welfare state', in: Stephen McBride and Bryan M. Evans (eds), *The Austerity State*, Toronto: University of Toronto Press, pp 25–43.

Thornton, Daniel. 2019. 'Can monetary policy stimulate economic growth?'. https://app.hedgeye.com/insights/76794

Tian, Nan, Alexandra Kiumova, Diego Lopes Da Silva, Pieter D. Wezemen and Siemon T. Wezeman. 2020. 'Trends in World Military Expenditure, 2019', *SPIRI Fact Sheet*. https://www.sipri.org/sites/default/files/2020-04/fs_2020_04_milex_0_0.pdf

Tobar, Marcela Rios. 2021. 'Chile's Constitutional Convention: A triumph of inclusion', UNDP Latin American and the Caribbean. https://www.latinamerica.undp.org/content/rblac/en/home/blog/2021/chile-s-constitutional-convention--a-triumph-of-inclusion.html

Tonby, Oliver et al. 2019. 'Globalization in Asia: Flows and networks shaping the Asian century', *McKinsey and Company*. https://www.mckinsey.com/featured-insights/asia-pacific/the-future-of-asia-asian-flows-and-networks-are-defining-the-next-phase-of-globalization

Tooze, Adam. 2018. *Crashed: How a Decade of Financial Crises Changed the World*, New York: Viking.

Tooze, Adam. 2021. 'Europe's decarbonisation challenge? "Wir scaffen das"', *Social Europe*, 22 March.

Trudell, Megan. 2016. 'Sanders, Trump and the US working class', *International Socialism*, 150: 17–30. http://isj.org.uk/sanders-trump-and-the-us-working-class/

TUAC (Trade Union Advisory Committee). 2018. *TUAC Assessment of the OECD's Revised Jobs Strategy*, Paris: Trade Union Advisory Committee on the OECD Commission. https://tuac.org/news/tuac-assesment-of-the-revised-jobs-strategy/

Uddin, Kamal. 2017. 'Climate change and global environmental politics: North–south divide', *Environmental Policy and Law*, 47(3): 106–14. doi:http://dx.doi.org.proxy.queensu.ca/10.3233/EPL-170022

UKIP. 2017. 'Britain Together: The UKIP 2017 Manifesto'. https://d3n8a8pro7vhmx.cloudfront.net/ukipdev/pages/3944/attachments/original/1495695469/UKIP_Manifesto_June2017opt.pdf?1495695469

Uldam, Julie. 2015. 'The electoral success of the Danish People's party: Something rotten in the state of Denmark?', *LSE Blog*. https://blogs.lse.ac.uk/eurocrisispress/2015/06/29/the-electoral-success-of-the-danish-peoples-party-something-rotten-in-the-state-of-denmark/

UNCTAD (United Nations Conference on Trade and Development). 2021. *Trade and Development Report Update: Out of the Frying Pan … Into the Fire?*, New York: UN.

Unity Task Force. 2020. *Biden–Sanders Unity Task Force Recommendations*. https://joebiden.com/wp-content/uploads/2020/08/UNITY-TASK-FORCE-RECOMMENDATIONS.pdf

Urban, Hans-Jurgen and Sebastian Kramer. 2021. 'Austerity after COVID-19: Towards inclusive economic governance in Europe', in: Stephen McBride, Bryan Evans and Dieter Plehwe (eds), *The Changing Politics and Policy of Austerity*, Bristol: Bristol University Press, pp 272–91.

Urra, Susana. 2018. 'Far-right Spanish political party Vox: What are its policies?', *El Pais*. https://english.elpais.com/elpais/2018/12/03/inenglish/1543832942_674971.html

Vallas, Steven. 2019. 'Platform capitalism: What's at stake for workers?', *New Labour Forum*, 28(1): 48–59.

Van Harten, Gus. 2005. '"Private authority and transnational governance", the contours of the international system of investor protection', *Review of International Political Economy*, 12(4): 600–23.

Van Harten, Gus and Dayna Nadine Scott. 2016. 'Investment treaties and the internal vetting of regulatory proposals: A case study from Canada', *Osgoode Legal Studies Research Paper Series*, p 151. https://digitalcommons.osgoode.yorku.ca/olsrps/151

Vanaerschot, Frank. 2019. 'Democratizing nationalized banks', in: Lavinia Steinfort and Satoko Kishimoto (eds), *Public Finance for the Future We Want*, Amsterdam: Transnational Institute. https://www.tni.org/files/publication-downloads/highres_public_finance_for_the_future_we_want_book_online_version_0307.pdf

Vergine, Stefano. 2020. 'Coronavirus: Are Italians losing faith in the EU?', *BBC News* [online], 17 May. https://www.bbc.com/news/world-europe-52666870

Vilches, Jose and Marcela Pizarro. 2019. 'Mass protests expose crack in Chile's economic success story', *Aljazeera*, 4 November. https://www.aljazeera.com/economy/2019/11/4/mass-protests-expose-cracks-in-chiles-economic-success-story

Vine, David. 2015. 'Where in the world is the U.S. military?', *Politico*. https://www.politico.com/magazine/story/2015/06/us-military-bases-around-the-world-119321

Voigts, Eckart and Alessandra Boller (eds). 2015. *Dystopia, Science Fiction, Post-Apocalypse: Classics, New Tendencies, Model Interpretations*, Trier: WVT Wissenschaftlicher Verlag Trier.

Waldman, Scott. 2021. 'Biden says infrastructure is the pillar of his climate plan', *Scientific America*, 8 April. https://www.scientificamerican.com/article/biden-says-infrastructure-is-the-pillar-of-his-climate-plan/

Walks, Alan. 2014. 'Canada's housing bubble story: Mortgage securitization, the state, and the global financial crisis', *International Journal of Urban and Regional Research*, 38(1): 256–84.

Walsh, Deirdre and Kelsey Snell. 2021. 'What stays and what's gone from Biden's spending bill (so far)', *NPR*, 16 November. https://www.npr.org/2021/10/22/1047975012/heres-what-we-know-is-in-the-scaled-back-biden-budget-bill-and-what-got-cut

Walsh, Mary Williams. 2020. 'A virus ravages budgets, states cut and borrow for balance', *The New York Times* [online], 14 May. https://www.nytimes.com/2020/05/14/business/virus-state-budgets.html

Warren, Mark E. 2002. 'What can democratic participation mean today?', *Political Theory*, 30(5): 677–701.

Watkins, Susan. 2021. 'Paradigm shifts', *New Left Review*, 128: 1–12.

Weber, Max. 1968. *Economy and Society*, Guenther Roth and Claus Wittich (eds), New York: Bedminster.

Weiss, Linda. 1998. *The Myth of the Powerless State*, New York: Cornell University Press.

West, Angus. 2015. '17 disturbing things Snowden has taught us (so far)', *PRI's The World*, 1 June. https://www.pri.org/stories/2013-07-09/17-disturbing-things-snowden-has-taught-us-so-far

Wherry, Aaron. 2020. 'Walking a "tightrope"': Bill Morneau and the path out of the pandemic economy', *CBC News*, 4 July. https://www.cbc.ca/news/politics/bill-morneau-pandemic-covid-coronavirus-debt-deficit-1.5636878

White House. 2021. 'President Biden and G7 leaders to announce steps to forge a more fair and inclusive global economy', United States Government. https://www.whitehouse.gov/briefing-room/statements-releases/2021/06/11/fact-sheet-president-biden-and-g7-leaders-to-announce-steps-to-forge-a-more-fair-and-inclusive-global-economy/

Whiteside, Heather. 2015. *Purchase for Profit: Public-Private Partnerships and Canada's Public Health Care System*, Toronto: University of Toronto Press.

Whiteside, Heather. 2021. 'Beyond austerity: Pro-public strategies versus public-private partnerships scandals', in: Stephen McBride, Bryan Evans and Dieter Plehwe (eds), *The Changing Politics and Policy of Austerity*, Bristol: Policy Press, pp 25–41.

Whiteside, Heather, Stephen McBride and Bryan Evans. 2021. *Varieties of Austerity*, Bristol: Bristol University Press.

WHO. 2021. *Vaccine Inequity Undermining Global Economic Recovery*, Geneva/New York City: World Health Organization.

Wiggan, Jay. 2017. 'Contesting the austerity and "welfare reform" narrative of the UK government: Forging a social democratic imaginary in Scotland', *International Journal of Sociology and Social Policy*, 37(11–12): 639–54.

Wilks, Stephen. 2013. *The Political Power of the Business Corporation*, Cheltenham: Edward Elgar.

Wolfe, Martin. 2016. 'Capitalism and democracy: The strain is showing', *Financial Times*, 30 August.

Woodman, Connor. 2018a. 'Spycops in context: Counter subversion, deep dissent and the logic of political policing', *Centre for Crime and Justice Studies*. https://www.crimeandjustice.org.uk/sites/crimeandjustice.org.uk/files/Spycops%20in%20context%20%E2%80%93%20counter-subversion%2C%20deep%20dissent%20and%20the%20logic%20of%20political%20policing.pdf

Woodman, Connor. 2018b. 'The infiltrator and the movement', *Politico*, 23 April. https://jacobinmag.com/2018/04/uk-infiltration-secret-police-mi5-special-branch-undercover

Wright, Thomas. 2018. 'The return to great-power rivalry was inevitable', *The Atlantic*, 18 September. https://www.theatlantic.com/international/archive/2018/09/liberal-international-order-free-world-trump-authoritarianism/569881/

Yakabuski, Konrad. 2020. 'Stephen Harper strikes back with a warning about big government', *The Globe and Mail* [online], 13 May. https://www.theglobeandmail.com/opinion/article-stephen-harper-strikes-back-with-a-warning-about-big-government/

Yellen, Janet. 2021. 'Remarks by Secretary of the Treasury Janet L. Yellen at the G20 Infrastructure Investors Dialogue: Challenges and opportunities in environment, social, and governance-aligned infrastructure investment', https://home.treasury.gov/news/press-releases/jy0210

Yilmazkuda, Demet and Hakan Yilmazkuda. 2014. 'Bilateral versus multilateral free trade agreements: A welfare analysis', *Review of International Economics*, 22(3): 513–35.

Zakaria, Fareed. 1997. 'The rise of illiberal democracy', *Foreign Affairs*, 7(6): 22–43.

Zehner, Ozzie. 2012. *Green Illusions: The Dirty Secrets of Clean Energy and the Future of Environmentalism*, Lincoln and London: University of Nebraska Press.

Zuboff, Shoshana. 2019. *The Age of Surveillance Capitalism*, London: Profile Books.

Zucman, Gabriel and Gus Wezerek. 2021. 'This is tax evasion, plain and simple', *The New York Times*, 7 July. https://www.nytimes.com/interactive/2021/07/07/opinion/minimum-corporate-tax.html

Index